GUIDE TO

MARINE FISHES

GUIDE

TO

MARINE

FISHES

By Alfred Perlmutter

New York University Press

DATE			

CONTENTS

Introduction   1

How to Identify Fishes and Fish-like Vertebrates   5

Identification Key   8

General Information   225

    Lampreys   227

    Sharks   228

    Sawfish, Skates and Rays   253

    True Fishes   271

Index

    Common Names   415

    Scientific Names   423

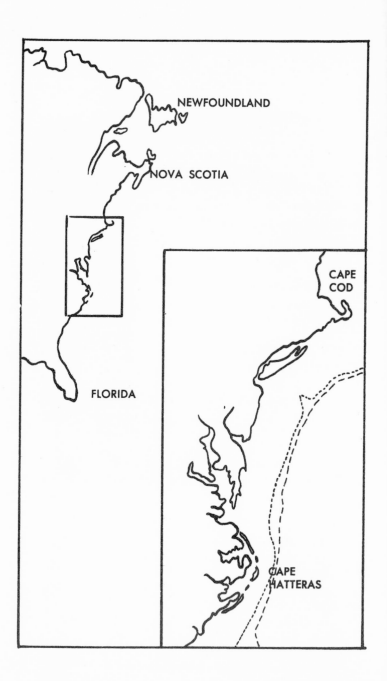

INTRODUCTION

The waters of our oceans teem with plant and animal life comprising numerous species, many as yet undiscovered. The animals may be divided into two main groups: invertebrates, that is, animals without backbones, such as the jellyfish, the starfish, clams and oysters, crabs and lobsters; and vertebrates, that is, animals with backbones, including lampreys, sharks, rays, skates, fishes, whales, and porpoises.

In popular language the term "fish" includes the lampreys, the sharks, the rays and skates, the bony fishes, and frequently even the whales and porpoises. With increased dissemination of scientific information, more people have come to recognize that the whales and porpoises are not fishes but belong to the class Mammalia which also includes man. However, few realize that the lampreys, sharks, rays, and skates are no more true fishes than are whales or porpoises. The lampreys are members of the class Cyclostomata, the sharks, rays, and skates of the class Chondricthyes, and the bony fishes, or true fishes, of the class Osteichthyes.

Without going into the technical reasons for assigning these various animals to different classes, it can be stated that the lampreys and the sharks, rays, and skates are as different from each other and from the bony or true fishes as are the whales and porpoises. However, traditionally the ichthyologist has accepted responsibility for the study of the lampreys, sharks, rays, and skates along with the true fishes, and they are accordingly included in this publication.

As far as the marine fishes and fish-like vertebrates are concerned, the American Atlantic coast may be divided into three zones: a cold-water zone north of Cape Cod,

Massachusetts; a warm-water zone south of Cape Hatteras, North Carolina; and a temperate-water zone between Cape Cod and Cape Hatteras.

The temperate-water zone borders the heavily populated states of Massachusetts, Rhode Island, Connecticut, New York, New Jersey, Pennsylvania, Delaware, Maryland, and Virginia. Along their shores each year millions of persons from these and adjoining states swim and fish, go water skiing, boating, or beachcombing. Often as not, while engaged in such pursuits, they see or catch unfamiliar marine fishes or fish-like vertebrates. The visitor is curious to know their names and habits.

Unfortunately, although a considerable amount of scientific literature is available on the fishes in the region from Cape Cod to Cape Hatteras, much of it is technical and difficult to follow for anyone other than a professional ichthyologist. While attempts have been made to bring this information to the general public in the form of field books or of faunal studies of a particular area, in my opinion they have had only limited success. The keys for identification of the various species have been restricted and complicated by adherence to natural biological groupings such as orders and families. Or they have been difficult to follow because the differentiating characters were obscure, poorly defined, or hard to determine.

In this guide, identification of the various species is based primarily on easily seen external characters which are employed for rapid identification of fishes in the field. Biological groupings are disregarded. Identifying characters are illustrated on silhouettes of the fish, according to the method used successfully by our Armed Forces to teach highly technical information to their men during World War II. Thus the amateur will be readily able to identify most species, not only in the adult sizes but also in the young, at least in those sizes most likely to be seen.

The species included in this guide are all of the marine fishes and fish-like vertebrates commonly found along the shores of the temperate-water zone from Cape Cod to

Cape Hatteras, together with some of the more common stragglers from the regions north of Cape Cod and south of Cape Hatteras and from the deep waters offshore.

In the sections of the book dealing with Species Information, both the most popular of the common names and the most generally accepted scientific name are given. The scientific name consists of three parts. The first italicized word, with the initial letter capitalized, is the genus; the second italicized word is the species; and the remaining word or words identify the person or persons who first described the fish. The genus given is always the one to which modern taxonomists assign the species. Where this assignment is still that of the original describer, his name follows the species without punctuation. Where the modern genus assignment differs from the original describer's, his name is enclosed in parentheses.

The higher categories of classification, the subfamilies, families, suborders, and orders, have been only briefly and incompletely indicated in the General Information section preceding descriptions for each of the various groups: lampreys; sharks; sawfish, skates, and rays; true fishes. The incompleteness was deliberate, in order to avoid entering upon an irrelevant scientific discussion of which of the many proposed systems of taxonomy (Jordan, Regan, Gregory, Berg) should be used.

While every attempt has been made to use nontechnical terminology in describing the various species and aspects of their life history, some technical terms could not be avoided. These are listed in the following paragraphs together with brief definitions.

FISH and FISHES: The term "fish" is used to describe one or more individuals belonging to a single species. If more than one species is being discussed, then the term "fishes" is used.

BLIND SIDE: The side of a flatfish on which there are no eyes.

EYED SIDE: The side of a flatfish on which there are two eyes.

DEMERSAL: Living on the bottom of the sea.

FIN RAY: The skeletal rods supporting the fins.

PELAGIC: Living in the open sea, commonly in the upper layers of the water.

LANDLOCKED: Applied to fishes normally residing in the sea which have become residents of coastal ponds and lakes formerly accessible to and now cut off from the sea.

PLANKTON: Microscopic and small plants and animals drifting freely in the open waters and carried by wind, tides, and currents.

HOW TO IDENTIFY FISHES AND
FISH-LIKE VERTEBRATES

Before attempting to identify a fish or fish-like vertebrate (lamprey, shark, ray), the reader should become familiar with the meaning of a few terms used in the identification key which are listed below and illustrated on p. 6.

1. DORSAL FIN: an unpaired (or single) fin on the upper surface of the body. If more than one dorsal fin is present, the fin nearest the head is called the first dorsal fin, the next one behind it the second dorsal fin, etc.

2. ANAL FIN: an unpaired fin on the lower surface of the body, near the rear end.

3. PELVIC FINS: a pair of fins located on the lower surface of the body in front of the anal fin.

4. PECTORAL FINS: a pair of fins located one on each side near the front of the body.

5. CAUDAL OR TAIL FIN: a single, tail-like fin located at the rear end of the body.

6. LATERAL LINE: a broken line of pores frequently found along the length of the sides of the body.

7. CAUDAL PEDUNCLE: the narrow region of the body between the rear of the dorsal and anal fins and the caudal fin.

8. SNOUT: the region in front of the eyes.

9. SPIRACLES: small openings located behind the eyes of some sharks and rays.

10. ORIGIN OF FIN: the front of the base of a fin.

11. OPERCULUM OR GILL COVER: the bony covering protecting the gill.

In identifying a specimen always start at page 8. The identification key is based on a system of multiple choice. On each page, characters separating two groups of fishes are described under the headings I and II. If your specimen fits the description under one of these headings you may

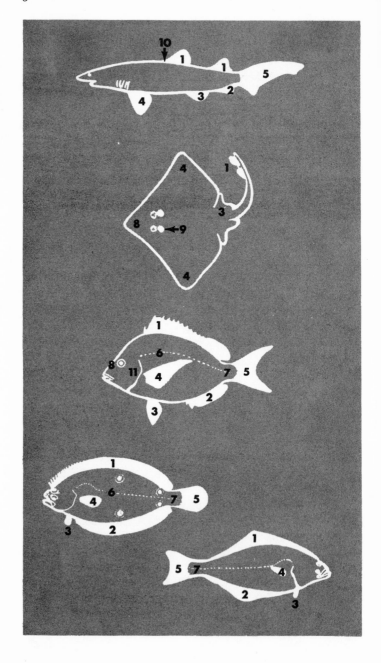

be referred to another page where again there will be offered a choice of characters under the headings I and II. Or you may be referred on the same page to a choice of characters under subheadings Ia and Ib, and possibly to still further subheadings 1 and 2, a and b. The differentiating characters described under the various headings are illustrated in silhouettes of fishes, usually on the page opposite.

After the fish has been identified the key refers the reader to a section in the rear part of the book (General Information), where the fish is illustrated and a description given of its color, distribution, size, habits, and economic importance.

ALFRED PERLMUTTER

HEAD—FISH-LIKE VERTEBRATES AND TRUE FISHES

I. *Numerous (5–7) gill openings on each side of head*
Page 9, figs. A–C

See Lampreys, Sharks, Rays, p. 10.

II. *One gill opening on each side of head*
Page 9, figs. D, E

See HEAD—TRUE FISHES, p. 52.

Numerous gill openings on each side of head

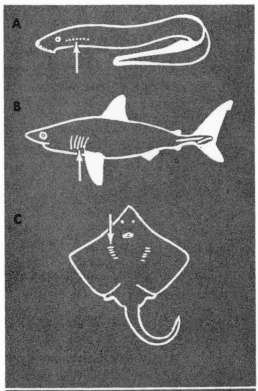

Single gill opening on each side of head

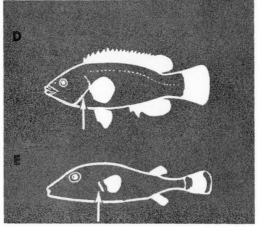

LAMPREYS, SHARKS, RAYS

I. *Body eel-shaped*
   Page 11, fig. A

   See Sea Lamprey, p. 227.

II. *Body not eel-shaped*
    Page 11, figs. B–E

   IIa. Body rounded and elongated; torpedo-shaped
        Page 11, fig. B

        See Hammerhead Sharks, Other Sharks, p. 12.

   IIb. Body broad and flat
        Page 11, figs. C–E

        See Sawfish, Angel Shark, Rays, Torpedo, Skates, p. 36.

Body eel-shaped

Sea lamprey

Body not eel-shaped

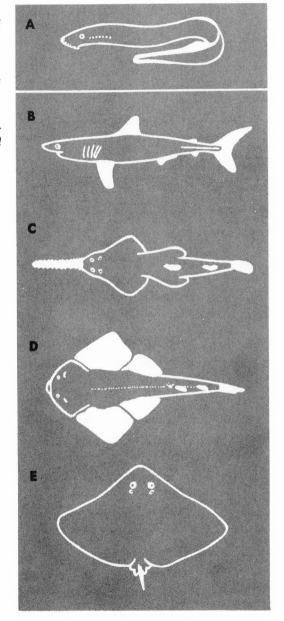

HAMMERHEAD SHARKS, OTHER SHARKS

I. *Head flattened laterally; shovel- or hammer-shaped*
Page 13, figs. A–D

Ia. Head shovel-shaped
Page 13, fig. B

See Shovelhead Shark, p. 247.

Ib. Head hammer-shaped
Page 13, figs. C, D

1. Front margin of head scalloped, notched at midline
Page 13, fig. C

See Southern Hammerhead Shark, p. 248.

2. Front margin of head rounded and not notched at midline
Page 13, fig. D

See Common Hammerhead Shark, p. 249.

II. *Head not flattened laterally*
Page 13, fig. E

See Thresher, Greenland, Other Sharks, p. 14.

Head flattened laterally

Shovelhead shark

Southern hammerhead shark

Common hammerhead shark

Head not flattened laterally

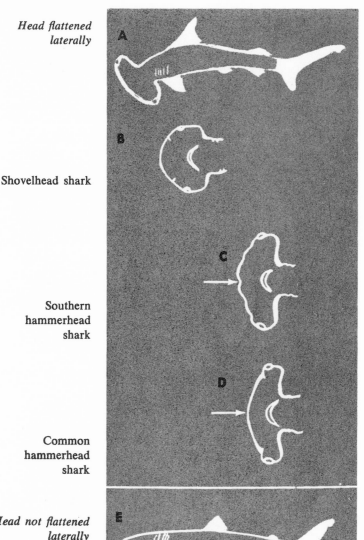

THRESHER, GREENLAND, OTHER SHARKS

I. *Tail long; about same length as body*
Page 15, fig. A

See Common Thresher Shark, p. 235.

II. *Tail shorter; length much less than that of body*
Page 15, figs. B–D

IIa. Lower surface of body with only one pair of fins, pelvics; anal fin absent
Page 15, figs. B, C

1. A spine in front of each dorsal fin
Page 15, fig. B

See Dogfishes, p. 32.

2. No spine in front of dorsal fins
Page 15, fig. C

See Greenland Shark, p. 251.

IIb. Lower surface of body with both pelvic fins and anal fin present
Page 15, fig. D

See Basking, Tiger, Mackerel, White, Other Sharks, p. 16.

Tail long

Common thresher
shark

Tail shorter

Greenland shark

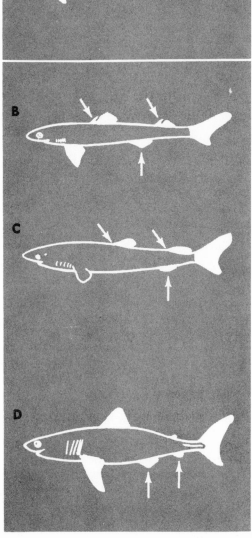

BASKING, TIGER, MACKEREL, WHITE, OTHER SHARKS

I. *Lateral keel or ridge on caudal peduncle*
Page 17, figs. A, C

    Ia. Gill slits very long; extend almost full height of head and onto lower surface of head
Page 17, figs. A, B

    See Basking Shark, p. 235.

    Ib. Gill slits shorter; do not extend full height of head or onto lower surface of head
Page 17, fig. C

    See Tiger, Mackerel, White Sharks, p. 34.

II. *No lateral keel or ridge on caudal peduncle*
Page 17, fig. D

See False Cat, Whale, Other Sharks, p. 18.

Lateral keel or ridge on caudal peduncle

Basking shark

No lateral keel or ridge on caudal peduncle

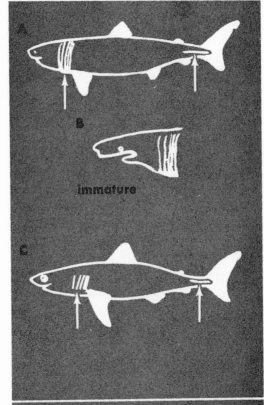

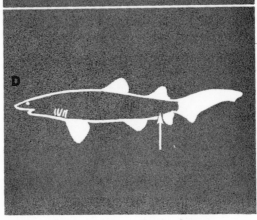

FALSE CAT, WHALE, OTHER SHARKS

I. *First dorsal fin very long; base length more than half
the distance from origin of pectoral fin to origin of
pelvic fin*
Page 19, fig. A

See False Cat Shark, p. 239.

II. *First dorsal fin much shorter; base length much less
than half the distance from origin of pectoral fin to
origin of pelvic fin*
Page 19, figs. B–D

IIa. Two distinct ridges on each side of the body extending from over gill slits to base of tail
Page 19, fig. B

See Whale Shark, p. 237.

IIb. No ridges on sides of body
Page 19, figs. C, D

See Nurse Shark, Chain Dogfish, Deep-Water Cat
Shark, Other Sharks, p. 20.

*First dorsal
fin very long*

False cat shark

*First dorsal fin
much shorter*

Whale shark

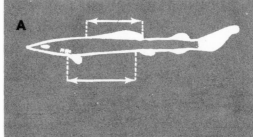

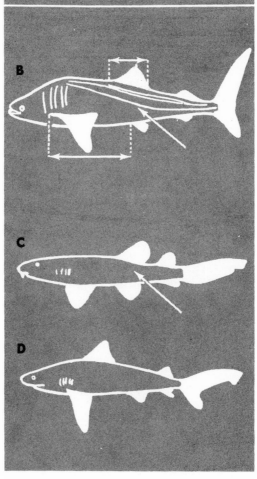

NURSE SHARK, CHAIN DOGFISH, DEEP-WATER CAT SHARK, OTHER SHARKS

I. *Origin of first dorsal fin over or behind origin of pelvic fin*
Page 21, figs. A–C

    Ia. Origin of first dorsal fin directly over origin of pelvic fin
Page 21, fig. A

    See Nurse Shark, p. 236.

    Ib. Origin of first dorsal fin well behind origin of pelvic fin
Page 21, figs. B, C

        1. Irregular chain-like markings on sides of body
Page 21, fig. B

        See Chain Dogfish, p. 238.

        2. No chain-like markings on sides of body
Page 21, fig. C

        See Deep-Water Cat Shark, p. 238.

II. *Origin of first dorsal fin well in front of origin of pelvic fin*
Page 21, figs. D, E

See Sand Shark, Smooth Dogfish, Other Sharks, p. 22.

*Origin of first
dorsal fin over or
behind origin of
pelvic fin*

Nurse shark

Chain dogfish

Deep-water
cat shark

*Origin of first
dorsal fin well in
front of origin of
pelvic fin*

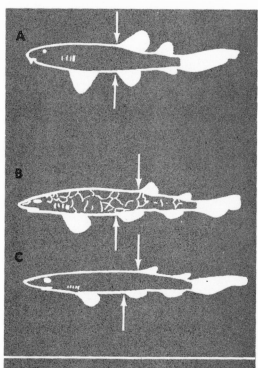
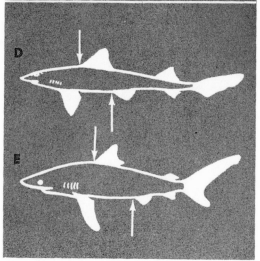

SAND SHARK, SMOOTH DOGFISH, OTHER SHARKS

I. *Rear end of base of first dorsal fin over origin of pelvic fin*
Page 23, fig. A

See Sand Shark, p. 231.

II. *Rear end of base of first dorsal fin far in front of origin of pelvic fin*
Page 23, figs. B–E

IIa. Origin of anal fin in center of base of second dorsal fin
Page 23, fig. B

See Smooth Dogfish, p. 239.

IIb. Origin of anal fin slightly behind, under, or in front of origin of second dorsal fin
Page 23, figs. C–E

See Blue, Other Sharks, p. 24.

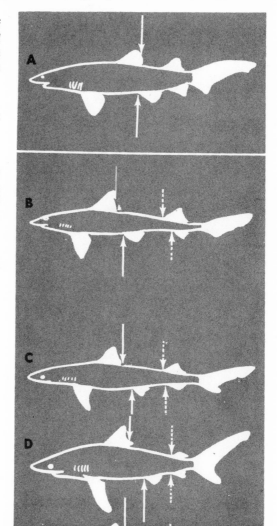

Rear end of base of first dorsal fin over origin of pelvic fin

Sand shark

Rear end of base of first dorsal fin far in front of origin of pelvic fin

Smooth dogfish

BLUE, OTHER SHARKS

I. *Long pectoral fins; length equal to distance from tip of snout to at least first gill slit*
Page 25, figs. A–D

    Ia. Origin of first dorsal fin far behind rear end of base of pectoral fin
    Page 25, fig. A

    See Blue Shark, p. 241.

    Ib. Origin of first dorsal fin over rear portion of base of pectoral fin
    Page 25, figs. B–D

    See Cub, Dusky, Brown Sharks, p. 26.

II. *Shorter pectoral fins; length less than distance from tip of snout to first gill slit*
Page 25, fig. E

See Paragaleus, Small Black-tipped, Lemon, Other Sharks, p. 28.

Long pectoral fins

Blue shark

Shorter pectoral fins

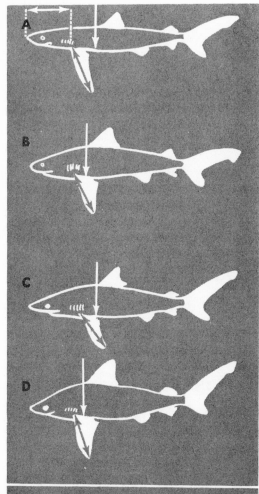

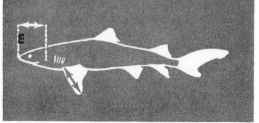

CUB, DUSKY, BROWN SHARKS

I. *Highest point of tail about on line with highest point of back*
Page 27, fig. A

See Cub Shark, p. 244.

II. *Highest point of tail much above highest point of back*
Page 27, figs. B, C

IIa. Length of front margin of first dorsal fin equal to distance from tip of snout to a point just back of eye
Page 27, fig. B

See Dusky Shark, p. 247.

IIb. Length of front margin of first dorsal fin equal to distance from tip of snout to first gill slit
Page 27, fig. C

See Brown Shark, p. 246.

*Highest point of
tail about on line
with highest point
of back*

Cub shark

*Highest point of
tail much above
highest point of
back*

Dusky shark

Brown shark

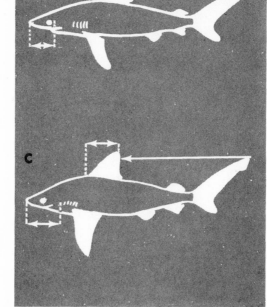

PARAGALEUS, SMALL BLACK-TIPPED, LEMON, OTHER SHARKS

I. *Length of front margin of pectoral fin equal to distance from tip of snout to a point just before first gill slit*
Page 29, figs. A–C

Ia. Base of first dorsal fin much longer than depth of head at third gill slit
Page 29, fig. A

See Paragaleus, p. 241.

Ib. Base of first dorsal fin about equal to or shorter than depth of head at third gill slit
Page 29, figs. B, C

1. Length of front margin of first dorsal fin over three times the length of front margin of second dorsal fin
Page 29, fig. B

See Small Black-tipped Shark, p. 245.

2. Length of front margin of first dorsal fin only slightly more than length of front margin of second dorsal fin
Page 29, fig. C

See Lemon Shark, p. 243.

II. *Length of front margin of pectoral fin equal to distance from tip of snout to a point about halfway between hind margin of eye and first gill slit*
Page 29, figs. D, E

See Sharp-nosed, Smooth-Tooth, Sickle-Shape Sharks, p. 30.

*Front margin of
pectoral fin equal
to distance from
tip of snout to a
point just before
first gill slit*

Paragaleus

Small black-tipped
shark

Lemon shark

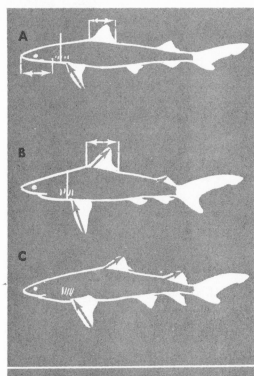

*Front margin of
pectoral fin equal to
distance from tip of
snout to point
halfway between
hind margin of eye
and first gill slit*

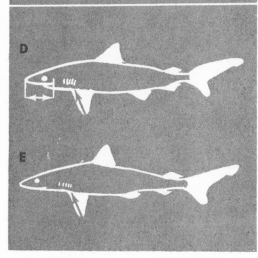

SHARP-NOSED, SMOOTH-TOOTH,
SICKLE-SHAPE SHARKS

I. *Origin of second dorsal fin about over midpoint of base of anal fin*
Page 31, fig. A

See Sharp-nosed Shark, p. 242.

II. *Origin of second dorsal fin almost directly over origin of anal fin*
Page 31, figs. B, C

IIa. Length of gill slits more than half the distance from tip of snout to front of eye
Page 31, fig. B

See Smooth-Tooth Shark, p. 243.

IIb. Length of gill slits less than half the distance from tip of snout to front of eye
Page 31, fig. C

See Sickle-Shape Shark, p. 244.

*Origin of second
dorsal over midpoint
of base of anal fin*

Sharp-nosed shark

*Origin of second
dorsal over origin of
anal fin*

Smooth-tooth shark

Sickle-shape shark

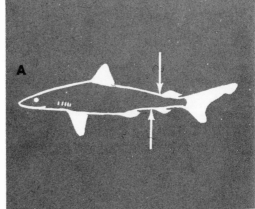

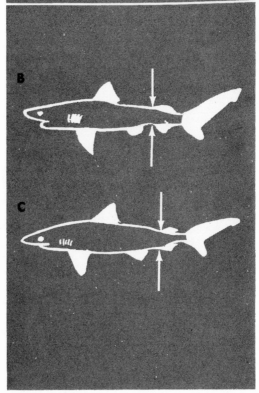

DOGFISHES

I. *Origin of second dorsal fin behind end of base of pelvic fin*
Page 33, fig. A

See Spiny Dogfish, p. 249.

II. *Origin of second dorsal fin over base of pelvic fin*
Page 33, figs. B, C

IIa. Upper margin of tail strongly arched; highest point of upper margin of tail lower than highest point of back
Page 33, fig. B

See Black Dogfish, p. 250.

IIb. Upper margin of tail concave; highest point of upper margin of tail above highest point of back
Page 33, fig. C

See Portuguese Shark, p. 251.

*Origin of second
dorsal fin behind
end of base of
pelvic fin*

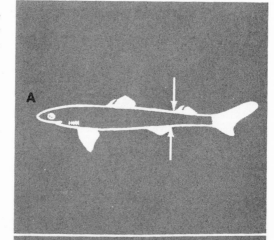

Spiny dogfish

*Origin of second
dorsal fin over base
of pelvic fin*

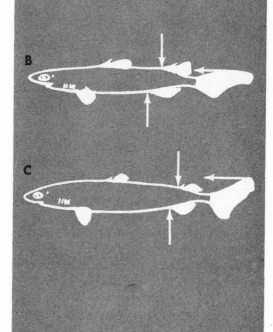

Black dogfish

Portuguese shark

TIGER, MACKEREL, WHITE SHARKS

I. *Upper lobe of tail much more than twice length of lower lobe*
Page 35, fig. A

See Tiger Shark, p. 240.

II. *Upper lobe of tail less than twice length of lower lobe*
Page 35, figs. B–D

    IIa. Caudal peduncle with a second keel below and to the rear of main keel
Page 35, fig. B

    See Mackerel Shark, p. 232.

    IIb. Caudal peduncle with only one keel
Page 35, figs. C, D

        1. Front margin of first dorsal fin longer than depth of head at first gill slit
Page 35, fig. C

        See Sharp-nosed Mackerel Shark, p. 233.

        2. Front margin of first dorsal fin about equal to depth of head at first gill slit
Page 35, fig. D

        See White Shark, p. 234.

Upper lobe of tail
much more than
twice length of
lower lobe

Tiger shark

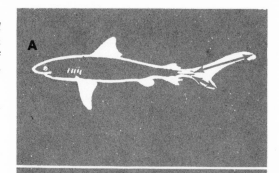

Upper lobe of tail
less than twice
length of lower lobe

Mackerel shark

Sharp-nosed
mackerel shark

White shark

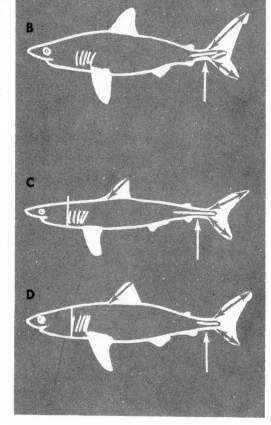

SHARKS, SAWFISH, SKATES, RAYS
TORPEDO, SKATES

I. *Long flat snout armed with teeth on each side*
Page 37, fig. A

See Common Sawfish, p. 256.

II. *No long flat snout*
Page 37, figs. B–E

IIa. Distinct notches between the head and front margins of the pectoral fin
Page 37, fig. B

See Angel Shark, p. 252.

IIb. No notches between the head and front margins of the pectoral fins
Page 37, figs. C–E

See Lesser Devil Ray, Giant Devil Ray, Other Rays, Torpedo, Skates, p. 38.

*Long flat snout
armed with teeth
on each side*

Sawfish

No long flat snout

Angel shark

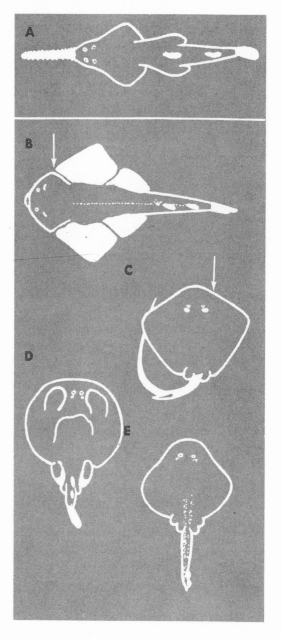

LESSER DEVIL RAY, GIANT DEVIL RAY, OTHER RAYS, TORPEDO, SKATES

I. *Two distinct fleshy lobes projecting from front of head*
Page 39, figs. A–D

Ia. Mouth on underside of head
Page 39, figs. A, B

See Lesser Devil Ray, p. 270.

Ib. Mouth extending along front of head
Page 39, figs. C, D

See Giant Devil Ray, p. 270.

II. *No fleshy lobes projecting from front of head*
Page 39, figs. E–G

See Giant Butterfly, Lesser Butterfly, Sting, Other Rays, Torpedo, Skates, p. 40.

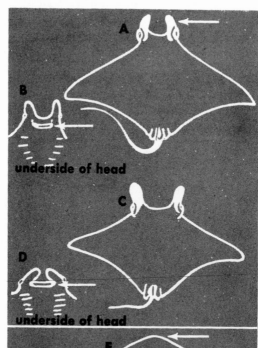

*Two distinct fleshy
lobes projecting
front of head*

Lesser devil ray

Giant devil ray

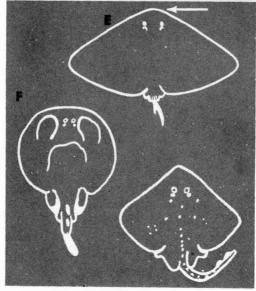

*No fleshy lobes
projecting from
front of head*

GIANT BUTTERFLY, LESSER BUTTERFLY, STING, OTHER RAYS, TORPEDO, SKATES

I. *No dorsal fin*
Page 41, fig. A

Ia. Width of body much greater than distance from tip of snout to end of tail
Page 41, figs. B, C

  1. Spine on tail
Page 41, fig. B
See Giant Butterfly Ray, p. 266.

  2. No spine on tail
Page 41, fig. C

See Lesser Butterfly Ray, p. 267.

Ib. Width of body much less than distance from tip of snout to end of tail
Page 41, fig. D

See Sting Rays, p. 50.

II. *One or two dorsal fins*
Page 41, figs. E–H

See Eagle Rays, Cow-nosed Ray, Torpedo, Skates, p. 42.

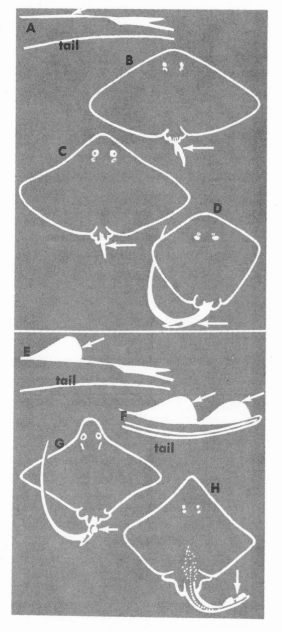

No dorsal fin

Giant butterfly ray

Lesser butterfly ray

One or two dorsal fins

EAGLE RAYS, COW-NOSED RAY,
TORPEDO, SKATES

I. *One dorsal fin*
Page 43, figs. A–D

    Ia. Snout elongated
    Page 43, figs. B, C

        1. Top surface of body covered with conspicuous spots
        Page 43, fig. B

        See Spotted Eagle Ray, p. 268.

        2. Top surface of body without conspicuous spots
        Page 43, fig. C

        See Eagle Ray, p. 267.

    Ib. Snout flat; indented at midpoint
    Page 43, fig. D

    See Cow-nosed Ray, p. 269.

II. *Two dorsal fins*
Page 43, figs. E–G

See Torpedo Ray, Barn-Door, Other Skates, p. 44.

One dorsal fin

Spotted eagle ray

Eagle ray

Cow-nosed ray

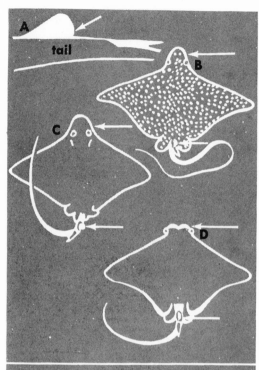

Two dorsal fins

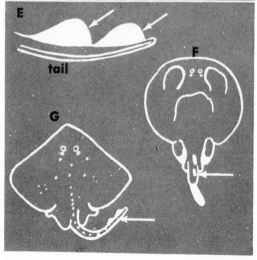

TORPEDO RAY, BARN-DOOR, OTHER SKATES

I. *Caudal fin large; depth much greater than height of dorsal fins*
Page 45, figs. A, B

See Torpedo, p. 257.

II. *Caudal fin very small or absent; when present, depth much less than height of dorsal fins*
Page 45, fig. C

IIa. Pores on undersurface of body marked by black lines or dots
Page 45, figs. D, E

See Barn-Door Skate, p. 260.

IIb. Pores on undersurface of body without black lines or dots
Page 45, fig. F

See Smooth-tailed, Rosetted, Other Skates, p. 46.

Caudal fin large

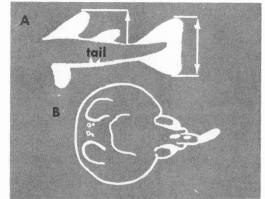

Torpedo

Caudal fin very
small or absent

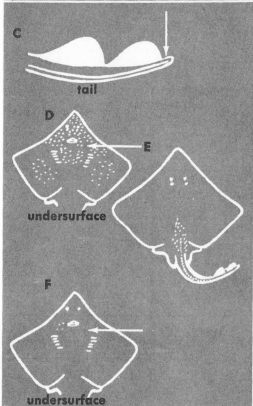

Barn-door skate

SMOOTH-TAILED, ROSETTED, OTHER SKATES

I. *No thorn-like spines on rear third or quarter of upper surface of tail*
Page 47, fig. A

See Smooth-tailed Skate, p. 263.

II. *One or more rows of thorn-like spines on entire upper surface of tail*
Page 47, figs. C–E

IIa. Conspicuous dark rosettes on upper surface of body
Page 47, figs. B, C

See Rosetted Skate, p. 260.

IIb. No conspicuous dark rosettes on upper surface of body (dots and blotches may be present)
Page 47, figs. D, E

See Thorny, Clear-nosed, Little, Big Skates, p. 48.

No thorn-like spines on rear portion of upper surface of tail

Smooth-tailed skate

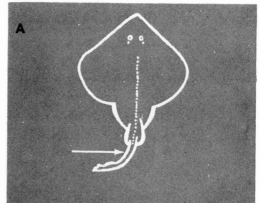

One or more rows of thorn-like spines on entire upper surface of tail

Rosetted skate

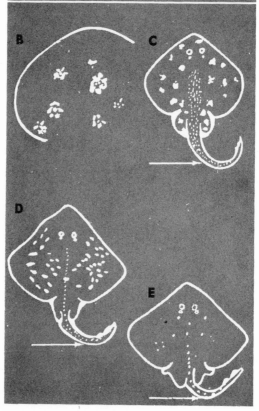

THORNY, CLEAR-NOSED, LITTLE, BIG SKATES

I. *A single row of thorn-like spines along the middle of the back*
Page 49, figs. A–C

    Ia. Mid-row thorns on tail considerably larger than other thorns on tail
Page 49, figs. A, B

    See Thorny Skate, p. 262.

    Ib. Mid-row thorns on tail about same size as other thorns on tail
Page 49, figs. C, D

    See Clear-nosed Skate, p. 258.

II. *More than one row of thorn-like spines along the middle of the back*
Page 49, figs. F, G

    IIa. Never more than 66 rows of teeth in upper jaw
Page 49, figs. E, F

    See Little Skate, p. 259.

    IIb. Never less than 80 rows of teeth in upper jaw
Page 49, figs. E–G

    See Big Skate, p. 261.

Single row of spines along middle of back

Thorny skate

Clear-nosed skate

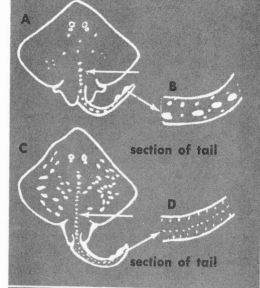

More than one row of spines along middle of back

Little skate

Big skate

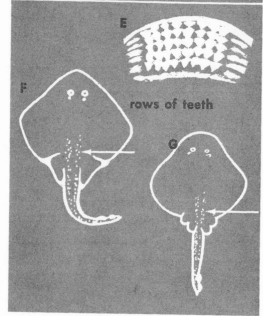

STING RAYS

I. *Outermost edge of pectoral fins broadly rounded*
Page 51, figs. A, B

Ia. Distance between spiracles equal to distance from
tip of snout to a point between the two eyes
Page 51, fig. A

See Say's Sting Ray, p. 265.

Ib. Distance between spiracles equal to distance from
tip of snout to a point well before eyes
Page 51, fig. B

See Stingaree, p. 265.

II. *Outermost edge of pectoral fins more angular*
Page 51, figs. C, D

IIa. Greatest diameter of orbit of eye much less than
length of spiracle
Page 51, fig. C

See Northern Sting Ray, p. 264.

IIb. Greatest diameter of orbit of eye equal to or
larger than length of spiracle
Page 51, fig. D

See Southern Sting Ray, p. 263.

Outermost edge of pectoral fins broadly rounded

Say's sting ray

Stingaree

Outermost edge of pectoral fins more angular

Northern sting ray

Southern sting ray

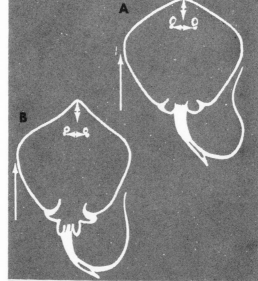
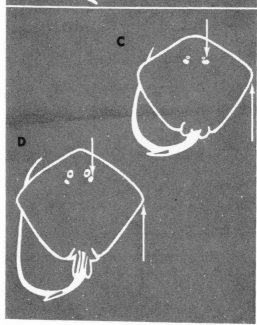

I. *Suction plate on top of head*
   Page 53, figs. A–E

   See Remoras, p. 100.

II. *No suction plate on top of head*

   See HEAD—TRUE FISHES, p. 54.

*Suction plate on
top of head*

Remoras

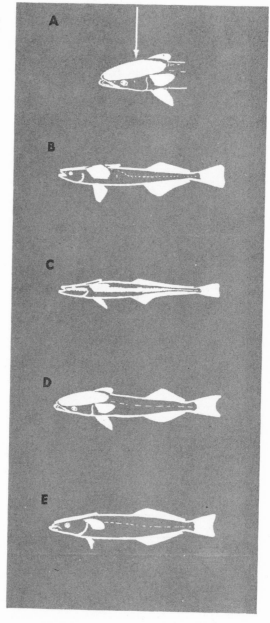

I. *Head horse-shaped*
  Page 55, figs. A, B

See Northern Sea Horse, p. 340.

II. *Head not horse-shaped*

See HEAD—TRUE FISHES, p. 56.

Horse-shaped head

Northern sea horse

I. *Snout tubular*
Page 57, figs. A, B

Ia. Tail fin rounded
Page 57, figs. C–E

See Pipefishes, p. 108.

Ib. Tail fin forked; long filament at center
Page 57, figs. F, G

See Trumpet Fish, p. 341.

II. *Snout not tubular*

See HEAD—TRUE FISHES, p. 58.

Tubular snout

Rounded tail fin

Pipefishes

Forked tail fin

Trumpet fish

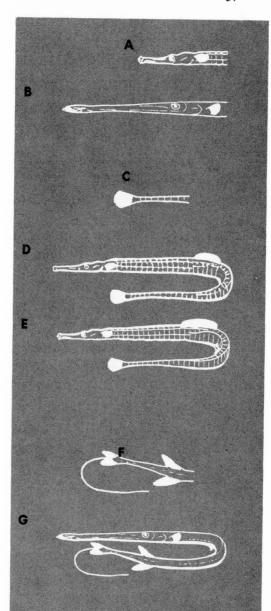

I. *One or both jaws elongated*
Page 59, figs. A–K

Ia. Both jaws elongated
Page 59, figs. A–D

See Needlefish, Billfishes, p. 102.

Ib. Only one jaw, upper or lower elongated
Page 59, figs. E–G, H–K

See HEAD—TRUE FISHES, p. 60.

II. *Jaws not elongated*

See HEAD—TRUE FISHES, p. 62.

Both jaws elongated

One jaw elongated

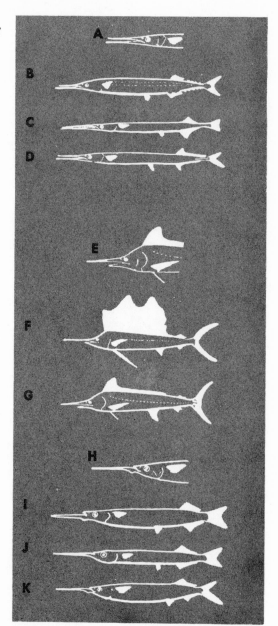

I. *Only upper jaw elongated*
   Page 61, figs. A–E

See Swordfish, Sailfish, Marlins, p. 104.

II. *Only lower jaw elongated*
    Page 61, figs. F–J

See Halfbeaks, p. 106.

Upper jaw elongated

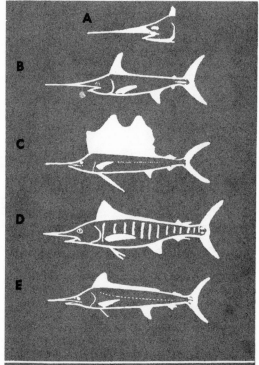

Lower jaw elongated

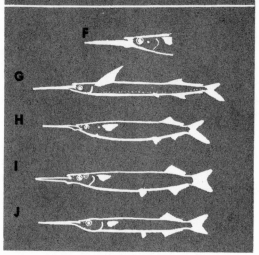

I. *Long ray, fleshy lobe, spine, or several spines on top of head*
Page 63, figs. A–E

Ia. Body flattened, wider than deep
Page 63, fig. A

See American Goosefish, p. 413.

Ib. Body not flattened, deeper than wide
Page 63, figs. B–E

See HEAD—TRUE FISHES, p. 64.

II. *No long ray, fleshy lobe, spine, or series of spines on top of head*

See TAIL REGION—TRUE FISHES, p. 66.

Ray, lobe, spine on head

Body flattened

American goosefish

Body not flattened

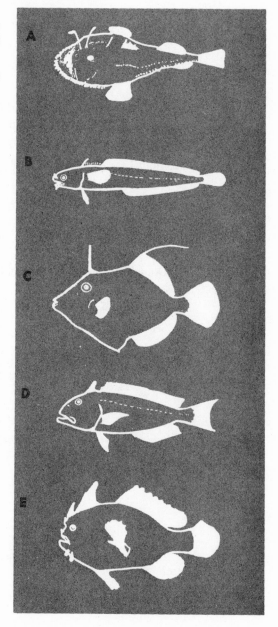

I. *Only one long ray, spine, or fleshy lobe on top of head*
Page 65, figs. A–C

Ia. A single ray on top of head followed by a series
of short hair-like rays continuing to the dorsal fin
Page 65, fig. A

See Four-bearded Rockling, p. 321.

Ib. A single spine or fleshy lobe on top of head, no
short hair-like rays following
Page 65, figs. B, C

1. Dorsal fin short, less than half the length of the
body
Page 65, fig. B

See Filefishes, p. 110.

2. Dorsal fin long, much more than half the length
of the body
Page 65, fig. C

See Tilefish, p. 385.

II. *More than one spine on top of head*
Page 65, fig. D

See Sargassum Fish, p. 414.

*One ray, spine, lobe
on top of head*

Four-bearded
rockling

Filefishes

Tilefish

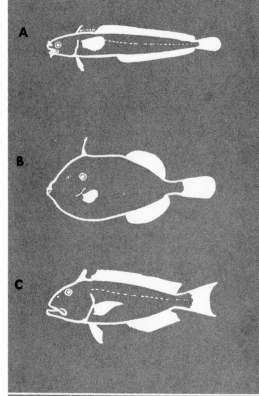

*More than one spine
on top of head*

Sargassum fish

I. *Tail whip-like, no caudal fin*
Page 67, figs. A, B

See Cutlass Fish, p. 350.

II. *Tail not whip-like, caudal fin present*
Page 67, figs. C–K

IIa. Caudal fin continuous with dorsal and anal fins
Page 67, figs. C–J

See TAIL REGION—TRUE FISHES, p. 68.

IIb. Caudal fin separated from dorsal and anal fins
Page 67, fig. K

See TAIL REGION—TRUE FISHES, p. 72.

Tail whip-like, no caudal fin

Cutlass fish

Tail not whip-like, caudal fin present

Caudal fin continuous with dorsal and anal fins

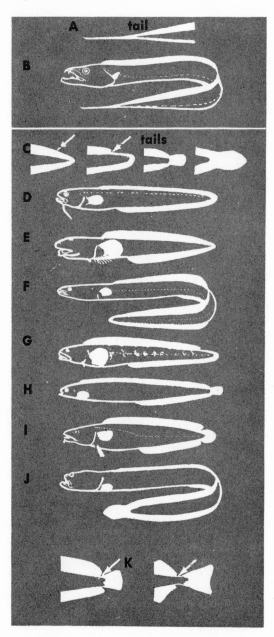

Caudal fin separated from dorsal and anal fins

I. *No notches between caudal fin and dorsal and anal fins*
Page 69, figs. A–E

See Cusk Eel, Arctic Eelpout, Tonguefish, American Eel, American Conger Eel, p. 116.

II. *Notch between caudal and dorsal fins or between caudal fin and both dorsal and anal fins*
Page 69, figs. F–J

See TAIL REGION—TRUE FISHES, p. 70.

No notches between caudal fin and dorsal and anal fins

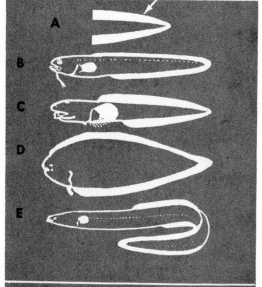

Notch between caudal and dorsal fins or between caudal fin and both dorsal and anal fins

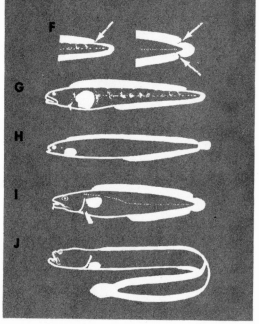

I. *Notch only between caudal and dorsal fin*
   Page 71, fig. A

See American Ocean Pout, p. 403.

II. *Notch between caudal fin and both dorsal and anal fins*
   Page 71, figs. B–D

See Rock Eel, Wrymouth, Cusk, p. 108.

Notch only between caudal and dorsal fins

American ocean pout

Notch between caudal fin and both dorsal and anal fins

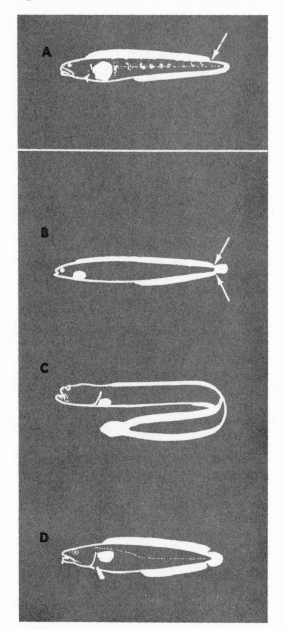

I. *Caudal fin consists of two lobes of unequal lengths*
Page 73, figs. A–D

Ia. Upper lobe of caudal fin longer than lower lobe
Page 73, figs. A–C

See Sturgeons, Sea Catfishes, Pigfish, p. 112.

Ib. Upper lobe of caudal fin shorter than lower lobe
Page 73, fig. D

See Flying Fishes, p. 114.

II. *Caudal fin consists of two lobes of equal length or of only one lobe*
Page 73, fig. E

See TAIL REGION—TRUE FISHES, p. 74.

*Caudal fin consists
of two lobes of
unequal length*

*Upper lobe longer
than lower lobe*

*Upper lobe shorter
than lower lobe*

*Caudal fin consists
of two lobes of equal
length or of only
one lobe*

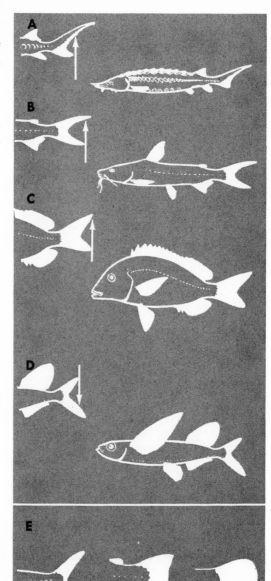

I. *Many small fins between the dorsal and caudal fins*
   Page 75, figs. A–E

See TAIL REGION—TRUE FISHES, p. 78.

II. *Only one, or no small fins between the dorsal and*
    caudal fins
    Page 75, figs. F–H

See TAIL REGION—TRUE FISHES, p. 76.

*Many small fins
between the dorsal
and caudal fins*

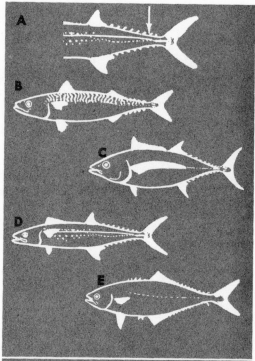

*Only one or no
small fins between
the dorsal and
caudal fins*

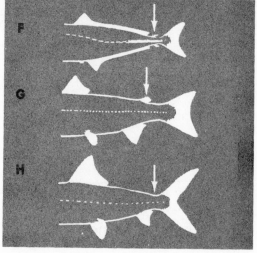

I. *One small fin between the dorsal and caudal fins*
Page 77, figs. A–G

    Ia. One small fin between the anal and caudal fins
    Page 77, figs. A–C

    See Round Scad. Mackerel Scad, p. 126.

    Ib. No small fin between the anal and caudal fins
    Page 77, figs. D–G

    See Smelt, Trout, Salmon, Lizard Fish, p. 124.

II. *No small fin between the dorsal and caudal fins*
Page 77, fig. H

See TAIL REGION—TRUE FISHES, p. 80.

One small fin between the dorsal and caudal fins

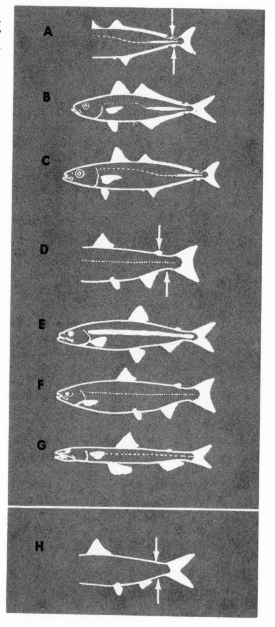

No small fin between the dorsal and caudal fins

I. *Keels on each side of the body near the tail, on the caudal peduncle*
Page 79, figs. A–F

Ia. No median keel; two keels, one above and the other below the center of the caudal peduncle; tail forked
Page 79, figs. A–C

See Mackerels, p. 126.

Ib. Median keel present; two other keels also present, one above and the other below the center of the caudal peduncle; tail crescent-shaped
Page 79, figs. D–F

See Frigate Mackerel, Bonito, Tunas, Spanish Mackerel, p. 118.

II. *No keels on each side of the body near the tail, on the caudal peduncle*
Page 79, figs. G, H

See Leatherjacket, p. 363.

Keels on caudal peduncle

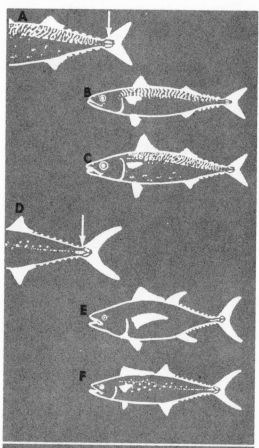

No keels on caudal peduncle

Leatherjacket

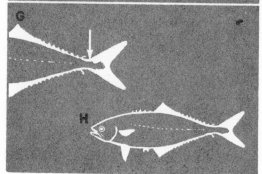

I. *Median keel on each side of the caudal peduncle*
Page 81, figs. A–F

See Amber Jack, Rudderfish, Pilot Fish, Three-spined Stickleback, Nine-spined Stickleback, p. 128.

II. *No median keel on each side of the caudal peduncle*
Page 81, fig. G

See TAIL REGION—TRUE FISHES, p. 82.

*Median keel on
caudal peduncle*

*No keel on
caudal peduncle*

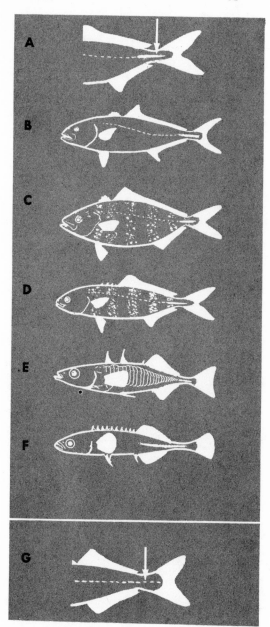

I. *Small bony shields centrally located on the caudal peduncle on each side of the body*
Page 83, figs. A–F

See Scads, Jacks, p. 130.

II. *No small bony shields centrally located on the caudal peduncle on each side of the body*
Page 83, fig. G

See DORSAL FINS—TRUE FISHES, p. 84.

Small bony shields on caudal peduncle

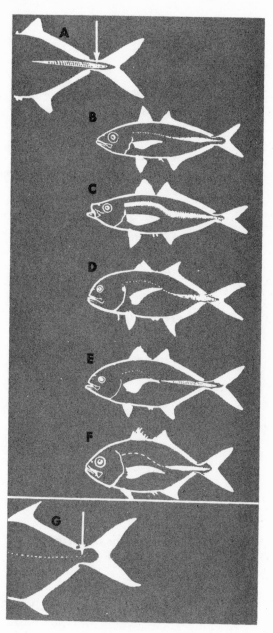

No small bony shields on caudal peduncle

I. *One dorsal fin, with or without a series of separate spines before it*
Page 85, figs. A–E

See DORSAL FINS—TRUE FISHES, p. 86.

II. *More than one dorsal fin*
Page 85, figs. F–H

See DORSAL FINS—TRUE FISHES, p. 94.

One dorsal fin, with or without separate spines before it

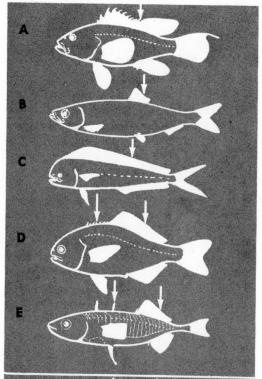

More than one dorsal fin

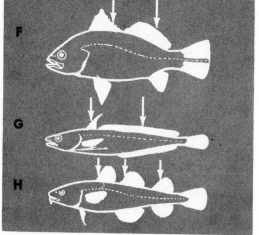

I. *Separate spines before the single dorsal fin*
    Page 87, figs. A–H

See Threadfish, Butterfish, Harvest Fish, Other, p. 188.

II. *No separate spines before the single dorsal fin*
     Page 89, figs. A–F

See DORSAL FINS—TRUE FISHES, p. 88.

*Separate spines
before single
dorsal fin*

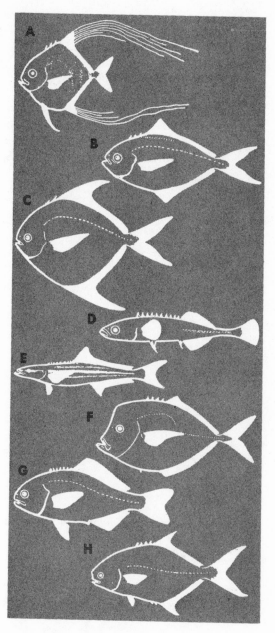

I. *Short dorsal fin; length of base about same as length of head or less*
Page 89, figs. A–C

See DORSAL FINS—TRUE FISHES, p. 90.

II. *Long dorsal fin; length of base much greater than length of head*
Page 89, figs. D–F

See Hogchoker, Flounders, Sand Launces, Other, p. 158.

Short dorsal fin

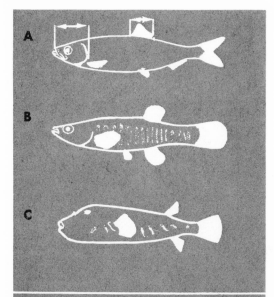

Long dorsal fin

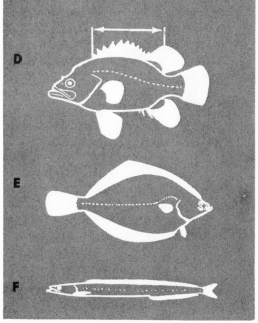

I. *Origin of dorsal fin near center of body*
Page 91, figs. A–D

See DORSAL FIN—TRUE FISHES, p. 92.

II. *Origin of dorsal fin near rear part of body*
Page 91, figs. E–I

See Trunkfishes, Lumpfish, Clingfish, Swellfishes, Box-fish, Porcupine Fish, p. 152.

Origin of dorsal fin near center of body

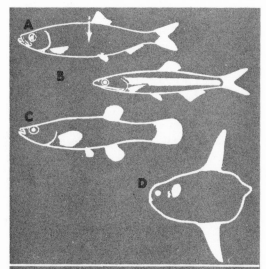

Origin of dorsal fin near rear part of body

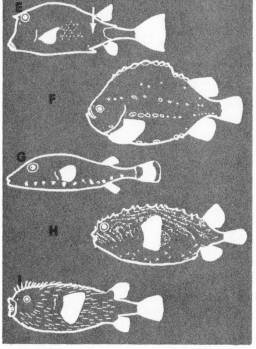

I. *Last ray of dorsal fin prolonged in a filament*
Page 93, figs. A–C

Ia. Mouth large; upper jaw reaches to well behind eye
Page 93, fig. A

See Tarpon, p. 286.

Ib. Mouth small; upper jaw reaches at most to front
portion of eye
Page 93, figs. B, C

1. Base length of anal fin much shorter than head
Page 93, fig. B

See Thread Herring, p. 292.

2. Base length of anal fin much longer than head
Page 93, fig. C

See Gizzard Shad, p. 294.

II. *Last ray of dorsal fin not prolonged in a filament*
Page 93, figs. D, E

See Ocean Sunfishes, Herrings, Anchovies, Killifishes,
Other, p. 132.

Last ray of dorsal fin a long filament

Tarpon

Thread herring

Gizzard shad

Last ray of dorsal fin not a long filament

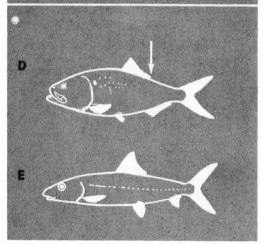

I. *Two dorsal fins*
Page 95, figs. A–E

See DORSAL FINS—TRUE FISHES, p. 96.

II. *Three dorsal fins*
Page 95, figs. F–H

See Haddock, Pollock, Cod, Tomcod, p. 98.

Two dorsal fins

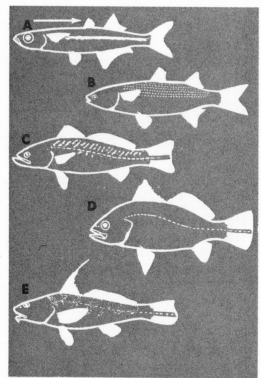

Three dorsal fins

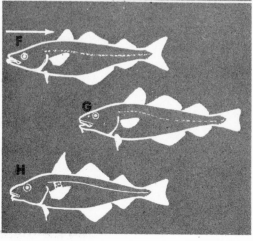

I. *Two dorsal fins separated by a space at least half the length of base of second dorsal fin*
Page 97, figs. A–D

See Goatfish, Barracudas, Silversides, Mullets, p. 196.

II. *Two dorsal fins separated by a space much less than half the length of base of second dorsal fin*
Page 97, figs. E, F

See Croakers, Drums, Other, p. 200.

Two dorsal fins separated by space at least half the length of base of second dorsal fin

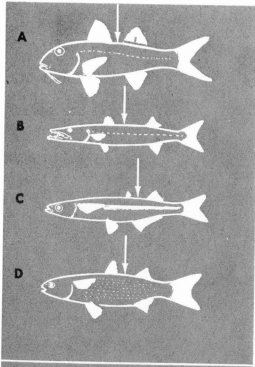

Two dorsal fins separated by space less than half the length of base of second dorsal fin

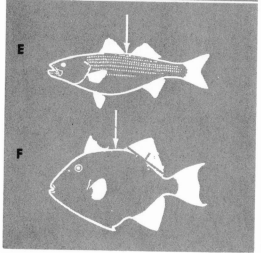

HADDOCK, POLLOCK, COD, TOMCOD

I. *Lateral line black; a dusky spot on body over pectoral fin*
Page 99, fig. A

See Haddock, p. 316.

II. *Lateral line not black; no dusky spot on body over pectoral fin*
Page 99, figs. C, E, F

IIa. Tip of lower jaw extends beyond tip of upper jaw; chin barbel, if present, very small
Page 99, figs. B, C

See Pollock, p. 317.

IIb. Tip of upper jaw extends beyond tip of lower jaw; conspicuous chin barbel
Page 99, figs. D–F

1. Filament of pelvic fin less than one-fourth the total length of the fin
Page 99, fig. E

See Cod, p. 315.

2. Filament of pelvic fin about half the total length of the fin
Page 99, fig. F

See Tomcod, p. 318.

Lateral line black

Haddock

Lateral line not black

Pollock

Cod

Tomcod

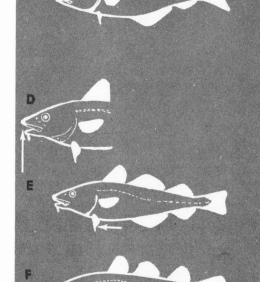

REMORAS

I. *Sucking plate large, more than twice length of head. Plate extends beyond tip of snout*
Page 101, figs. A, B

See Spearfish Remora, p. 397.

II. *Sucking plate small, less than twice length of head. Plate does not extend beyond tip of snout*
Page 101, figs. C–F

IIa. A conspicuous, longitudinal, sooty-brown stripe with white edges on each side of body
Page 101, fig. D

See Shark Remora, p. 396.

IIb. No stripes on sides
Page 101, figs. E, F

1. Head plate longer than base of dorsal fin
Page 101, fig. E

See Offshore Remora, p. 396.

2. Head plate shorter than base of dorsal fin
Page 101, fig. F

See Swordfish Remora, p. 396.

Large sucking plate

Spearfish remora

Small sucking plate

Shark remora

Offshore remora

Swordfish remora

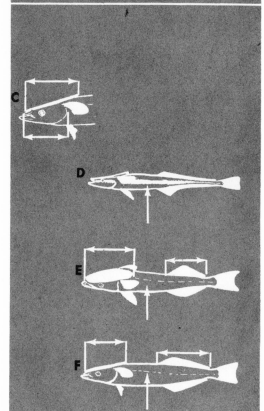

NEEDLEFISH, BILLFISHES

I. *A series of small fins between dorsal and anal fins*
Page 103, fig. A

See Needlefish, p. 312.

II. *No small fins between dorsal and anal fins*
Page 103, figs. C, E, F

IIa. Body less than one-half as thick as it is deep
Page 103, figs. B, C

See Flat Billfish, p. 310.

IIb. Body as thick as it is deep
Page 103, figs. D–F

1. Caudal fin only slightly concave
Page 103, fig. E

See Billfish, p. 309.

2. Caudal fin deeply forked
Page 103, fig. F

See Agujon, p. 309.

Series of small fins between dorsal and anal fins

Needlefish

No small fins between dorsal and anal fins

Flat billfish

Billfish

Agujon

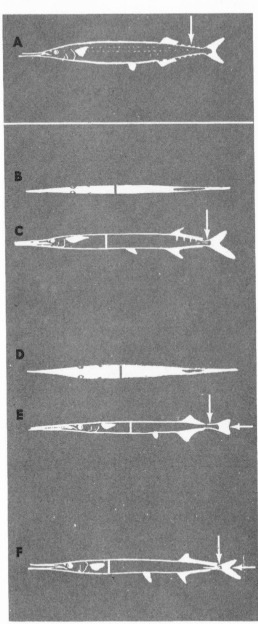

SWORDFISH, SAILFISH, MARLINS

I. *First dorsal fin short; base of fin shorter than distance from tip of sword to rear edge of gill slit*
Page 105, fig. A

See Swordfish, p. 352.

II. *First dorsal fin long; base of fin longer than distance from tip of sword to rear edge of gill slit*
Page 105, figs. B–D

IIa. Height of first dorsal fin much greater than depth of body
Page 105, fig. B

See Atlantic Sailfish, p. 352.

IIb. Height of first dorsal fin less than depth of body
Page 105, figs. C, D

1. First dorsal fin pointed at apex; lateral line not visible
Page 105, fig. C

See Blue Marlin, p. 350.

2. First dorsal fin rounded at apex; lateral line conspicuous
Page 105, fig. D

See White Marlin, p. 351.

Short first dorsal fin

Swordfish

Long first dorsal fin

Atlantic sailfish

Blue marlin

White marlin

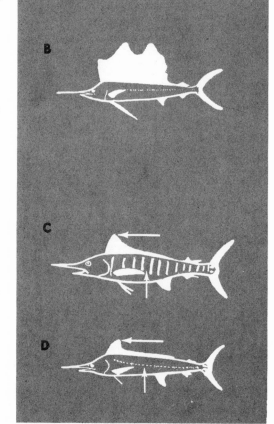
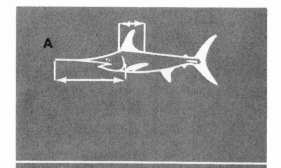

HALFBEAKS

I. *Pectoral fins longer than distance from tip of snout to rear edge of operculum*
Page 107, fig. A

See Flying Halfbeak, p. 311.

II. *Pectoral fins shorter than distance from tip of snout to rear edge of operculum*
Page 107, figs. B–D

IIa. Pelvic fins located just before dorsal fin
Page 107, fig. B

See Balao, p. 311.

IIb. Pelvic fins located far in front of dorsal fin
Page 107, figs. C, D

1. Body deep; depth about one-sixth the distance from tip of upper jaw to base of tail
Page 107, fig. C

See Halfbeak, p. 310.

2. Body slender; depth about one-eighth the distance from tip of upper jaw to base of tail
Page 107, fig. D

See Pajarito, p. 311.

Long pectoral fins

A

Flying halfbeak

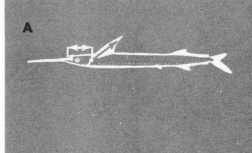

Short pectoral fins

B

Balao

C

Halfbeak

D

Pajarito

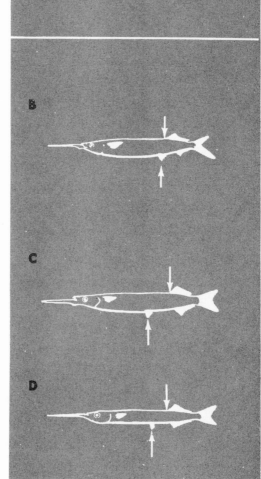

PIPEFISHES

I. *Snout short; half or less length of head*
Page 109, figs. A, B

See Northern Pipefish, p. 339.

II. *Snout long; more than half length of head*
Page 109, figs. C, D

See Florida Pipefish, p. 340.

ROCK EEL, WRYMOUTH, CUSK

I. *Pelvic fins absent*
Page 109, figs. E, F

Ia. Head small; about equal to depth of body
Page 109, fig. E

See Rock Eel, p. 400.

Ib. Head larger; about twice the depth of the body
Page 109, fig. F

See Wrymouth, p. 401.

II. *Pelvic fins present*
Page 109, fig. G

See Cusk, p. 321.

Snout short

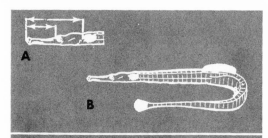

A

Northern pipefish

B

Snout long

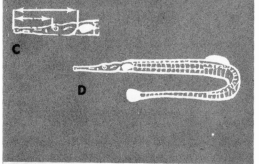

C

Florida pipefish

D

Pelvic fins absent

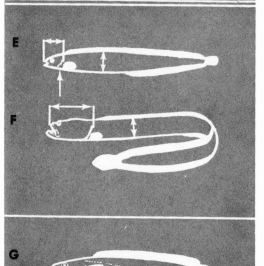

E

Rock eel

F

Wrymouth

Pelvic fins present

G

Cusk

FILEFISHES

I. *Small spine on ventral flap; gill slits nearly vertical*
Page 111, figs. A, B

    Ia. Ventral flap well developed; extends beyond the ventral spine
Page 111, fig. A

    See Fringed Filefish, p. 407.

    Ib. Ventral flap small; does not reach beyond the ventral spine
Page 111, fig. B

    See Common Filefish, p. 406.

II. *No spine on ventral flap; gill slits oblique*
Page 111, figs. C, D

    IIa. Length of base of dorsal fin greater than distance from origin of dorsal spine to origin of dorsal fin
Page 111, fig. C

    See Unicorn Filefish, p. 408.

    IIb. Length of base of dorsal fin about equal to distance from origin of dorsal spine to origin of dorsal fin
Page 111, fig. D

    See Orange Filefish, p. 407.

*Small spine on
ventral flap*

Fringed filefish

Common filefish

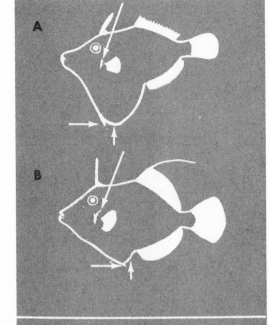

*No spine on
ventral flap*

Unicorn filefish

Orange filefish

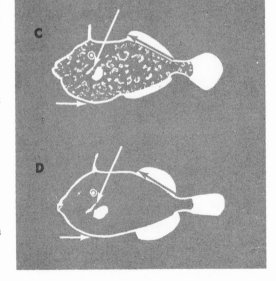

STURGEONS, SEA CATFISHES, PIGFISH

I. *Barbels on mouth*
Page 113, figs. A–D

    Ia. Bony plates on various parts of the body
    Page 113, figs. A, B

        1. Plates on back touching or overlapping
        Page 113, fig. A

        See Common Sturgeon, p. 284.

        2. Plates on back separated from each other
        Page 113, fig. B

        See Short-nosed Sturgeon, p. 285.

    Ib. No bony plates on body; skin naked
    Page 113, figs. C, D

        1. Lower jaw with a single barbel on each side of head; barbels on upper jaw flat and much longer than head
        Page 113, fig. C

        See Gaff-Topsail Catfish, p. 299.

        2. Lower jaw with two barbels on each side of head; barbels on upper jaw round and shorter than head
        Page 113, fig. D

        See Sea Catfish, p. 299.

II. *No barbels on mouth*
Page 113, fig. E

See Pigfish, p. 371.

Barbels on mouth

Common sturgeon

Short-nosed sturgeon

Gaff-topsail
catfish

Sea catfish

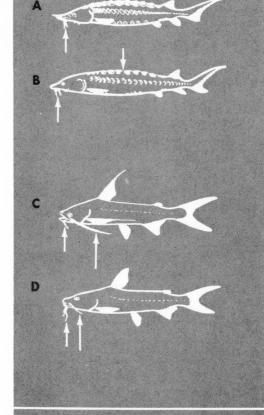

*No barbels
on mouth*

Pigfish

FLYING FISHES

I. *Pectoral fins long; reach beyond rear part of base of dorsal fin*
Page 115, fig. A

See Atlantic Flying Fish, p. 312.

II. *Pectoral fins shorter; do not reach as far as rear part of base of dorsal fin*
Page 115, figs. B, C

IIa. Dorsal fin directly over anal fin; base length of two fins almost equal
Page 115, fig. B

See Short-winged Flying Fish, p. 313.

IIb. Dorsal fin more forward on body than anal fin; base length of dorsal fin over twice that of anal fin
Page 115, fig. C

See Spot-Fin Flying Fish, p. 313.

Long pectoral fins

Atlantic flying fish

Short pectoral fins

Short-winged
flying fish

Spot-fin
flying fish

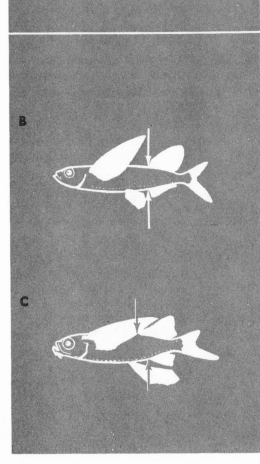

CUSK EEL, ARCTIC EELPOUT, TONGUEFISH, AMERICAN EEL, AMERICAN CONGER EEL

I. *Pelvic fins present*
Page 117, figs. A–C

    Ia. Pelvic fins attached at throat beneath eyes; each fin consists of a single barbel split at the end into two filaments
Page 117, fig. A

    See Margined Cusk Eel, p. 404.

    Ib. Pelvic fins attached at throat far behind eyes, in front of lower rear margin of operculum
Page 117, figs. B, C

        1. One eye on each side of head; body rounded
Page 117, fig. B

        See Reticulated Eelpout, p. 404.

        2. Both eyes on same side of head; body flattened
Page 117, fig. C

        See Tonguefish, p. 330.

II. *Pelvic fins absent*
Page 117, figs. D, E

    IIa. Origin of dorsal fin far behind pectoral fin
Page 117, fig. D

    See American Eel, p. 300.

    IIb. Origin of dorsal fin immediately behind rear edges of pectoral fins
Page 117, fig. E

    See American Conger Eel, p. 301.

Pelvic fins present

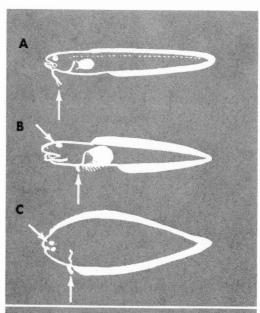

Margined cusk eel

Reticulated eel-
pout

Tonguefish

Pelvic fins absent

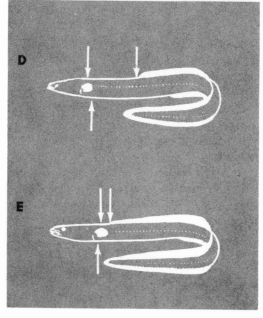

American eel

American
conger eel

FRIGATE MACKEREL, BONITO, TUNAS, SPANISH MACKEREL

I. *Two dorsal fins far apart; space between more than half length of head*
Page 119, fig. A

See Frigate Mackerel, p. 344.

II. *Two dorsal fins close together; space between much less than half length of head*
Page 119, figs. B–F

IIa. No scales on rear part of body below lateral line
Page 119, figs. B, C

1. Lateral line with a distinct downward curve under second dorsal fin; four to six longitudinal stripes on side of body below lateral line
Page 119, fig. B

See Ocean Bonito, p. 345.

2. Lateral line without a distinct curve; dark, wavy, longitudinal bands in varied patterns above lateral line
Page 119, fig. C

See Little Tuna, p. 345.

IIb. Scales on entire body
Page 119, figs. D–F

See Tunas, Bonito, Spanish Mackerel, p. 120.

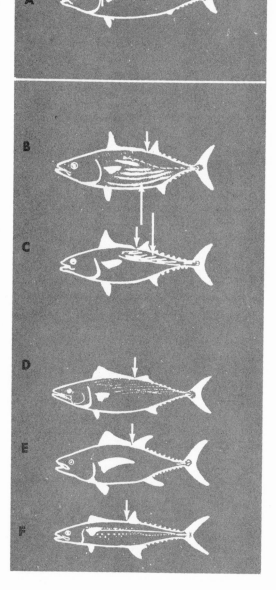

*Two dorsal
fins far apart*

Frigate mackerel

*Two dorsal fins
close together*

Ocean bonito

Little tuna

TUNAS, BONITO, SPANISH MACKEREL

I. *Pectoral fin much longer than head*
Page 121, figs. A, B

    Ia. Longest rays of second dorsal fin shorter than head
        Page 121, fig. A

        See Albacore, p. 348.

    Ib. Longest rays of second dorsal fin much longer than
        head
        Page 121, fig. B

        See Yellowfin Tuna, p. 347.

II. *Pectoral fin about equal to or shorter than head*
Page 121, figs. C–E

    IIa. Horizontal black stripes on upper portion of sides
        of body
        Page 121, fig. C

        See Common Bonito, p. 344.

    IIb. No horizontal black stripes on upper portion of
        sides of body
        Page 121, figs. D, E

        See Tunas, Cavalla, King Mackerel, Spanish
        Mackerel, p. 122.

*Pectoral fin longer
than head*

Albacore

*Pectoral fin shorter
than head*

Common bonito

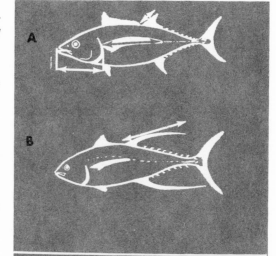
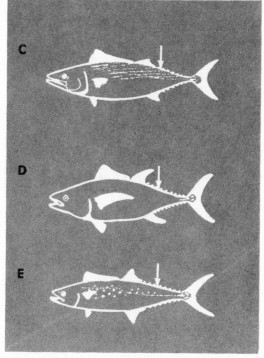

TUNAS, KING MACKEREL, CERO
SPANISH MACKEREL

I. *Base of first dorsal fin shorter than head*
   Page 123, figs. A, B

   Ia. Pectoral fin reaches to at least the origin of second dorsal fin
   Page 123, fig. A

   See Blackfin Tuna, p. 347.

   Ib. Pectoral fin reaches to at most the rear portion of first dorsal fin
   Page 123, fig. B

   See Bluefin Tuna, p. 346.

II. *Base of first dorsal fin longer than head*
   Page 123, figs. C–E

   IIa. Lateral line dips sharply under second dorsal fin
   Page 123, fig. C

   See King Mackerel, p. 349.

   IIb. Lateral line descends gradually under second dorsal fin
   Page 123, figs. D, E

      1. Origin of pelvic fins below origin of first dorsal fin; side with one or two longitudinal dark stripes
      Page 123, fig. D

      See Cero, p. 349.

      2. Origin of pelvic fins behind origin of first dorsal fin; no longitudinal dark stripes on sides
      Page 123, fig. E

      See Spanish Mackerel, p. 348.

Base of first dorsal fin shorter than head

Blackfin tuna

Bluefin tuna

Base of first dorsal fin longer than head

King mackerel

Cero

Spanish mackerel

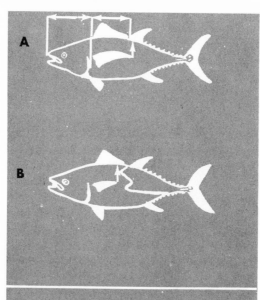
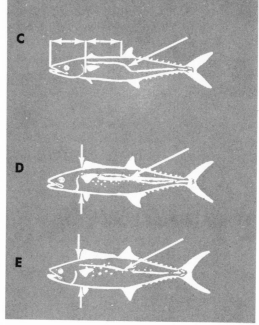

SMELT, TROUT, SALMON, LIZARD FISH

I. *Origin of pelvic fins about in center of body*
Page 125, figs. A–C

    Ia. Origin of pelvic fins under origin of dorsal fin
    Page 125, fig. A

    See Smelt, p. 297.

    Ib. Origin of pelvic fins well behind origin of dorsal fin
    Page 125, figs. B, C

        1. Origin of pelvic fins under center of base of dorsal fin
        Page 125, fig. B

        See Rainbow Trout, p. 297.

        2. Origin of pelvic fins under end of base of dorsal fin
        Page 125, fig. C

        See Atlantic Salmon, p. 296.

II. *Origin of pelvic fins far in front of center of body*
Page 125, fig. D

See Lizard Fish, p. 302.

Origin of pelvic fins about in center of body

Smelt

Rainbow trout

Atlantic salmon

Origin of pelvic fins far in front of center of body

Lizard fish

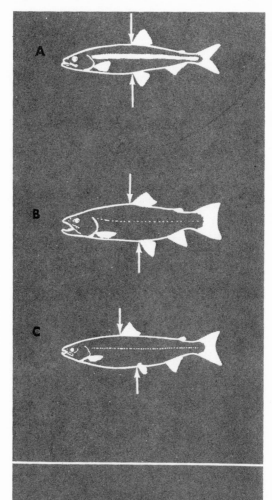

MACKERELS

I. *Sides of body below lateral line have many light spots*
Page 127, fig. A

See Chub Mackerel, p. 343.

II. *Sides of body below lateral line have no spots*
Page 127, fig. B

See Common Mackerel, p. 342.

ROUND SCAD, MACKEREL SCAD

I. *Shields on lateral line start under front part of second dorsal fin*
Page 127, fig. C

See Round Scad, p. 356.

II. *Shields on lateral line start under rear part of second dorsal fin*
Page 127, fig. D

See Mackerel Scad, p. 357.

Spots on lower sides of body

Chub mackerel

No spots on lower sides of body

Common mackerel

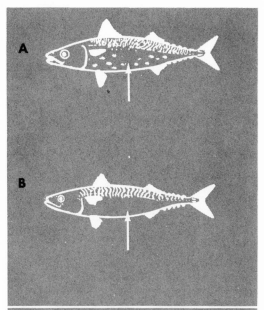

Lateral line shields start under front of second dorsal fin

Round scad

Lateral line shields start under rear of second dorsal fin

Mackerel scad

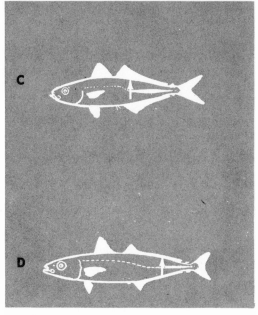

AMBER JACK, BANDED RUDDER FISH,
PILOT FISH, THREE-SPINED STICKLEBACK,
NINE-SPINED STICKLEBACK

I. *Two dorsal fins*
Page 129, figs. A, B

   Ia. Origin of anal fin well in front of center of base
of second dorsal fin
Page 129, fig. A

     See Amber Jack, p. 362.

   Ib. Origin of anal fin at or behind center of base of
second dorsal fin
Page 129, fig. B

     See Banded Rudder Fish, p. 361.

II. *A single dorsal fin preceded by a series of free spines*
Page 129, figs. C–E

   IIa. Base of dorsal fin much longer than head
Page 129, fig. C

     See Pilot Fish, p. 362.

   IIb. Base of dorsal fin about equal to head
Page 129, figs. D, E

     1. Usually three spines before dorsal fin; some-
times four or five
Page 129, fig. D

       See Three-spined Stickleback, p. 337.

     2. Usually nine spines before dorsal fin; may vary
from seven to twelve
Page 129, fig. E

       See Nine-spined Stickleback, p. 338.

Two dorsal fins

Amber jack

Banded rudder fish

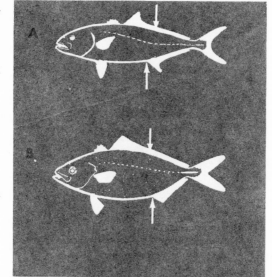

Single dorsal fin preceded by free spines

Pilot fish

Three-spined stickleback

Nine-spined stickleback

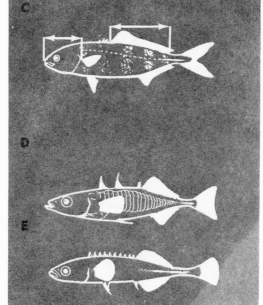

SCADS, JACKS

I. *Bony shields extend whole length of lateral line from behind head to base of tail*
Page 131, fig. A

See Rough Scad, p. 357.

II. *Bony shields only on rear part of lateral line*
Page 131, figs. B–E

IIa. Front portion of lateral line barely arched
Page 131, fig. B

See Goggle-eyed Scad, p. 356.

IIb. Front portion of lateral line strongly arched
Page 131, figs. C–E

1. Breast without scales
Page 131, fig. C

See Common Jack, p. 357.

2. Breast with small scales
Page 131, figs. D, E

a. Straight part of lateral line starts under origin of second dorsal fin
Page 131, fig. D

See Blue Runner, p. 358.

b. Straight part of lateral line starts beneath a point well back of origin of second dorsal fin
Page 131, fig. E

See Horse-Eye Jack, p. 359.

Bony shields along
whole lateral line

Rough scad

Bony shields only on
rear part of lateral
line

Goggle-eyed scad

Common jack

Blue runner

Horse-eye jack

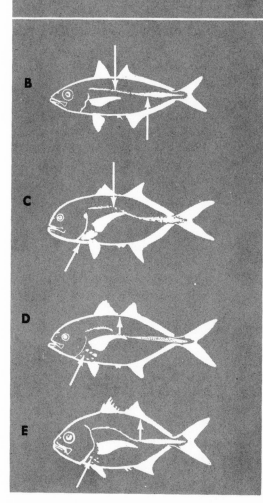

OCEAN SUNFISHES, HERRINGS, ANCHOVIES, KILLIFISHES, OTHER

I. *No pelvic fins*
   Page 133, figs. A, B

   Ia. Rear end of body with a lobe-like projection near
       center
       Page 133, fig. A

       See Sharp-tailed Ocean Sunfish, p. 413.

   Ib. Rear end of body rounded and without a lobe-like
       projection
       Page 133, fig. B

       See Ocean Sunfish, p. 412.

II. *Pelvic fins present*
    Page 133, figs. C–G

    See Herrings, Anchovies, Killifishes, Other, p. 134.

No pelvic fins

Sharp-tailed ocean
sunfish

Ocean sunfish

Pelvic fins present

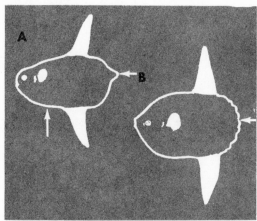
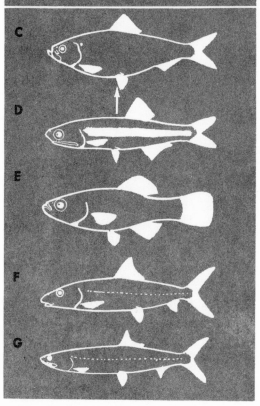

HERRINGS, ANCHOVIES, KILLIFISHES, OTHER

I. *Pelvic fins under dorsal fin*
Page 135, figs. A–D

See Herrings, Sheepshead Minnow, Ten-Pounder, Bone-fish, p. 136.

II. *Pelvic fins before or behind dorsal fin*
Page 135, figs. E–G

See Round Herring, Anchovies, Killifishes, p. 142.

Pelvic fins under dorsal fin

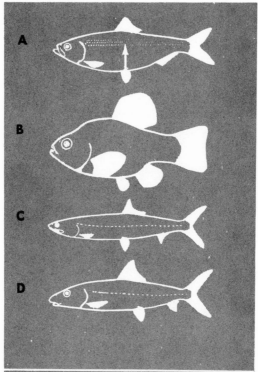

Pelvic fins before or behind dorsal fin

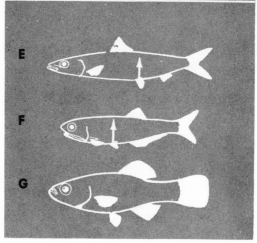

HERRINGS, SHEEPSHEAD MINNOW, TEN-POUNDER, BONEFISH

I. *Base length of dorsal fin about equal to base length of anal fin*
Page 137, fig. A

See Menhaden, Sea Herring, Shad, Other Herrings, p. 138.

II. *Base length of dorsal fin about two or two-and-a-half times the base length of the anal fin*
Page 137, figs. B–D

IIa. Origin of anal fin under rear part of base of dorsal fin
Page 137, fig. B

See Sheepshead Minnow, p. 305.

IIb. Origin of anal fin far back on body beyond end of base of dorsal fin
Page 137, figs. C, D

1. Base of pelvic fins under front half of dorsal fin
Page 137, fig. C

See Ten-Pounder, p. 285.

2. Base of pelvic fins under rear half of dorsal fin
Page 137, fig. D

See Bonefish, p. 286.

*Base length of
dorsal and anal
fins about equal*

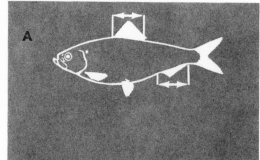

*Base length of
dorsal fin about
two or two-and-a-
half times the base
length of anal fin*

Sheepshead minnow

Ten-pounder

Bonefish

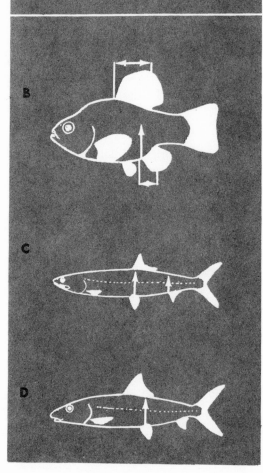

MENHADEN, SEA HERRING, SHAD,
OTHER HERRINGS

I. *Head large; about one-third the distance from snout to end of body*
   Page 139, fig. A

   See Menhaden, p. 293.

II. *Head smaller; between one-fourth and one-fifth the distance from snout to end of body*
   Page 139, figs. B, D, F

   IIa. Origin of dorsal fin about halfway between tip of snout and end of body
   Page 139, fig. B

   See Sea Herring, p. 288.

   IIb. Origin of dorsal fin much nearer to tip of snout than to end of body
   Page 139, figs. D, F

      1. Upper jaw long; reaches to rear half of eye
      Page 139, figs. C, D

      See Shad, p. 291.

      2. Upper jaw shorter; reaches to front half of eye
      Page 139, figs. E, F

      See Hickory Shad, Blueback, Alewife, p. 140.

Head large

Menhaden

Head smaller

Sea herring

Shad

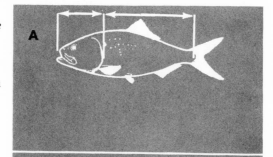
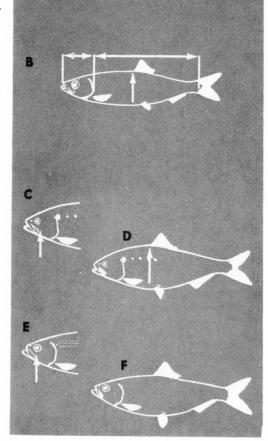

HICKORY SHAD, BLUEBACK, ALEWIFE

I. *A straight line from tip of snout to origin of dorsal fin would pass well above eye*
Page 141, fig. A

See Hickory Shad, p. 289.

II. *A straight line from tip of snout to origin of dorsal fin would pass through top of eye*
Page 141, figs. B, D, F

IIa. Diameter of eye about equal to distance from tip of snout to front of eye; back, dark blue. Inner abdominal wall blackish
Page 141, figs. C, D

See Blueback, p. 289.

IIb. Diameter of eye longer than distance from tip of snout to front of eye; back, grayish green. Inner abdominal wall white
Page 141, figs. E, F

See Alewife, p. 290.

Straight line from snout tip to dorsal fin origin passes above eye

Hickory shad

Straight line from snout tip to dorsal fin origin passes through top of eye

Blueback

Alewife

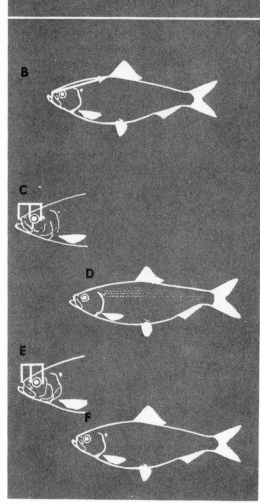

ROUND HERRING, ANCHOVIES, KILLIFISHES

I. *Origin of pelvic fins to rear of dorsal fin*
Page 143, fig. A

See Round Herring, p. 287.

II. *Origin of pelvic fins before dorsal fin*
Page 143, figs. C–E, G–I

IIa. Large upper jaw; reaches far past hind margin of eye, almost to rear margin of operculum
Page 143, figs. B–E

See Anchovies, p. 144.

IIb. Small upper jaw; at most barely reaches front of eye
Page 143, figs. F–I

See Top Minnow, Lucy's Killifish, Other Killifishes, p. 146.

Origin of pelvic fins to rear of dorsal fin

Round herring

Origin of pelvic fins before dorsal fin

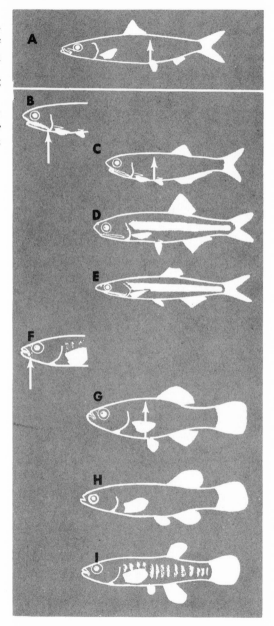

ANCHOVIES

I. *Origin of dorsal fin directly over origin of anal fin*
Page 145, fig. A

See Common Anchovy, p. 294.

II. *Origin of dorsal fin farther forward on body than origin of anal fin*
Page 145, figs. B, C

IIa. Origin of anal fin under rear half of base of dorsal fin
Page 145, fig. B

See Striped Anchovy, p. 295.

IIb. Origin of anal fin to rear of end of base of dorsal fin
Page 145, fig. C

See Silvery Anchovy, p. 295.

*Origin of dorsal fin
over origin of
anal fin*

Common anchovy

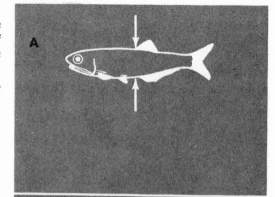

*Origin of dorsal fin
farther forward
on body than
origin of anal fin*

Striped anchovy

Silvery anchovy

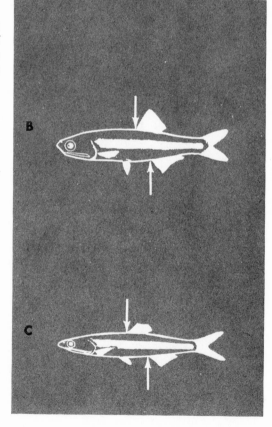

TOP MINNOW, LUCY'S KILLIFISH,
OTHER KILLIFISHES

I. *Origin of dorsal fin over or behind rear end of base of anal fin*
Page 147, figs. A, B

See Top Minnow, p. 308.

II. *Origin of dorsal fin in front of, over, or slightly behind origin of anal fin*
Page 147, figs. C–G

IIa. Base of dorsal fin shorter than base of anal fin
Page 147, fig. C

See Lucy's Killifish, p. 306.

IIb. Base of dorsal fin equal to or longer than base of anal fin
Page 147, figs. D–G

See Rain-Water Fish, Fresh-Water Killifish, Other Killifishes, p. 148.

Origin of dorsal fin over or behind rear end of base of anal fin

Top minnow

Origin of dorsal fin in front of, over, or slightly behind origin of anal fin

Lucy's killifish

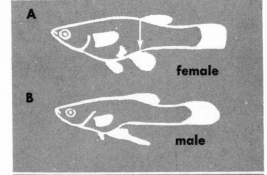
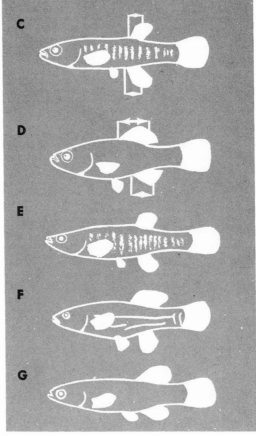

RAIN-WATER FISH, FRESH-WATER KILLIFISH, OTHER KILLIFISHES

I. *Rear tip of pectoral fin beneath origin of dorsal fin*
Page 149, fig. A

See Rain-Water Fish, p. 306.

II. *Rear tip of pectoral fin well in front of origin of dorsal fin*
Page 149, figs. B–F

IIa. Base length of dorsal fin equal to distance from
tip of snout to rear part of eye
Page 149, fig. B

See Fresh-Water Killifish, p. 307.

IIb. Base length of dorsal fin equal to distance from
tip of snout to a point well behind eye
Page 149, figs. C–F

See Striped, Common, Ocellated Killifishes, p. 150

Rear tip of pectoral fin beneath origin of dorsal fin

Rain-water fish

Rear tip of pectoral fin point well in front of origin of dorsal fin

Fresh-water killifish

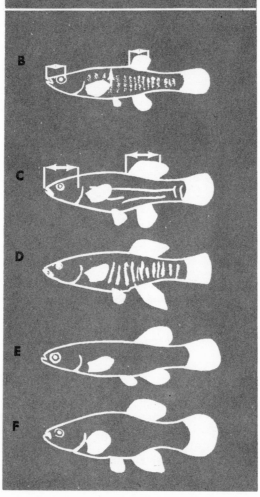

STRIPED, COMMON, OCELLATED KILLIFISHES

I. *Snout long; distance from tip of snout to front of eye much longer than diameter of eye. Dorsal rays: 13–15*
Page 151, figs. A, B

See Striped Killifish, p. 304.

II. *Snout short; distance from tip of snout to front of eye about equal to or less than diameter of eye. Dorsal rays: 10–12*
Page 151, figs. C, D

IIa. Anal rays: 10–12. Common fish in middle Atlantic and southern New England regions
Page 151, fig. C

See Common Killifish, p. 302.

IIb. Anal rays: 9–10. Found only in Chesapeake Bay and farther south
Page 151, fig. D

See Ocellated Killifish, p. 307.

Snout long

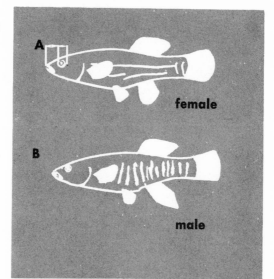

Striped killifish

Snout short

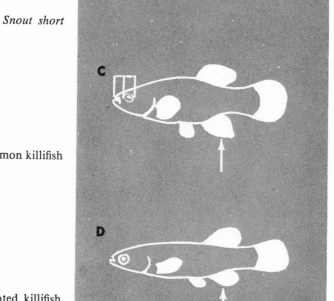

Common killifish

Ocellated killifish

TRUNKFISHES, LUMPFISH, CLINGFISH, SWELLFISHES, BOXFISH, PORCUPINE FISH

I. *A hard shell covers most of body*
Page 153, figs. A–C

    Ia. A spine on each side of shell before anal fin and
pointing to it
Page 153, figs. A, B

        1. A single spine before each eye
Page 153, fig. A

        See Cowfish, p. 409.

        2. No spines before eyes
Page 153, fig. B

        See Common Trunkfish, p. 408.

    Ib. No spines on any part of body
Page 153, fig. C

    See Smooth Trunkfish, p. 408.

II. *No hard shell covering body*
Page 153, figs. D–G

See Lumpfish, Clingfish, Swellfishes, Boxfish, Porcupine
Fish, p. 154.

*Hard shell covers
most of body*

Cowfish

Common trunkfish

Smooth trunkfish

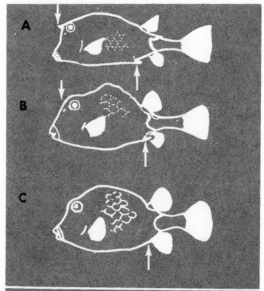

*No hard shell
covering body*

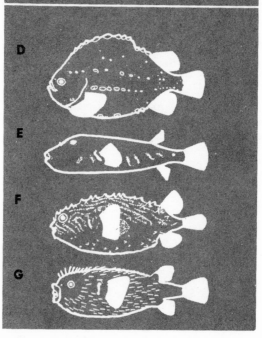

LUMPFISH, CLINGFISH, SWELLFISHES,
BOXFISH, PORCUPINE FISH

I. *Gill opening large: equal to half depth of body at rear*
   margin of operculum
   Page 155, figs. A, B

   Ia. Head shorter than depth of body
         Page 155, fig. A

         See Lumpfish, p. 389.

   Ib. Head longer than depth of body
         Page 155, fig. B

         See Clingfish, p. 405.

II. *Gill opening small: only a slit before pectoral fin and*
    shorter than base of pectoral fin
    Page 155, figs. C–G

    See Swellfishes, Boxfish, Porcupine Fish, p. 156.

Gill opening large

Lumpfish

Clingfish

Gill opening small

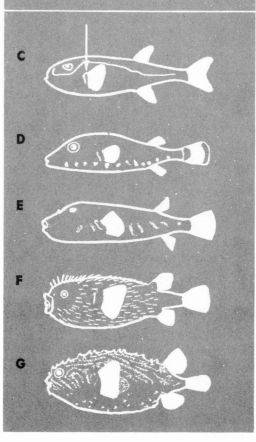

SWELLFISHES, BOXFISH, PORCUPINE FISH

I. *Entire body, including back, covered with prickles or spines*
Page 157, figs. A–F

Ia. Small prickles on body making skin rough to touch
Page 157, figs. A, B

1. Front and rear portion of tail has a broad dusky band
Page 157, fig. A

See Southern Swellfish, p. 410.

2. No bands on tail
Page 157, fig. B

See Northern Swellfish, p. 410.

Ib. Large spines on body
Page 157, figs. C–F

1. Spines thick, not movable
Page 157, figs. C, D

See Spiny Boxfish, p. 411.

2. Spines slender, movable
Page 157, figs. E, F

See Porcupine Fish, p. 412.

II. *Back smooth, no prickles or spines*
Page 157, fig. G

See Smooth Swellfish, p. 409.

Entire body covered with prickles or spines

Southern swellfish

Northern swellfish

Spiny boxfish

Porcupine fish

No prickles or spines on back

Smooth swellfish

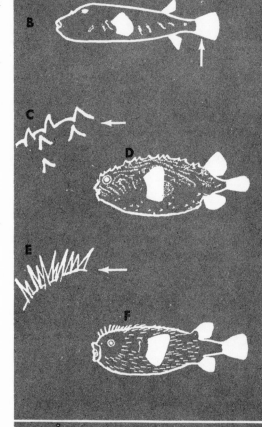

HOGCHOKER, FLOUNDERS, SAND
LAUNCES, OTHER

I. *Both eyes on the same side of head*
Page 159, figs. A–C

See Hogchoker, Flounders, p. 162.

II. *A single eye on each side of head*
Page 159, figs. D–G

    IIa. Body elongated, eel-like; length from tip of snout
        to end of tail over eleven times the greatest body
        depth
        Page 159, figs. D, E

        1. Dorsal rays: 50–60, mostly 53–59
           Page 159, fig. D

           See American Sand Launce, p. 397.

        2. Dorsal rays: 57–63, mostly 59–62
           Page 159, fig. E

           See Ocean Sand Launce, p. 398.

    IIb. Body deeper; length from tip of snout to end of
        tail less than six times the greatest body depth
        Page 159, figs. F, G

        See Dolphin, Deep Big-Eye, Blennies, Other, p.
        160.

Both eyes on same side of head

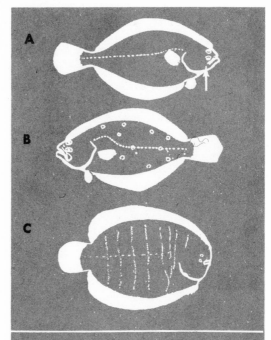

Single eye on each side of head

American sand launce

Ocean sand launce

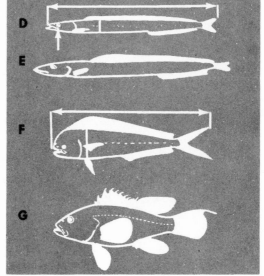

DOLPHIN, DEEP BIG-EYE, BLENNIES, OTHER

I. *Origin of dorsal fin closer to rear margin of eye than to rear edge of operculum*
Page 161, figs. A–D

See Dolphin, Deep Big-Eye, Blennies, p. 172.

II. *Origin of dorsal fin closer to rear edge of operculum than to rear margin of eye; or on body in back of head*
Page 161, figs. E–G

See Wolf Fish, Common Big-Eye, Wreckfish, Other, p. 174.

*Origin of dorsal fin
closer to eye than
to edge of
operculum*

*Origin of dorsal fin
closer to edge of
operculum than
to eye*

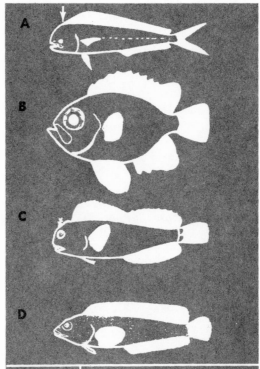

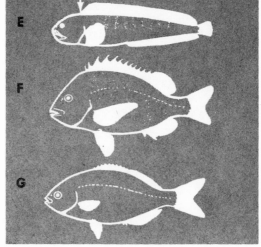

HOGCHOKER, FLOUNDERS

I. *No pectoral fins*
Page 163, fig. A

See Hogchoker, p. 331.

II. *Pectoral fins present*
Page 163, figs. B–D

IIa. Tail fin concave
Page 163, fig. B

See Atlantic Halibut, p. 322.

IIb. Tail fin rounded
Page 163, figs. C, D

1. Fish heading toward the right when eyed side is up and gut section is toward observer
Page 163, fig. C

See Dab, Yellowtail Flounder, Other Flounders, p. 164.

2. Fish heading toward the left when eyed side is up and gut section is toward observer
Page 163, fig. D

See Eyed, Small-Mouth, Other Flounders, p. 168.

No pectoral fins

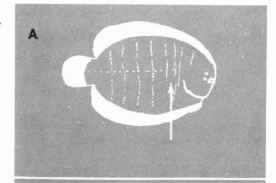

Hogchoker

Pectoral fins present

Atlantic halibut

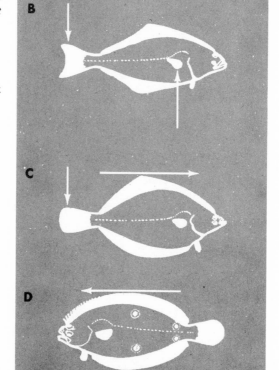

DAB, YELLOWTAIL FLOUNDER,
OTHER FLOUNDERS

I. *Mouth large; upper jaw extends back to center of eye*
Page 165, fig. A

See Dab, p. 323.

II. *Mouth smaller; upper jaw extends at most back to front of eye*
Page 165, figs. B–E

IIa. Lateral line well arched in region over pectoral fin
Page 165, fig. B

See Yellowtail Flounder, p. 325.

IIb. Lateral line straight or only slightly arched over pectoral fin
Page 165, figs. C–E

See Gray Sole, Blackback Flounder, Smooth Flounder, p. 166.

Mouth large

Dab

Mouth smaller

Yellowtail
flounder

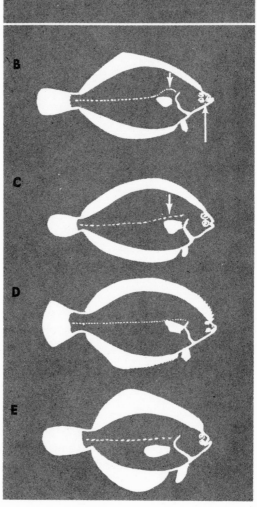
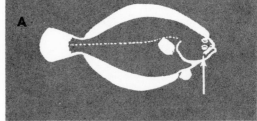

GRAY SOLE, BLACKBACK FLOUNDER,
SMOOTH FLOUNDER

I. *Depth of caudal peduncle about equal to distance between outer margins of eyes*
Page 167, fig. A

See Gray Sole, p. 326.

II. *Depth of caudal peduncle much more than distance between outer margins of eyes*
Page 167, figs. C, E

    IIa. Scales on area between eyes. Depth of caudal peduncle much more than length of pelvic fin
    Page 167, figs. B, C

    See Blackback Flounder, p. 324.

    IIb. No scales on area between eyes. Depth of caudal peduncle about equal to length of pelvic fin
    Page 167, fig. D, E

    See Smooth Flounder, p. 325.

Depth of caudal peduncle about equal to distance between outer margins of eyes

Gray sole

Depth of caudal peduncle much more than distance between outer margins of eyes

Blackback flounder

Smooth flounder

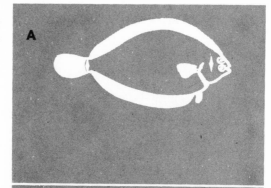
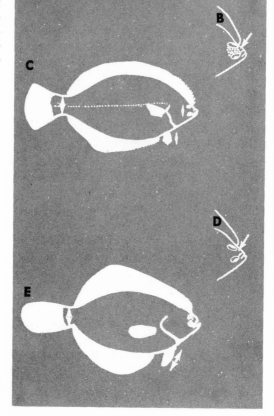

EYED, SMALL-MOUTH, OTHER FLOUNDERS

I. *Mouth small; upper jaw reaches at most to front of eye*
Page 169, figs. A, B

   Ia. Lateral line highly arched in front
      Page 169, fig. A

      See Eyed Flounder, p. 330.

   Ib. Lateral line barely arched in front
      Page 169, fig. B

      See Small-Mouth Flounder, p. 329.

II. *Mouth larger; upper jaw reaches back beyond front of
eye*
Page 169, figs. C–E

   See Sundial, Four-spotted Fluke, Northern Fluke, p.
170.

Mouth small

Eyed flounder

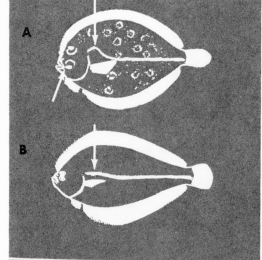

Small-mouth
flounder

Mouth large

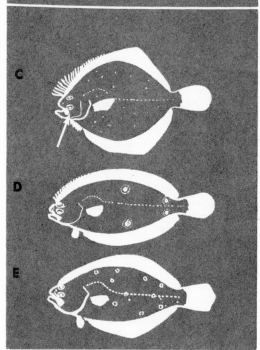

SUNDIAL, FOUR-SPOTTED FLUKE,
NORTHERN FLUKE

I. *Front part of dorsal fin has long fringe-like rays*
Page 171, fig. A

See Sundial, p. 327.

II. *Front part of dorsal fin has no long fringe-like rays*
Page 171, figs. B, C

    IIa. Four conspicuous black eye-spots on dark side of body. Only a narrow ridge between the eyes
Page 171, fig. B

    See Four-spotted Fluke, p. 329.

    IIb. Many black eye-spots on dark side of body. Space between eyes almost equal to diameter of eye
Page 171, fig. C

    See Northern Fluke, p. 328.

*Front of dorsal fin
has long fringe-
like rays*

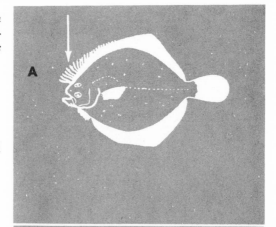

Sundial

*Front of dorsal fin
has no long fringe-
like rays*

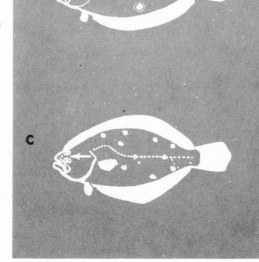

Four-spotted fluke

Northern fluke

DOLPHIN, DEEP BIG-EYE, BLENNIES

I. *Origin of dorsal fin over eye*
   Page 173, fig. A

   See Dolphin, p. 353.

II. *Origin of dorsal fin behind eye*
    Page 173, figs. B–D

    IIa. Base of anal fin about equal to distance from tip of snout to rear edge of operculum
Page 173, fig. B

         See Deep Big-Eye, p. 369.

    IIb. Base of anal fin about twice the distance from tip of snout to rear edge of operculum
Page 173, figs. C, D

        1. Body deep; greatest depth more than length of head
Page 173, fig. C

           See Carolina Blenny. p. 400.

        2. Body more slender; greatest depth less than length of head
Page 173, fig. D

           See Striped Blenny, p. 399.

Origin of dorsal fin over eye

Dolphin

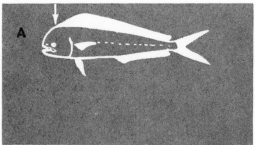

Origin of dorsal fin behind eye

Deep big-eye

Carolina blenny

Striped blenny

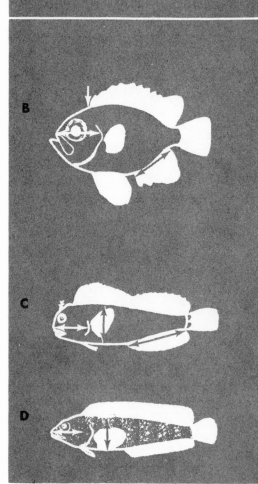

WOLF FISH, COMMON BIG-EYE,
WRECKFISH, OTHER

I. *Base of anal fin about half or more the length of base of dorsal fin*
Page 175, figs. A–D

See Wolf Fish, Sea Snails, Common Big-Eye, Butterfly Fishes, p. 176.

II. *Base of anal fin much less than half length of base of dorsal fin*
Page 175, figs. E, F

See Wreckfish, Other, p. 178.

Base of anal fin about half or more length of base of dorsal fin

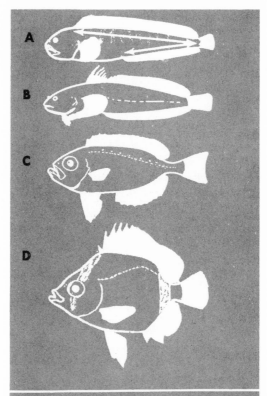

Base of anal fin much less than half length of base of dorsal fin

WOLF FISH, SEA SNAILS, COMMON BIG-EYE, BUTTERFLY FISHES

I. *Body elongated; total length over four times greatest depth of body*
   Page 177, figs. A–C
   Ia. Origin of dorsal fin on top of head
       Page 177, fig. A
       See Common Wolf Fish, p. 402.
   Ib. Origin of dorsal fin in back of head over pectoral fin
       Page 177, figs. B, C
       1. Front part of dorsal fin separated by a notch from rest of fin
          Page 177, fig. B
          See Sea Snail, p. 389.
       2. Front part of dorsal fin not separated by a notch from rest of fin
          Page 177, fig. C
          See Striped Sea Snail, p. 390.

II. *Body deeper; total length less than four times greatest depth of body*
    Page 177, figs. D–F
    IIa. Tail fin concave
        Page 177, fig. D
        See Common Big-Eye, p. 370.
    IIb. Tail fin rounded
        Page 177, figs. E, F
        1. A large spot on body below rear part of dorsal fin
           Page 177, fig. E
           See Four-eyed Butterfly Fish, p. 384.
        2. No large spot on body below rear part of dorsal fin
           Page 177, fig. F
           See Common Butterfly Fish, p. 383.

Body elongated

Common wolf fish

Sea snail

Striped sea snail

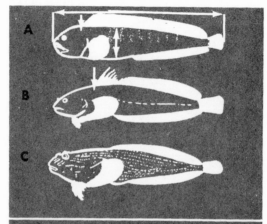

Body deeper

Common big-eye

Four-eyed
butterfly fish

Common
butterfly fish

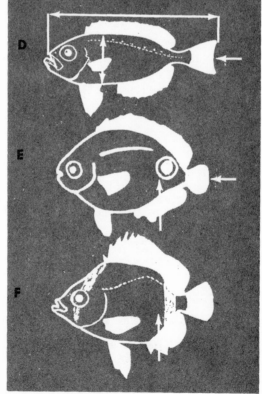

WRECKFISH, OTHER

I. *Tail rounded*
   Page 179, figs. A–C

    Ia. Mouth large; upper jaw reaches to rear margin of eye
   Page 179, fig. A

    See Wreckfish, p. 369.
    Ib. Mouth smaller; upper jaw reaches at most to center of eye
   Page 179, figs. B, C

    See Sea Bass, Tripletail, Cunner, Tautog, p. 180.

II. *Tail concave or forked*
   Page 179, figs. D–F

    See Gray Snapper, White Grunt, Bermuda Chub, Other, p. 182.

Tail rounded

Wreckfish

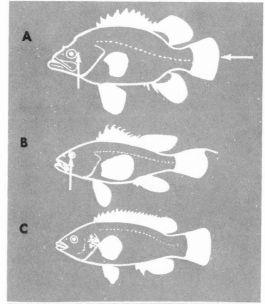

*Tail concave
or forked*

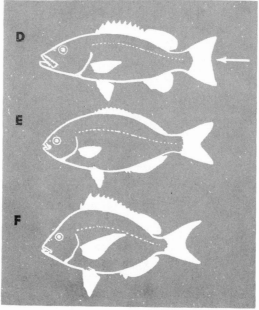

COMMON SEA BASS, TRIPLETAIL,
CUNNER, TAUTOG

I. *Pectoral fin long; hind tip reaches to about origin of anal fin*
Page 181, fig. A

See Common Sea Bass, p. 368.

II. *Pectoral fin shorter; hind tip reaches a point far in front of origin of anal fin*
Page 181, figs. B–D

IIa. Mouth large; upper jaw reaches beyond front margin of eye
Page 181, fig. B

See Tripletail, p. 370.

IIb. Mouth smaller; upper jaw does not reach front margin of eye
Page 181, figs. C, D

1. Snout pointed; scales on rear part of operculum
Page 181, fig. C

See Cunner, p. 93.

2. Snout rounded; no scales on rear part of operculum
Page 181, fig. D

See Tautog, p. 393.

Pectoral fins long

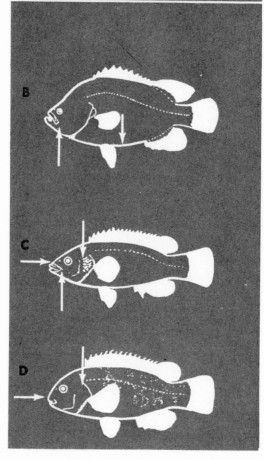

Common sea bass

Pectoral fins shorter

Tripletail

Cunner

Tautog

GRAY SNAPPER, WHITE GRUNT,
BERMUDA CHUB, OTHER

I. *Tail Concave*
Page 183, fig. A

See Gray Snapper, p. 371.

II. *Tail forked*
Page 183, figs. B–F

IIa. Mouth large; upper jaw reaches to center of eye
Page 183, fig. B

See White Grunt, p. 372.

IIb. Mouth smaller; upper jaw reaches at most to front of eye
Page 183, figs. C–F

1. Origin of dorsal fin well behind base of pectoral fin
Page 183, fig. C

See Bermuda Chub, p. 375.

2. Origin of dorsal fin over or before base of pectoral fin
Page 183, figs. D–F

See Northern and Southern Porgy, Other, p. 184.

Tail concave

Gray snapper

Tail forked

White grunt

Bermuda chub

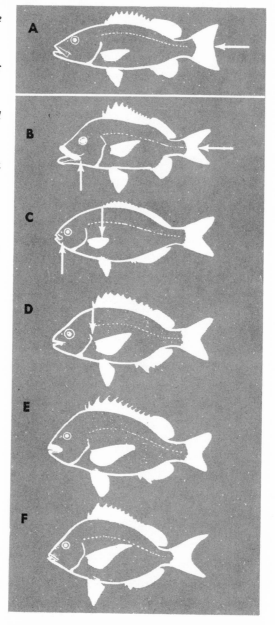

NORTHERN AND SOUTHERN PORGY, OTHER

I. *Dorsal spines long; third spine half or more length of head*
   Page 185, figs. A–C

   Ia. Depth of body unchanging between origin of dorsal fin to origin of anal fin
       Page 185, fig. B

       See Northern Porgy, p. 372.

   Ib. Depth of body gradually decreases in the region from origin of dorsal fin to origin of anal fin
       Page 185, fig. C

       See Southern Porgy, p. 373.

II. *Dorsal spines shorter; third spine less than half length of head*
    Page 185, figs. D, E

    See Holbrook's Porgy, Pinfish, Sheepshead, p. 186.

Dorsal spines long

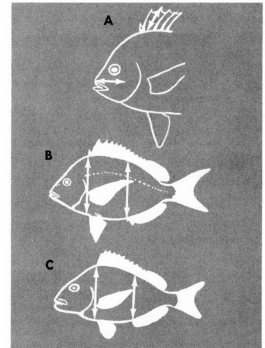

Northern porgy

Southern porgy

Dorsal spines shorter

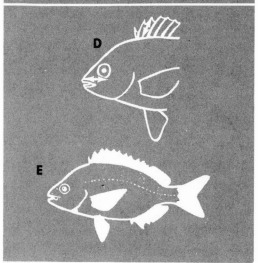

HOLBROOK'S PORGY, PINFISH, SHEEPSHEAD

I. *A conspicuous black saddle on the caudal peduncle*
Page 187, fig. A

See Holbrook's Porgy, p. 373.

II. *No conspicuous black saddle on the caudal peduncle*
Page 187, figs. B, C

IIa. Base of anal fin about equal to depth of head at
center of eye
Page 187, fig. B

See Pinfish, p. 374.

IIb. Base of anal fin much less than depth of head at
center of eye
Page 187, fig. C

See Sheepshead, p. 374.

*Black saddle on
caudal peduncle*

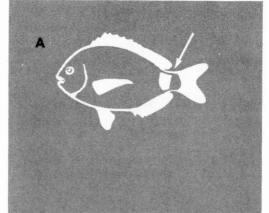

Holbrook's porgy

*No black saddle on
caudal peduncle*

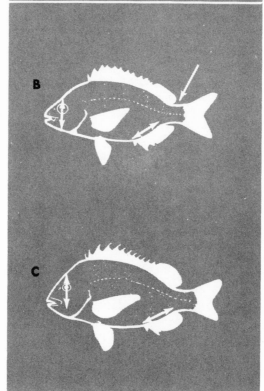

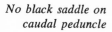

Pinfish

Sheepshead

THREADFISH, BUTTERFISH, HARVEST FISH, OTHER

I. *Front rays of dorsal and anal fins extended in long streamers*
   Page 189, fig. A

   See Threadfish, p. 359.

II. *Front rays of dorsal and anal fins not extended in long streamers*
    Page 189, figs. B–H

   IIa. No pelvic fins
        Page 189, figs. B, C

        1. Row of large pores on back near base of dorsal fin
           Page 189, fig. B

           See Butterfish, p. 353.

        2. No row of pores on back
           Page 189, fig. C

           See Harvest Fish, p. 354.

   IIb. Pelvic fins present
        Page 189, figs. D–H

        See Cobia, Sticklebacks, Other, p. 190.

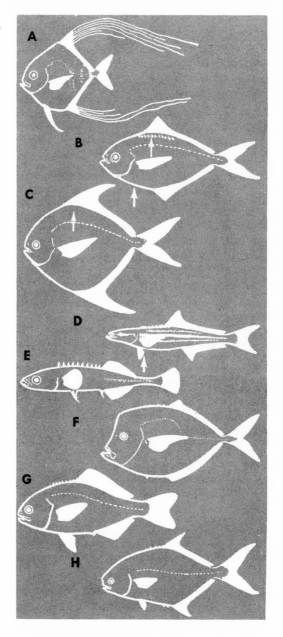

Front rays of dorsal and anal fins long streamers

Threadfish

Front rays of dorsal and anal fins not long streamers

Butterfish

Harvest fish

COBIA, STICKLEBACKS, OTHER

I. *Body slender; greatest depth about equal to or less than length of head*
Page 191, figs. A–C

Ia. Dorsal fin long; extends from above rear tip of pectoral fin to about caudal peduncle
Page 191, fig. A

See Cobia, p. 365.

Ib. Dorsal fin short; extends from far behind the rear tip of the pectoral fin to before the caudal peduncle
Page 191, figs. B, C

See Sticklebacks, p. 192.

II. *Body deep; greatest depth much longer than length of head*
Page 191, figs. D–G

See Moonfish, Black Rudder Fish, Round Pompano, Common Pompano, p. 194.

Body slender

Cobia

Body deep

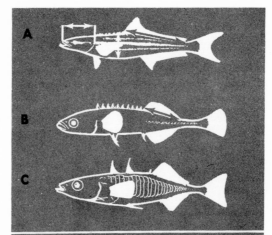
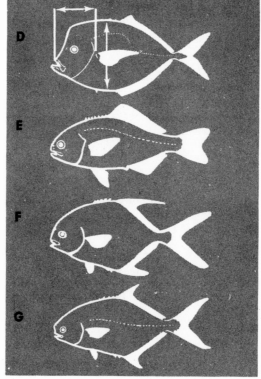

STICKLEBACKS

I. *Seven or more dorsal spines*
Page 193, fig. A

See Nine-spined Stickleback, p. 338.

II. *Less than seven dorsal spines*
Page 193, figs. B, D, F

    IIa. Bony ridge on each side of belly. Sides without plates
Page 193, fig. B

        See Four-spined Stickleback, p. 336.

    IIb. No bony ridge on each side of belly. Sides usually have plates
Page 193, figs. D, F

        1. A strong cusp at the base of each pelvic spine
Page 193, figs. C, D

           See Two-spined Stickleback, p. 338.

        2. No strong cusp at the base of each pelvic spine
Page 193, figs. E, F

           See Three-spined Stickleback, p. 337.

*Seven or more
dorsal spines*

Nine-spined
stickleback

*Less than seven
dorsal spines*

Four-spined
stickleback

Two-spined
stickleback

Three-spined
stickleback

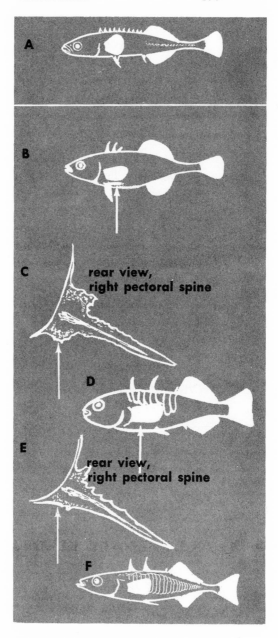

A

B

C rear view,
right pectoral spine

D

E rear view,
right pectoral spine

F

MOONFISH, BLACK RUDDER FISH, ROUND POMPANO, COMMON POMPANO

I. *Origin of dorsal fin above the pectoral fin*
Page 195, figs. A, B

    Ia. Pelvic fin short; length less than diameter of eye
        Page 195, fig. A

        See Moonfish, p. 360.

    Ib. Pelvic fin long; length more than half length of head
        Page 195, fig. B

        See Black Rudder Fish, p. 355.

II. *Origin of dorsal fin well back of rear tip of pectoral fin*
Page 195, figs. C, D

    IIa. Greatest height of dorsal fin longer than length of head; 19–20 rays in dorsal fin
        Page 195, fig. C

        See Round Pompano, p. 364.

    IIb. Greatest height of dorsal fin shorter than length of head; 23–24 rays in dorsal fin
        Page 195, fig. D

        See Common Pompano, p. 363.

*Origin of dorsal fin
above pectoral fin*

Moonfish

Black rudder fish

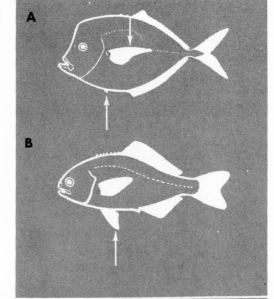

*Origin of dorsal fin
behind rear tip of
pectoral fin*

Round pompano

Common pompano

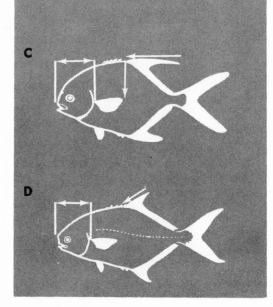

GOATFISH, BARRACUDAS, SILVERSIDES,
MULLETS

I. *Origin of first dorsal fin about over origin of pelvic fin*
Page 197, figs. A–C

    Ia. Double barbel on chin
        Page 197, fig. A

        See Northern Goatfish, p. 342.

    Ib. No barbel on chin
        Page 197, figs. B, C

        1. Origin of first dorsal fin over rear portion of
           pectoral fin
           Page 197, fig. B

           See Great Barracuda, p. 336.

        2. Origin of first dorsal fin over a point well in
           back of pectoral fin
           Page 197, fig. C

           See Northern Barracuda, p. 335.

II. *Origin of first dorsal fin above a point well behind
rear end of base of pelvic fin*
Page 197, figs. D–H

See Silversides, Mullets, p. 198.

Origin of first dorsal fin about over origin of pelvic fin

Northern goatfish

Great barracuda

Northern barracuda

Origin of first dorsal fin over point well behind rear end of base of pelvic fin

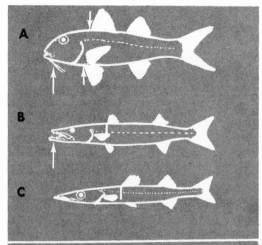

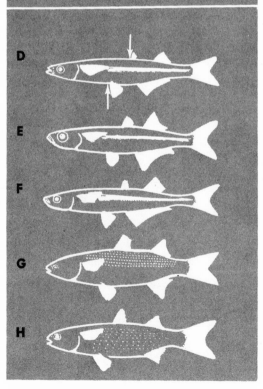

SILVERSIDES, MULLETS

I. *Origin of second dorsal fin well behind origin of anal fin. A silver streak on the sides*
Page 199, figs. A–C

  Ia. Body rough to touch when stroked from tail toward head
Page 199, fig. A

    See Rough Silverside, p. 333.

  Ib. Body smooth to touch when stroked from tail toward head
Page 199, figs. B, C

    1. Origin of anal fin under first dorsal fin
Page 199, fig. B

      See Northern Silverside, p. 332.

    2. Origin of anal fin at a point behind first dorsal fin
Page 199, fig. C

      See Tide-Water Silverside, p. 332.

II. *Origin of second dorsal fin almost directly over origin of anal fin. No silver streak on sides*
Page 199, figs. D, E

  IIa. Conspicuous dark stripes along rows of scales on sides of body. Eleven anal spines plus rays
Page 199, fig. D

    See Striped Mullet, p. 334.

  IIb. No dark stripes on sides of body. Twelve anal spines plus rays
Page 199, fig. E

    See White Mullet, p. 334.

*Origin of second
dorsal fin well
behind origin
of anal fin*

Rough silverside

Northern silverside

Tide-water
silverside

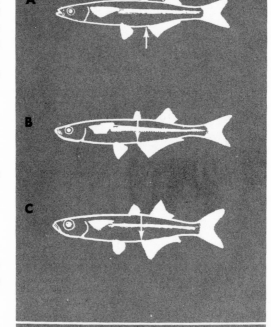

*Origin of second
dorsal fin almost
directly over origin
of anal fin*

Striped mullet

White mullet

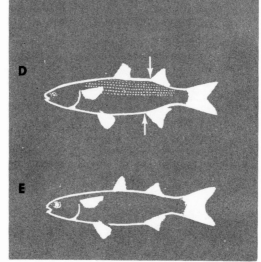

CROAKERS, DRUMS, OTHER

I. *Lateral line continues onto tail*
   Page 201, figs. A–D

See Croaker, Black Drum, Other, p. 202.

II. *Lateral line does not continue onto tail*
    Page 201, figs. E–G

See Sea Raven, Look-down, Common Trigger Fish, Other, p. 210.

*Lateral line
continues onto tail*

*Lateral line does not
continue onto tail*

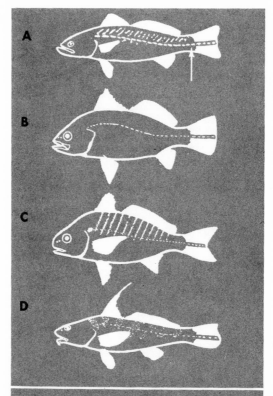
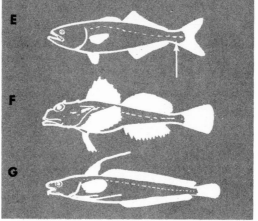

CROAKER, BLACK DRUM, OTHER

I. *One to many barbels on lower jaw*
Page 203, figs. A–C

Ia. A single barbel on lower jaw
Page 203, fig. A

See King Whitings, p. 204.

Ib. Many barbels on lower jaw
Page 203, figs. B, C

1. A row of short, slender barbels located only on each side of chin
Page 203, fig. B

See Croaker, p. 380.

2. Numerous small barbels located all along lower jaw from chin to region below center of eye
Page 203, fig. C

See Black Drum, p. 381.

II. *No barbels on lower jaw*
Page 203, figs. D, E

See Channel Bass, Spot, Banded Croaker, Other, p. 206.

One to many barbels on lower jaw

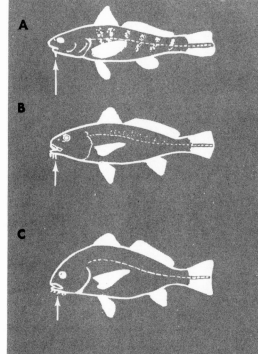

Croaker

Black drum

No barbels on lower jaw

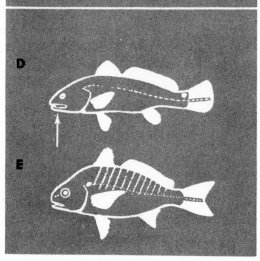

KING WHITINGS

I. *Scales on chest much smaller than scales on sides*
Page 205, figs. A, B

See Gulf King Whiting, p. 379.

II. *Scales on chest about same size as scales on sides*
Page 205, fig. C

IIa. Sides have dark oblique bands, the last band on back of head and the first band on body forming a V. Length of front spine of first dorsal fin equal to distance from origin of first dorsal fin to well behind origin of second dorsal fin
Page 205, fig. D

See Northern King Whiting, p. 377.

IIb. Sides plain or with obscure oblique bands which do not form a V at back of head. Length of front spine of first dorsal fin equal to distance from origin of first dorsal fin to about origin of second dorsal fin
Page 205, fig. E

See Southern King Whiting, p. 378.

Scales on chest much smaller than scales on sides

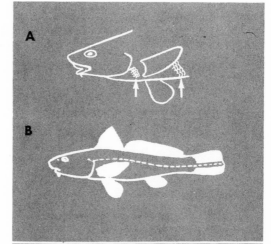

Gulf king whiting

Scales on chest about same size as scales on sides

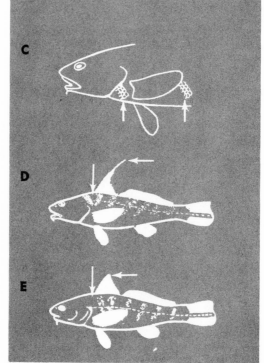

Northern king whiting

Southern king whiting

CHANNEL BASS, SPOT,
BANDED CROAKER, OTHER

I. *One or more spots on upper side of caudal peduncle*
Page 207, fig. A

See Channel Bass, p. 381.

II. *No spots on caudal peduncle*
Page 207, figs. B–E

IIa. Dark spot on body just behind upper edge of operculum
Page 207, fig. B

See Spot, p. 379.

IIb. No dark spot on body behind upper edge of operculum
Page 207, figs. C–E

1. Upper parts of sides have 7–9 dark vertical bars
Page 207, fig. C

See Banded Croaker, p. 382.

2. No dark vertical bars on sides
Page 207, figs. D, E

See Silver Perch, Silver Sea Trout, Spotted Sea Trout, Gray Sea Trout, p. 208.

One or more spots on upper side of caudal peduncle

Channel bass

No spots on caudal peduncle

Spot

Banded croaker

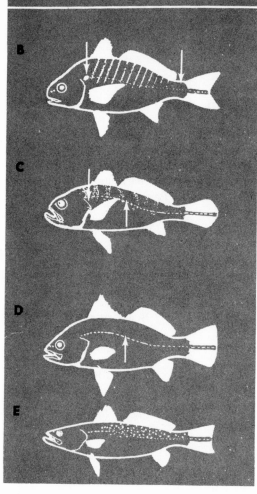

SILVER PERCH, SILVER SEA TROUT, SPOTTED SEA TROUT, GRAY SEA TROUT

I. *Body depth greater than length of head*
Page 209, fig. A

See Silver Perch, p. 383.

II. *Body depth less than length of head*
Page 209, figs. B–D

IIa. No dark spots or marks on body
Page 209, fig. B

See Silver Sea Trout, p. 377.

IIb. Dark spots or marks on body
Page 209, figs. C, D

1. Black spots on upper sides and on dorsal and caudal fins
Page 209, fig. C

See Spotted Sea Trout, p. 376.

2. Upper portion of sides has black, wavy oblique lines. No black spots on dorsal or caudal fins
Page 209, fig. D

See Gray Sea Trout, p. 375.

*Body depth
greater than length
of head*

Silver perch

*Body depth less
than length of head*

Silver sea trout

Spotted sea trout

Gray sea trout

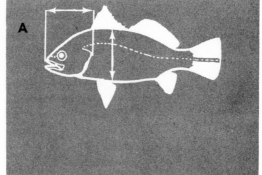
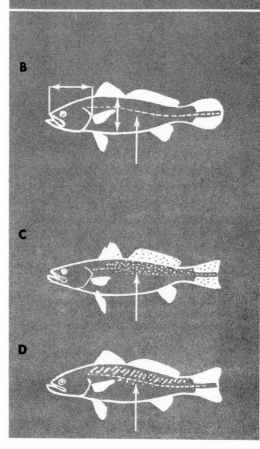

SEA RAVEN, LOOK-DOWN,
COMMON TRIGGERFISH, OTHER

I. *Base of first dorsal fin about twice length of base of second dorsal fin*
Page 211, fig. A

See Sea Raven, p. 388.

II. *Base of first dorsal fin only slightly longer or much shorter than base of second dorsal fin*
Page 211, fig. B–E

    IIa. Front portion of second dorsal and anal fins greatly elongated
Page 211, fig. B

    See Look-down, p. 361.

    IIb. Front portion of second dorsal and anal fins not greatly elongated
Page 211, figs. C–E

        1. Pelvic fins poorly developed, represented by a single spine
Page 211, fig. C

        See Common Triggerfish, p. 406.

        2. Pelvic fins well developed
Page 211, figs. D, E

        See Spotted, Red, and White Hakes, Toadfish, Other, p. 212.

Base of first dorsal
fin about twice
length of base of
second dorsal fin

Sea raven

Base of first dorsal
fin only slightly
longer or much
shorter than base of
second dorsal fin

Look-down

Common triggerfish

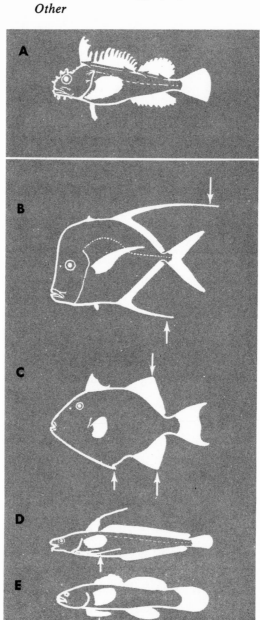

SPOTTED, RED, AND WHITE HAKES,
TOADFISH, OTHER

I. *Each pelvic fin consists of one long filament forked at end*
   Page 213, figs. A–C

   Ia. First dorsal fin has a conspicuous black dot. Both dorsal fins about same height
   Page 213, fig. A

   See Spotted Hake, p. 319.

   Ib. First dorsal fin has no black dot. First dorsal fin higher than second
   Page 213, figs. B, C

   1. Upper jaw reaches to slightly behind center of eye
      Page 213, fig. B

      See Red Hake, p. 320.

   2. Upper jaw reaches to rear margin of eye
      Page 213, fig. C

      See White Hake, p. 319.

II. *Pelvic fins not filamentous*
    Page 213, figs. D–G

    IIa. Fleshy irregular flaps on various parts of head
    Page 213, fig. D

    See Toadfish, p. 404.

    IIb. No fleshy irregular flaps on head
    Page 213, figs. E–G

    See Sea-green, Naked, and Ginsburg's Gobies, Other, p. 214.

*Pelvic fin a long
   forked filament*

Spotted hake

Red hake

White hake

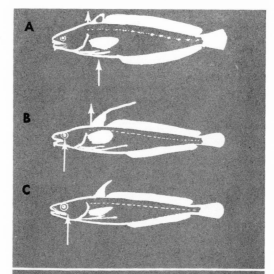

*Pelvic fin not
   filamentous*

Toadfish

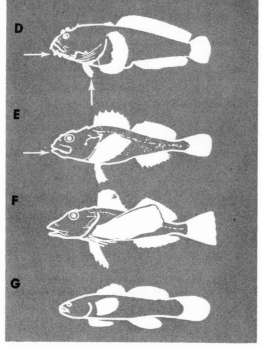

SEA-GREEN, NAKED, AND
GINSBURG'S GOBIES, OTHER

I. *Pelvic fins united to form a suction cup*
Page 215, fig. A

    Ia. Pectoral fin reaches to a point behind origin of second dorsal fin
Page 215, fig. B

    See Sea-green Goby, p. 395.

    Ib. Pectoral fin reaches to a point under rear part of first dorsal fin
Page 215, figs. C, D

        1. Pelvic fin cup extends about half the distance from its base to the vent
Page 215, fig. C

        See Naked Goby, p. 394.

        2. Pelvic fin cup extends two-thirds of the distance from its base to the vent
Page 215, fig. D

        See Ginsburg's Goby, p. 395.

II. *Two pelvic fins, not united to form a suction cup*
Page 215, fig. E
See Sea Robins, Sculpins, Other, p. 216.

Pelvic fins united to form a suction cup

Sea-green goby

Naked goby

Ginsburg's goby

Pelvic fins not united to form a suction cup

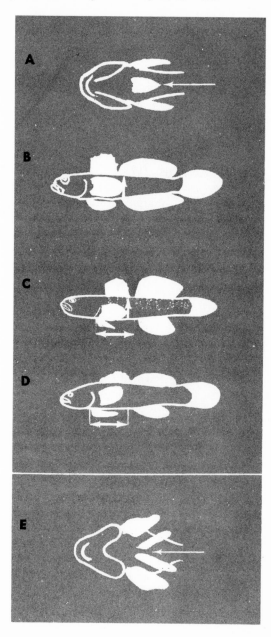

SEA ROBINS, SCULPINS, OTHER

I. *Base of pectoral fin wide; at least half depth of body at rear edge of operculum*
   Page 217, figs. A–D

   Ia. Pectoral fin long; reaches back to a point well beyond origin of second dorsal fin
       Page 217, figs. A–C
       1. No long spine-like projections at the lower rear margin of the operculum
          Page 217, figs. A, B
          a. Dusky or brownish stripe along length of lower part of sides
             Page 217, fig. A
             See Striped Sea Robin, p. 392.
          b. No stripe on sides
             Page 217, fig. B
             See Common Sea Robin, p. 391.
       2. A long spine-like projection at the lower rear margin of the operculum
          Page 217, fig. C
          See Flying Gurnard, p. 391.

   Ib. Pectoral fin shorter; reaches back to a point about under origin of second dorsal fin
       Page 217, fig. D
       See Sculpins, p. 218.

II. *Base of pectoral fin narrow; much less than half depth of body at rear edge of operculum*
    Page 217, figs. E–H
    See Stargazer, Striped Bass, White Perch, Other, p. 220.

*Base of pectoral
fin wide*

Striped sea robin

Common sea robin

Flying gurnard

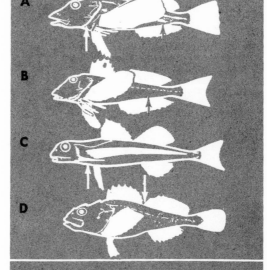

*Base of pectoral
fin not wide*

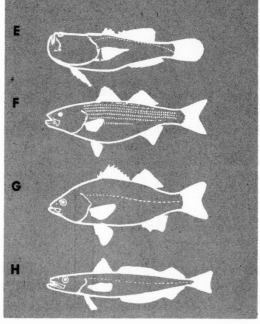

SCULPINS

I. *Uppermost cheek spine short; reaches back to a point less than half the distance from its base to the rear edge of the operculum*
Page 219, figs. A–D

    Ia. Total length more than nine inches
       Page 219, fig. C

       See Shorthorn Sculpin, p. 386.

    Ib. Total length less than nine inches
       Page 219, figs. C, D

       1. 13–14 anal rays
         Page 219, fig. C

         See Shorthorn Sculpin, p. 386.

       2. 10–11 anal rays
         Page 219, fig. D

         See Little Sculpin, p. 386.

II. *Uppermost cheek spine long; reaches back almost to rear edge of operculum*
Page 219, figs. E, F

   See Longhorn Sculpin, p. 387.

*Uppermost cheek
spine short*

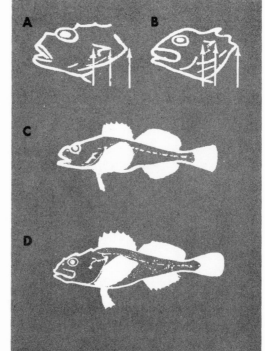

Shorthorn sculpin

Little sculpin

*Uppermost cheek
spine long*

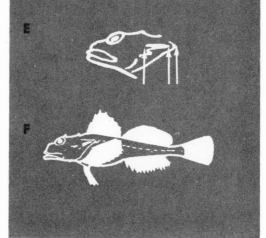

Longhorn sculpin

STARGAZER, STRIPED BASS,
WHITE PERCH, OTHER

I. *Base of second dorsal fin shorter than head*
Page 221, figs. A–C

Ia. Mouth opening on top of head
Page 221, fig. A

See Northen Stargazer, p. 398.

Ib. Mouth opening about in center of front of head
Page 221, figs. B, C

1. Sides have dusky, longitudinal stripes
Page 221, fig. B

See Striped Bass, p. 366.

2. Sides have no stripes
Page 221, fig. C

See White Perch, p. 367.

II. *Base of second dorsal fin longer than head*
Page 221, figs. D–G

See Whiting, Bluefish, Spadefish, Bumper, p. 222.

Base of second dorsal fin shorter than head

Stargazer

Striped bass

White perch

Base of second dorsal fin longer than head

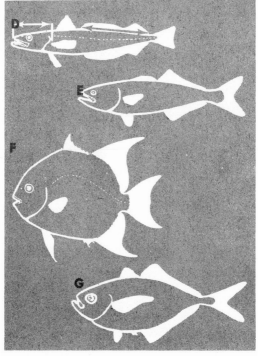

WHITING, BLUEFISH, SPADEFISH, BUMPER

I. *Greatest depth of body about equal to or less than length of head*
Page 223, figs. B, D, E

  Ia. Pectoral fin reaches back to a point beneath space between the two dorsal fins or front part of second dorsal fin
Page 223, figs. B, D

    1. Side of head mostly scaled
Page 223, figs. A, B

    See Offshore Whiting, p. 315.

    2. Side of head only partly scaled
Page 223, figs. C, D

    See Whiting, p. 314.

  Ib. Pectoral fin reaches back to a point beneath center of first dorsal fin
Page 223, fig. E

  See Bluefish, p. 364.

II. *Greatest depth of body at least twice length of head*
Page 223, figs. F, G

  IIa. Pectoral fin reaches back to a point about under the front part of first dorsal fin
Page 223, fig. F

  See Spadefish, p. 384.

  IIb. Pectoral fin reaches back to a point well past origin of second dorsal fin
Page 223, fig. G

  See Bumper, p. 360.

*Greatest depth of
body about equal to
or less than length
of head*

Offshore whiting

Whiting

Bluefish

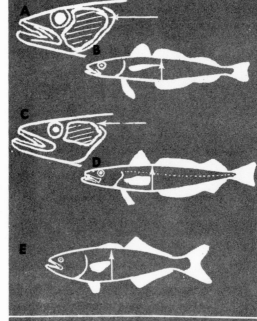

*Greatest depth of
body at least twice
length of head*

Spadefish

Bumper

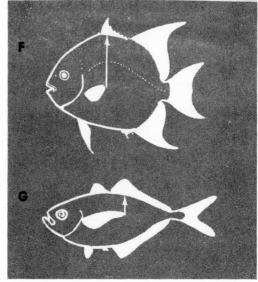

PART TWO

GENERAL INFORMATION

LAMPREYS

The lampreys are primitive aquatic fish-like vertebrates belonging in the Class Cyclostomata. Their skeletons are cartilagenous and the skull is very simple and barely different from the vertebral column. They have no true jaws, ribs, or paired fins. Only a single species, the sea lamprey, occurs in the marine waters of the American Atlantic coast.

Sea Lamprey
Petromyzon marinus Linnaeus

Color: Adults: ground color of upper surface of body various shades of brown, green, red, or blue, with mottles of a darker shade of the same color. Belly white, gray, or lighter shade of ground color of upper surface of the body. Young: silvery blackish blue above, white beneath.
Distribution: Occurs on both sides of the Atlantic. In the western Atlantic it is found from Greenland to Florida and in a landlocked form in some of the American lakes.
Size: Reaches a length of about 3 feet and a weight of over 2¼ pounds.
General Information: Specimens of Sea Lamprey found in salt water are not mature. In this stage it obtains nourishment by fastening to the sides of various marine fishes with its sucker-like mouth and by movement of the horny-toothed tongue rasping away at the flesh of the fish to encourage the flow of blood which is its food. This blood-feeding form remains in the sea from one to two years, then runs up coastal streams and rivers to fresh water, where it

spawns. Spawning takes place on stony or pebbly bottoms. The male and female make a "nest" for the eggs by removing pebbles from the nesting site with their sucker-like mouths until an irregular depression about 6 inches deep and 2 or more feet in diameter is formed. The adults die after spawning. Actually, once they enter the streams and rivers and their gonads ripen, their digestive system degenerates and they can no longer assimilate food.

The eggs hatch into small, blind, toothless animals called ammocoetes. These ammocoetes burrow into the mud and live on the microscopic animals in the upper part of the bottom mud. They remain in the mud for about 3 to 4 years, reaching a length of about 6 inches. About this time the eyes develop and the sucking mouth is formed, and the lamprey now moves down to sea and starts to feed on the blood of fish.

Economic Importance: Impassable dams have drastically reduced the population of Sea Lampreys along the coast. Formerly this species was used for food, but few are now taken for this purpose. In recent years the landlocked form of this animal has spread through man-made channels into the Great Lakes where it has reportedly reduced the populations of the most important food fishes, particularly the lake trout.

SHARKS

Characters: Sharks are fish-like vertebrates with well developed jaws and bony teeth. The skeleton consists of cartilage. The skin is covered with small, tooth-like enamel projections (denticles). There are 5–7 gill slits on each side of the head. The gill slits open separately to the outside of the body. All or part of the gill openings are on the sides of the body.

General Information: The body is usually torpedo-like but in a few exceptional species is flattened. Sharks are widely distributed from the subpolar to the tropical zones. They are mostly found in salt water, but some species enter brackish and even fresh water.

Fertilization is internal. Located on the inner edges of the pelvic fins of the male is a pair of organs (claspers) used to introduce the sperm or sexual products of the male into the two sexual openings of the female. These female sexual openings are located within the one large opening on the ventral surface of the body, the so-called cloacal opening. Both intestinal and urinary wastes and young are discharged through the cloacal opening.

Only a few species of sharks lay eggs. In most species the young are born alive. Compared with the true fishes, the number of young born at any one time is small, usually considerably less than 80. In the true fishes the number of eggs laid may range from several hundred into the millions.

Sharks are mostly flesh eaters. The larger, more active species may feed on other sharks, seals, and sea turtles, as well as on fish. Some with crushing teeth regularly eat crabs, lobsters, and shellfish. The whale shark and the basking shark, two of the largest species, feed on small shrimp-like animals and on small fishes. Most sharks are scavengers, and they will often concentrate in areas where garbage is being dumped. The sense of smell is well developed in sharks. Blood appears to excite them, and an injured, bleeding person is more likely to be attacked by some of the more aggressive species (such as the tiger, white, or hammerhead sharks) than is a casual swimmer. Shark attacks are most common in tropical waters and are more liable to occur at night than in the day. They are also more apt to happen in deep waters offshore than along shallow beaches.

Economic Importance: There is a limited fishery for sharks throughout the world in areas where they are abundant. The hide is used for leather; the liver oil of some species is a source of Vitamin A. The fins of certain species are considered a delicacy in the Far East. Many kinds of shark are regularly sold for human consumption, or are processed for use as feed for poultry and livestock.

Classification: The scientific classification of the sharks found in the area from Cape Cod to Cape Hatteras is as follows:

Class: Chondrichthyes (Elasmobranchs and Chimaeroids)
Subclass: Elasmobranchii (Sharks, Rays, Skates)
Order: Selachii (Modern Sharks)
Suborder: Galeoidea
Family: Carchariidae (Sand Sharks)
Carcharias taurus—sand shark

Family: Isuridae (Mackerel Sharks)
Lamna nasus—mackerel shark, porbeagle
Isurus oxyrinchus—mako, sharp-nosed mackerel shark
Carcharodon carcharias—white shark, man-eater

Family: Cetorhinidae (Basking Sharks)
Cetorhinus maximus—basking shark

Family: Alopiidae (Thresher Sharks)
Alopias vulpinus—common thresher shark

Family: Orectolobidae (Carpet Sharks)
Ginglymostoma cirratum—nurse shark

Family: Rhincodontidae (Whale Sharks)
Rhincodon typus—whale shark

Family: Scyliorhinidae (Cat Sharks)
Scyliorhinus retifer—chain dogfish
Apristurus profundorum—deep-water cat shark

Family: Pseudotriakidae (False Cat Sharks)
Pseudotriakis microdon—false cat shark

Family: Triakidae (Smooth Dogfishes)
Mustelus canis—smooth dogfish

Family: Carcharhinidae
Galeocerdo cuvier—tiger shark
Paragaleus pectoralis—Paragaleus
Prionace glauca—blue shark
Scoliodon terrae-novae—sharp-nosed shark
Aprionodon isodon—smooth-tooth shark
Negaprion brevirostris—lemon shark

Carcharhinus falciformis—sickle-shape shark
Carcharhinus leucas—cub, ground, bull shark
Carcharhinus limbatus—spot-fin ground shark, small black-tipped shark
Carcharhinus milberti—brown shark
Carcharhinus obscurus—dusky shark

Family: Sphyrnidae (Hammerhead Sharks)
Sphyrna tibura—shovelhead, bonnet shark
Sphyrna diplana—southern hammerhead shark
Sphyrna zygaena—common hammerhead shark

Suborder: Squaloidea
  Family: Squalidae (Spiny Dogfishes)
Squalus acanthias—spiny dogfish
Centroscyllium fabricii—black dogfish
Centroscymnus coelolepis—Portuguese shark

  Family: Dalatiidae
Somniosus microcephalus—Greenland shark

Suborder: Squatinoidea
  Family: Aquatinidae
Squatina dumeril—angel shark

Sand Shark
Carcharias taurus Rafinesque

Color: Gray-brown on upper surface of body, gray-white on belly; yellow-brown oval or round spots on sides of body and caudal and dorsal fins.

Distribution: Cape Verdes, Canaries, tropical West Africa and the Mediterranean. In the western Atlantic from the Gulf of Maine to southern Brazil.

Size: May reach about 10 feet in length and weigh more than 250 pounds. A fish almost 9 feet long weighed about 250 pounds.

General Information: Very common. The most abundant shark on the coast from Cape Cod to Delaware Bay. A sluggish shark living near the bottom close to shore. Often found in less than 6 feet of water off beaches. Feeds mainly on small fish, crabs, and squid. Matures when over 7 feet long. Most sand sharks caught are between 4 and 6 feet and are immature.

Economic Importance: Not important in the commercial fisheries. Frequently taken by the sport fisherman while surf casting.

Mackerel Shark, Porbeagle
Lamna nasus (Bonnaterre)

Color: Dark blue-gray above, becoming white on lower sides and undersurface.

Distribution: From the Murman coast and Norway south to the Mediterranean and northwestern Africa. In the western Atlantic from the Newfoundland Banks to South Carolina. Most common north of Cape Cod. Appears as a stray from New York south.

Size: Reported to reach almost 13 feet in length. Most common size, 4–5 feet.

General Information: An active species ranging from the bottom to the surface of the water. It has been taken in depths down to 480 feet and may go deeper. Feeds largely on schools of herrings and mackerel but also on other available fishes. Young are large at birth and may be over 2 feet long and weigh over 25 pounds. From 1 to 5 young are born at a time.

Economic Importance: Of minor importance in the commercial fisheries. It is of little interest to the angler because of its sluggishness when hooked.

Sharp-nosed Mackerel Shark, Mako
Isurus oxyrinchus Rafinesque

Color: Deep cobalt to blue-gray on the upper parts of the body, snowy white below.

Distribution: Mediterranean, tropical West Africa, and north to Norway. In the western Atlantic from the Gulf of Maine south to Brazil. Common offshore from southern New England to Maryland.

Size: Reported to reach a length of 13 feet. Recorded weights of specimens: 8 feet, about 300 pounds; 9 feet, 700–800 pounds; 10½ feet, 1,000 pounds.

General Information: An active, strong-swimming shark often found offshore near the surface of the water. Feeds mostly on fish, both the smaller school types such as herrings and mackerels and larger fish such as the swordfish.

Economic Importance: Of limited value in the commercial fisheries. Some are marketed. Its habit of leaping when hooked makes it one of the most desirable of sharks for sport fishing.

White Shark, Man-Eater
Carcharodon carcharias (Linnaeus)

Color: Color of upper part of body varies among individuals. May be gray-brown, gray-blue, dark gray, or almost black. Lower part of body dirty white. A black spot near rear part of base of pectoral fin.

Distribution: World-wide in tropical and subtropical zones and warmer waters of temperate zone. Not abundant in any particular region. Occurs erratically. Has been taken on the western Atlantic from Newfoundland to Brazil.

Size: It is said to reach a length of 40 feet. Fish at 13 feet may weigh 1,300 pounds and at 21 feet 7,100 pounds.

General Information: Typically an oceanic form, it frequently comes into shallow inshore waters, where it has been known to attack man and has therefore earned the title of "man-eater shark." An active, voracious species. It feeds on a wide variety of small fish and marine animals but is also known to swallow almost whole other sharks, seals, turtles, sturgeons, and tunas. Probably matures when over 13 feet long.

Economic Importance: This species is too infrequently encountered to be of much importance to the commercial or recreational fisheries. Its active, pugnacious nature makes it a dangerous adversary when hooked or harpooned.

Basking Shark
Cetorhinus maximus (Gunnerus)

Color: Brown-gray, medium gray, or nearly black on upper surface of body. Undersurface may be same color as upper surface, a lighter shade, or almost white.

Distribution: World-wide in northern and temperate waters. Recorded in the western Atlantic from Newfoundland to the Falkland Islands, but nowhere abundant.

Size: Reported to reach a length of 50 feet. Recorded as weighing 8,600 pounds at 30 feet. Immature fish under 13 feet have a long-drawn-out snout which gives them an entirely different appearance from the adult.

General Information: A sluggish, harmless shark often found swimming slowly at the surface with its mouth open to collect the plankton in the water, its chief source of food. The plankton is carried into the open mouth with the water and sifted by fine comb-like gill rakers from the water as it passes over the gills and out of the gill slits.

Economic Importance: Now of little importance on the western Atlantic coast. Formerly, when animal oils were used for lighting, the liver oil was extracted for fuel for lamps.

Common Thresher Shark
Alopias vulpinus (Bonnaterre)

Color: Upper side and back variable; brown, blue-gray, dark gray or almost black. Lower sides a lighter shade of back color. Lower surface mostly white, sometimes mottled with gray.

Distribution: World-wide in the subtropical zone and warmer waters of the temperate zone. In the western Atlantic, reported from the Gulf of St. Lawrence to northern Argentina, with most appearances recorded off southern New England.

Size: May grow to over 20 feet in length. Fish 13–16 feet common. A fish 13 feet long weighs about 400 pounds.

General Information: Usually found a few miles offshore swimming near the surface. Feeds on smaller schooling fishes including mackerel, bluefish, herring, bonito, and menhaden. The long, whip-like tail is used to splash the water to frighten the schools of fish into a concentrated mass while the shark gradually swims in a narrowing circle around them. Occasionally, two thresher sharks may work together. Sometimes the tail is used to lash out and stun the prey.

Economic Importance: Of little importance in the commercial fisheries. Frequently caught by sport fishermen off the New York and New Jersey coasts.

Nurse Shark
Ginglymostoma cirratum (Bonnaterre)

Color: Upper surface of body yellow-brown to gray-brown. Remainder of body lighter shade of same color.

Distribution: Found on both sides of the Atlantic and in the American Pacific oceans in tropical and subtropical waters. In the western Atlantic most common in the

Caribbean-West Indian regions, but extending its range in summer to North Carolina. Occurs only as strays north of North Carolina.

Size: Maximum length recorded, 14 feet. Sharks 8½ feet in length weigh from 330 to 370 pounds.

General Information: Chiefly found inshore in shallow waters, often less than 10 feet deep. A sluggish species commonly seen in small schools resting on the bottom. Feeds mostly on crabs, shrimp, squid, sea urchins, and small fish.

Economic Importance: Where it is common, the skin may be used for leather.

Whale Shark
Rhincodon typus Smith

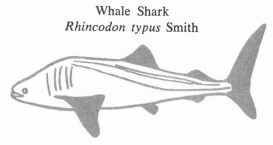

Color: Back and sides red or greenish brown to dark gray and covered with scattered white or yellow spots; also some transverse white or yellow stripes. Lower surface of body white or yellow.

Distribution: Widely distributed offshore in tropical waters of all oceans. In the western Atlantic found from New York to Brazil, but most abundant in the Caribbean-West Indian region.

Size: The largest of the sharks. Reported to reach a length of 60 feet or more. A 38-foot specimen has been estimated to weigh 26,594 pounds.

General Information: Little is known about its life history. It is often found in schools basking at the surface of the water. Like the basking shark, the whale shark feeds on plankton. Small fish, squid, and small shrimp-like forms are also eaten.

Economic Importance: None.

Chain Dogfish
Scyliorhinus retifer (Garman)

Color: Upper part of body red-brown, lower part yellowish. Series of chain-like black markings over body.
Distribution: Found on the outer part of the Continental Shelf from New York to North Carolina in depths of 250–750 feet.
Size: Probably does not grow longer than 2½ feet. Most caught smaller than 1½ feet.
General Information: Little is known about this species. It appears to be most abundant along the Continental Shelf off Chesapeake Bay.
Economic Importance: None.

Deep-water Cat Shark
Apristurus profundorum (Goode and Bean)

Color: Grayish brown.
Distribution: Deep water off Delaware Bay.
Size: Largest specimen taken about 20 inches. Maximum size not known.
General Information: A rare deep-sea shark about which little is known.
Economic Importance: None.

False Cat Shark
Pseudotriakis microdon Brito Capello

Color: Body a uniform brown-gray.
Distribution: Both sides of the North Atlantic. Rare. In western Atlantic a single specimen reported washed ashore near Amagansett, Long Island, New York.
Size: Maximum length recorded, 9⅔ feet.
General Information: Has been captured in the eastern Atlantic at depths of 980–4,840 feet.
Economic Importance: None.

Smooth Dogfish
Mustelus canis (Mitchill)

Color: Upper part of body olive-gray, slate gray, or brown. Lower part yellow, white, or gray-white.
Distribution: Mouth of Bay of Fundy south to Uruguay. Most common from Cape Cod to Virginia.
Size: Attains a maximum length of about 5 feet, but 3–4-foot specimens are more common.
General Information: This is one of the most numerous sharks in the southern New England and Middle Atlantic areas. It is commonly caught in bays and estuaries and along ocean beaches in depths of 60 feet or less. Crabs are its chief food. Also eats small fish, squid, shellfish, and

worms. In some areas lobsters comprise a large part of its diet. The spiny dogfish matures when about 3 feet long. Normally 10–20 young are born at one time, but smaller litters have been reported. Young are born in summer in the northern part of the species' range.

Economic Importance: Frequently taken in large numbers by the commercial fisheries, but only a limited quantity is marketed. A common catch of the surf-caster and recreational boat fisherman.

Tiger Shark
Galeocerdo cuvier (LeSueur)

Color: Body gray or brown-gray, lighter hued on sides and belly than on back. Specimens under 6 feet marked with brown spots fusing into irregular bars on sides.

Distribution: World-wide in tropical and subtropical waters. In the western Atlantic recorded from Cape Cod to Uruguay. Most abundant in the Caribbean-South Florida region. Only a few recorded north of Florida as summer visitors.

Size: Reported to reach a length of 30 feet. Most specimens taken are less than 14 feet. A tiger shark 13–14 feet long weighs 1,000–1,400 pounds.

General Information: The tiger shark is found in both inshore and offshore waters. It often enters bays and river mouths in the south. A noted scavenger, it feeds on animal debris thrown from ships or dumped from shore. Eats a wide variety of foods. Crabs, horse-shoe crabs, spiny lobsters, fish, other sharks, skates, and sting rays have been found in stomach of this shark. Gravid females have been found to carry 10–80 young.

Economic Importance: The skin of this shark has been used for leather. In some localities it is taken incidentally by anglers fishing for other species.

Paragaleus
Paragaleus pectoralis (Garman)

Color: Brown-gray.
Distribution: Known from only a single specimen caught off the coast of southern New England.
Size: Specimen was slightly over 25½ inches long.
General Information: Nothing is known about this shark.
Economic Importance: None.

Blue Shark
Prionace glauca (Linnaeus)

Color: Dark blue along the back, clear brilliant blue on sides. Belly, clear white.
Distribution: World-wide in subtropical and temperate waters of all oceans. In the western Atlantic from Newfoundland Banks to Argentina. Infrequent visitor in sum-

mer in the southern New England and middle Atlantic area.
Size: Reported to reach a length of 20 feet.
A 9-foot blue shark weighed 164 pounds.
General Information: Usually found offshore but often comes inshore. Feeds on small fishes, particularly herring and mackerel, and is also an active scavenger. Probably does not mature until over 7 feet long. From 28 to 54 young have been counted in gravid females.
Economic Importance: Of limited commercial value. A few are eaten. A powerful swimmer, prone to make repeated rushes when hooked, it is a desirable species for the recreational fisherman.

Sharp-nosed Shark
Scoliodon terrae-novae (Richardson)

Color: Upper part of body brown to olive-gray. Lower part of body white.
Distribution: Tropical and subtropical waters on both sides of the Atlantic. In the western Atlantic from the Gulf of Maine to Uruguay. Most abundant in the Caribbean and Gulf of Mexico. Common summer visitor along the coast of South Carolina. Rare from Chesapeake Bay north.
Size: Maximum size reported, about 3 feet.
General Information: Commonly found in shallow waters along beaches, in bays, and in estuaries. Feeds chiefly on small fish. Also eats shellfish and shrimp. Matures when 26–30 inches long. Newborn sharks are 11–16 inches long.
Economic Importance: Too rare a species from Chesapeake Bay north to be of any importance.

Smooth-tooth Shark
Aprionodon isodon (Müller and Henle)

Color: Blue-gray above, gray-white on lower sides, and pure white below.
Distribution: Tropical waters on both sides of the Atlantic. In the western Atlantic, off Cuba, in the Gulf of Mexico and as a stray along the east coast of the United States as far north as New York.
Size: Maximum length reported, 4 feet.
General Information: Nothing is known of its life history. Rare in the region from Cape Cod to Cape Hatteras.
Economic Importance: None.

Lemon Shark
Negaprion brevirostris (Poey)

Color: Upper part of body usually yellow-brown, sometimes dark brown or blue-gray. Lower sides yellowish or olive-green. Lower part of body olive-gray or pale yellow.
Distribution: Northern Brazil to North Carolina, and, rarely, north to New Jersey.
Size: Maximum length about 11 feet. A 9½-foot specimen is reported to weigh 265 pounds.

General Information: Common around docks, in creeks, and in sounds from Florida to North Carolina. Probably feeds on fish. Matures at 7–7½ feet. Breeds in spring and summer in Florida waters.

Economic Importance: Part of the commercial catch of sharks in Florida waters.

Sickle-shape Shark
Carcharhinus falciformis (Müller and Henle)

Color: Upper surface of body dark gray, underside gray-white.

Distribution: Both sides of the Atlantic in subtropical and tropical waters. In the western Atlantic most common in the Caribbean region, but reported as a stray on the Continental Shelf off Delaware Bay.

Size: Maximum size not known. A 10-foot specimen has been reported.

General Information: Little is known about this species.

Economic Importance: None.

Cub Shark, Ground Shark, Bull Shark
Carcharhinus leucas (Müller and Henle)

Color: Light to dark gray on upper parts of body; white below.

Distribution: The western Atlantic from southern Brazil to North Carolina, and as a stray north to New York.

Size: Maximum size probably more than 10 feet. A 10-foot specimen weighs about 400 pounds.

General Information: A slow-swimming species most frequently found in shoal, inshore waters. Feeds on crabs, fish, and any animal refuse. Matures at about 7 feet. Birth probably occurs in late winter and early spring. From 5 to 6 young are born at one time.

Economic Importance: Common in the catch of the commercial shark fishery in Florida.

Small Black-tipped Shark, Spot-fin Ground Shark
Carcharhinus limbatus (Müller and Henle)

Color: Grayish brown, brayish blue, or dark gray on upper parts of body. Lower part of body white or yellow-white. Pectoral fins tipped with black.

Distribution: Possibly world-wide in tropical and subtropical waters. In the western Atlantic found from southern Brazil to North Carolina, and as a stray off the coasts of New York and southern New England.

Size: Maximum length probably 8 feet. A 5½-foot specimen weighed slightly over 68 pounds.

General Information: Found both near the shore and offshore. An active, fast-swimming shark, often appearing in schools at the surface of the water. When surfaced it frequently will leap clear of the water. Fish appears to be principal food. In Florida waters young are born in spring. From 3 to 6 are produced at one time, and they are about feet long at birth.

Economic Importance: Of minor importance in the commercial and recreational fisheries of Florida.

Brown Shark
Carcharhinus milberti (Müller and Henle)

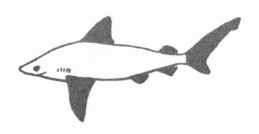

Color: Brown, brown-gray, or slate gray on upper part of body. Lower part of body lighter shades of these colors or white.

Distribution: Reported from the Mediterranean Sea and European Atlantic. In the western Atlantic from southern Brazil to southern New England. Occasionally abundant off the coasts of New York and New Jersey during the summer.

Size: Maximum length about 8 feet; weight at this length was near 200 pounds.

General Information: Fairly abundant near shore in the Middle Atlantic area. Found commonly in shoal water of harbors, bays, and estuaries. Feeds chiefly on fish, shellfish, crabs, and other crustaceans. Matures at about 6 feet. On the coast of New York young are released from June to August. From 6 to 13 young are born at a time, 2 inches long and weighing 2½ pounds at birth.

Economic Importance: Of limited commercial value. Caught incidentally by the angler.

Dusky Shark
Carcharhinus obscurus (LeSueur)

Color: Back and upper sides light to dark gray or blue-gray; lower sides and belly white.

Distribution: Both sides of the Atlantic in tropical and warm temperate waters. In the western Atlantic from southern Massachusetts to the Bahamas. Taken frequently from Delaware Bay north to Woods Hole, Massachusetts, but often confused with the Brown Shark or the Cub Shark.

Size: Reported as reaching a length of 14 feet.

General Information: Little is known about this shark. It probably is most common offshore but frequently is found in shoal waters inshore.

Economic Importance: None.

Shovelhead, Bonnet Shark
Sphyrna tibura (Linnaeus)

Color: Upper part of body gray or brown-gray; a lighter shade of same color below.

Distribution: Reported from both sides of the Atlantic and on the American Pacific coast. In the western Atlantic found from Massachusetts Bay to southern Brazil. Uncommon north of North Carolina.

Size: Reported to reach a length of 6 feet.

General Information: Frequents shallow waters along the coast. A sluggish species feeding largely on crabs and other crustaceans. Also eats shellfish and small fish. Matures when 3½–4 feet long. From 6 to 9 young are born at a time.

Economic Importance: None.

Southern Hammerhead Shark
Sphyrna diplana Springer

Color: Upper surface of body light gray, shading to white below.

Distribution: Tropical and warm temperate waters of the Atlantic Ocean. In the western Atlantic, recorded from southern New Jersey to Brazil.

Size: Grows to at least 10 feet.

General Information: First described in 1941, it has been confused in the past with the Common Hammerhead. Little is known about this shark.

Economic Importance: None.

Common Hammerhead Shark
Sphyrna zygaena (Linnaeus)

Color: Upper part of body dark olive-gray or brown-gray, sides lighter. Undersurface gray-white.
Distribution: World-wide in warm and temperate waters. In the western Atlantic found from Uruguay to southern New England and as a stray as far north as Nova Scotia.
Size: May grow to 13 feet and over 900 pounds.
General Information: Often seen near the surface of the water both offshore and inshore. In summer, large schools are frequently reported moving along the shores of New York and New Jersey. Feeds mainly on fish, but squid, crabs, and shrimp are also eaten. Matures at 7–8 feet. From 29 to 37 young have been counted in a single gravid female. The young are probably 19–20 inches long at birth.
Economic Importance: Used to some extent for meal, oil, and leather in Florida and the West Indies. Readily takes a bait and is frequently caught by the angler.

Spiny Dogfish
Squalus acanthias Linnaeus

Color: Upper portion of body slate gray; lower portion pale gray to white. Scattered white spots over body of smaller specimens.

Distribution: World-wide, chiefly in temperate and sub-arctic waters. In the western Atlantic, found from south-eastern Labrador to North Carolina.

Size: Maximum length about 4 feet with a weight of 15–20 pounds. Most fish range between 2 and 3½ feet in length and weigh 7–10 pounds.

General Information: A rather sluggish shark often occurring in large schools. Common inshore but likely to be found anywhere between the surface of the water and the bottom to depths of 600 feet. The dorsal spines are used for defense. The fish curls itself into a bow-like position in striking. The spines are thought to be slightly poisonous. Chief food is fish, although squid, worms, crabs, and shrimp are also eaten. Males mature at 24–31 inches and females at 27–39 inches. Birth occurs in the Middle Atlantic region in late winter. From 2 to 11 young are born at a time, with 4–6 the average. Newborn young range from 6½ to 13 inches in length.

Economic Importance: Widely utilized in Europe as a food. Unsuccessful attempts have been made in the United States to market the Spiny Dogfish, both as a food and as fish meal and oil. Although frequently they are so abundant locally as to hamper commercial fishing, only a small quantity can be marketed. While not an active enough species to attract a recreational fishery, the Spiny Dogfish is often caught incidentally by the angler.

Black Dogfish
Centroscyllium fabricii (Reinhardt)

Color: Upper surface of body chocolate brown; darker almost black, below.

Distribution: Both sides of the North Atlantic in depths over 900 feet. In the western Atlantic, common from southwestern Greenland to the eastern end of Georges Bank off the coast of Massachusetts. Extent of range south unknown, but occurrences reported in the deep waters off the coast of New York.

Size: Reported to reach a length of 3½ feet.

General Information: A deep-water species found at 900–3,500 feet. Little is known about this species. It feeds on small shrimp-like animals, squids, octopi, and jellyfishes.

Economic Importance: None.

Portuguese Shark
Centroscymnus coelolepis Bocage and Capello

Color: Entire body a dark chocolate brown.

Distribution: Both sides of the North Atlantic in depths over 1,100 feet. In the western Atlantic, specimens have been taken from the Newfoundland Grand Banks south to the Continental Slope off Nantucket, Massachusetts.

Size: Length of largest specimen taken slightly less than 4 feet.

General Information: Little is known about this shark.

Economic Importance: None.

Greenland Shark
Somniosus microcephalus (Black and Schneider)

Color: Whole body the same color, but variable from one specimen to another. Color of body may be dark brown, black, or different shades of gray. Sides may or may not be tinged with violet and may or may not have faint dark bands or faint white spots.

Distribution: On both sides of the Atlantic, mostly in arctic and subarctic waters. In the western Atlantic, found from Hudson Strait to the tip of Cape Cod, but most common in the north.

Size: Said to reach a length of 24 feet. A 21-foot specimen is reported to have weighed 2,250 pounds.

General Information: In Greenland and Labrador it is reported as coming to the surface in winter. In summer it has been caught in depths of more than 3,900 feet. Food consists of a wide variety of fishes, including herring, salmon, pollock, cod, haddock, and halibut. Seals and sea birds as well as a varied assortment of other forms of sea animals have been found in the stomachs of Greenland Sharks. It is also reported to be an active scavenger.

Economic Importance: The liver oil is used in Europe and the dried meat is fed to dogs in Greenland. Not utilized on the American Atlantic coast.

Angel Shark
Squatina dumeril (LeSueur)

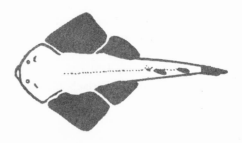

Color: Upper surface of body light gray or blue-gray; head tinted with red. Lower surface of body white; a

reddish spot on the throat, on the belly, and near the tail.
Distribution: Found from southern New England to
Jamaica. Sometimes common off the coasts of Maryland
and Virginia.
Size: Maximum length reported, about 5 feet. A 4-foot
specimen weighed 60 pounds.
General Information: Most frequently found in only a
few feet of water, but it has been taken in depths down
to 4,200 feet. Feeds on crabs, shellfish, and fish. Probably
matures when 3–3½ feet long.
Economic Importance: None.

SAWFISH, SKATES, AND RAYS

Characters: The sawfish, skates, and rays are fish-like
vertebrates with well-developed jaws and bony teeth. The
skeleton consists of cartilage. The skin is covered with
small, tooth-like, enamel projections. There are 5 pairs of
gill slits, all located on the lower surface of the body. The
front edges of the pectoral fins are united with the head.
General Information: Most of the forms in this group have
a flattened, disc-like body. The Sawfish, however, is more
shark-like in body form. The various species are widely
distributed from the subpolar to tropical zones. In the
cooler waters of the temperate and subpolar zones, Skates
are most numerous both in number of species and in individuals. In the warm waters of the tropical and subtropical
zones the Sawfish and Rays predominate.

Like the sharks, the males of this group of fish-like
vertebrates possess a pair of copulatory organs (claspers),
elongated appendages situated along the inner margins of
the pelvic fins. Fertilization is internal. Members of the
Skate family lay eggs enclosed in a horny capsule (p. 254,
fig. 1). In all of the other families the young are born
alive.

In general the members of this group are sluggish animals living on or near the bottom and frequently burying

themselves partially or completely in the mud or sand. The species that commonly act in such fashion have large openings (*spiracles*) behind the eyes. In breathing, water passes into the spiracles over the gills and out of the gill slits. Little or no water is taken into the mouth as is characteristic of species with small spiracles. Some exceptional species such as the Eagle and Cow-nosed Rays and the Devil Rays are active animals and are frequently seen vigorously swimming near the surface of the water or leaping clear of the water. Shellfish, crabs, worms, small shrimp-like animals comprise the bulk of the food of the sawfish, skates, and rays.

The Torpedo Ray has two electric organs, one on each side of the front third of the body. These may possibly be used for defense or for stunning their prey. Among the Sting Rays, the long, whip-like tail is armed with one or more poisonous spines. Spines are also present on the tails of some of the Butterfly Rays, the Cow-nosed Ray and the Eagle Rays. The spine may be as long as 5 inches in some species. Sting Rays can be dangerous when accidentally disturbed by the swimmer or when captured. The long tail can be lashed vigorously and a severe wound inflicted by the poisonous spines.

Economic Importance: The pectoral fins (wings or saddles) of some of the larger species are marketed for food. Many species are used for bait in crab and lobster traps, and more recently as a source of fish meal. The spines of the Sting Rays have been used by primitive tribes for needles and spear tips.

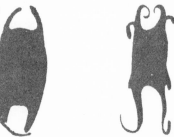

Fig. 1. Egg cases of Skates

Classification: The scientific classification of the sawfish, skates, and rays in the area from Cape Cod to Cape Hatteras is as follows:

Class: Chondrichthyes (Elasmobranchs and Chimaeroids)
Subclass: Elasmobranchii (Sharks, Sawfish, Skates, Rays)
Order: Batoidei (Sawfish, Skates, Rays)
Suborder: Pristoidea
    Family: Pristidae (Sawfishes)
    Pristis pectinatus—common sawfish

Suborder: Torpedinoidea
    Family: Torpedinidae (Torpedoes)
    Torpedo nobliana—electric ray, torpedo

Suborder: Rajoidea
    Family: Rajidae (Skates)
    Raja eglanteria—clear-nosed, brier skate
    Raja erinacea—little skate
    Raja garmani—rosetted skate, leopard skate
    Raja laevis—barn-door skate
    Raja ocellata—big skate
    Raja radiata—thorny skate
    Raja senta—smooth-tailed skate

Suborder: Myliobatoidea
    Family: Dasyatidae (Sting Rays)
    Dasyatis americana—southern sting ray
    Dasyatis centroura—northern sting ray
    Dasyatis sabina—stingaree
    Dasyatis say—Say's sting ray

    Family: Gymnuridae (Butterfly Rays)
    Gymnura altavela—giant butterfly ray
    Gymnura micrura—lesser butterfly ray

    Family: Myliobatidae (Eagle Rays)
    Myliobatis freminvillii—eagle ray
    Aetobatus narinari—spotted eagle ray

    Family: Rhinopteridae (Cow-nosed Rays)
    Rhinoptera bonasus—cow-nosed ray

Family: Mobulidae (Devil Rays)
Mobula hypostoma—lesser devil ray
Manta birostris—giant devil ray

Common Sawfish
Pristis pectinatus Latham

Color: Upper portion of body dark gray to black-brown; light yellow, white, or gray-white below.
Distribution: Tropical and subtropical waters on both sides of the Atlantic and in the eastern Mediterranean. In the western Atlantic, commonly found from Brazil to northern Florida. A summer visitor to the north as far as New York.
Size: Maximum size over 18 feet. A specimen about 16 feet long weighed 700 pounds.
General Information: The Common Sawfish almost always occurs near land, in a few feet of water, often in bays and estuaries. It is found in brackish as well as salt water and will ascend rivers into fresh water. Observations in Texas indicate that at least in this locality birth takes place from late spring through autumn. The young are about 2 feet at birth. From 15 to 20 young are carried by a gravid female.
Economic Importance: None. A nuisance to the commercial fishermen in southern waters, often becoming entangled in their nets.

Torpedo, Electric Ray
Torpedo nobliana Bonaparte

Color: Dark chocolate brown to purple-brown or almost black on upper surface of body. White below.
Distribution: Both sides of the Atlantic and in the Mediterranean. In the western Atlantic, from Cuba to southern Nova Scotia.
Size: The largest specimen reported almost 6 feet long. Relationship of length to weight varies greatly depending on fatness of fish. Heaviest fish recorded has been estimated at 200 pounds.
General Information: Little is known about this ray. It probably lives on the bottom partly buried in the sand or mud. Chief food is fish. The electric organs, located in the front third of the body, are able to discharge moderate amounts of electricity by means of which it is believed fish are stunned for more ready capture. While some specimens of the Electric Ray have been taken near shore in only a few feet of water, it is likely that they are most numerous in waters of 60–360 feet or deeper.
Economic Importance: None.

Clear-nosed Skate, Brier Skate
Raja eglanteria Bosc

Color: Upper surface of body light and dark brown; brown spots and bars. Lower surface white.

Distribution: Massachusetts Bay to Florida.

Size: Maximum length recorded slightly over 3 feet. A specimen 31 inches long weighed 6½ pounds.

General Information: Abundant seasonally from New York to Virginia. It occurs in shallow waters along beaches and out to depths of 400 feet. Feeds on crabs, shrimp, squid, and fish. In the north, matures when 2–3 feet long. The eggs are probably laid in spring. Young are about 5½ inches long when hatched.

Economic Importance: Common in the commercial catch of the fisheries in the Middle Atlantic area. The pectoral fins or "wings" of the largest specimens are occasionally used for food. The Clear-nosed Skate is frequently caught by the surf-caster fishing off the shores of New York and New Jersey.

Little Skate
Raja erinacea Mitchill

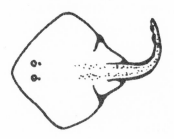

Color: Upper surface of body light to dark brown; scattered dark brown spots. Lower surface white or light gray.
Distribution: Massachusetts Bay to Florida.
Size: Largest size recorded about 21 inches long. A specimen of this length weighs about 2 pounds.
General Information: Common in shallow waters along the coast, but has been taken in depths down to 480 feet. Crabs and shrimp form an important part of its diet. It also feeds on squid, shellfish, worms, and small fishes including the silversides, sand launces, and herrings. The Little Skate matures when 18–20 inches long. The eggs are laid in early spring and summer. Newborn young are 3½–4 inches long.
Economic Importance: One of the commonest skates along the coasts of New England and the Middle Atlantic. Often taken in quantity by the commercial fisheries, but most of the catch is discarded. Small quantities are used as bait in eel and lobster traps. The Little Skate is probably the species of skate most frequently caught by the angler.

Rosetted Skate, Leopard Skate
Raja garmani Whitley

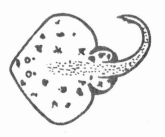

Color: Upper surface of body.light to dark brown; scattered small light and dark brown spots; also conspicuous dark rosettes formed of a half dozen or more dark brown or brown-black spots arranged around a central spot.
Distribution: From southern New England to Florida in the deep waters of the Continental Shelf.
Size: A specimen 17 inches long has been recorded. Maximum length is not known.
General Information: Little is known about this skate. It appears to inhabit waters deeper than 240 feet.
Economic Importance: None.

Barn-Door Skate
Raja laevis Mitchill

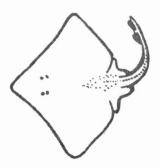

Color: Upper surface of body brown, with darker spots of various sizes scattered over its surface. Lower surface white, often with gray blotches; mucous pores in snout region with black dots.

Distribution: Grand Banks of Newfoundland south to North Carolina.

Size: Reported to reach a length of 6 feet. Specimens 4–4½ feet weigh 30–38 pounds.

General Information: The Barn-Door Skate is often found close to shore but is most common offshore in depths of 30–500 feet and has been taken in depths down to 1,400 feet. It feeds chiefly on crabs, shrimp, and lobsters but also eats shellfish, squid, worms, and a wide variety of fishes. The eggs are laid in winter, and the young are about 7 inches long at hatching.

Economic Importance: A common species growing to a large size, it comprises the bulk of the commercial catch of skates marketed on the American Atlantic coast. Barn-Door Skates are frequently caught by anglers "deep-sea" fishing off the coasts of New York and New Jersey.

Big Skate
Raja ocellata Mitchill

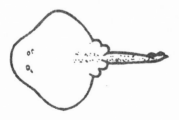

Color: Upper surface of body light brown with scattered round, black spots. Outer or hind part of pectoral fin often has 1–4 dark brown or blackish spots edged with white. Lower surface white, with irregular brown patches.

Distribution: Grand Banks of Newfoundland south to North Carolina.

Size: Maximum length about 3½ feet. A specimen 2½ feet long weighs about 7 pounds.

General Information: Commonly found both in the shoal waters along the shore and down to depths of 240 feet. It has been recorded at a depth of 360 feet. The main food of this skate is crabs, but worms, shrimp, shellfish, and small fishes are also eaten. In southern New England the eggs appear to be laid throughout the year. Newly hatched young are 4½–5 inches long.

Economic Importance: Fairly common in the catch of the offshore otter trawl fishery. The larger specimens are sometimes marketed for food. Some are processed into fish meal.

Thorny Skate
Raja radiata Donovan

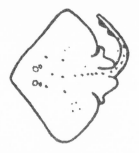

Color: Upper surface of body brown. Lower surface white, sometimes with brown or gray blotches.

Distribution: Both sides of the North Atlantic Ocean. In the western Atlantic, found from Labrador to South Carolina. South of Cape Cod occurs mostly in depths of 900–1,800 feet along the Continental Slope.

Size: Maximum length recorded slightly less than 3½ feet.

General Information: Most common north of Cape Cod. Feeds on crabs, shrimp, worms, and small fishes. Eggs appear to be deposited throughout the year. Newly hatched young are about 4 inches long.

Economic Importance: None.

Smooth-tailed Skate
Raja senta Garman

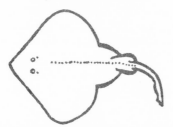

Color: Upper surface of body pale brown with numerous dark spots. Lower surface white.
Distribution: Gulf of St. Lawrence to South Carolina.
Size: Maximum length recorded is 2 feet.
General Information: A deep-water species. South of Cape Cod it has been taken in depths of from 300 to 2,800 feet. Little is known about this skate.
Economic Importance: None.

Southern Sting Ray
Dasyatis americana Hildebrand and Schroeder

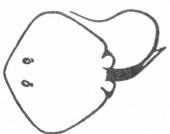

Color: Upper surface of body gray, brown, or brownish green; a gray or white spot on center line of snout immediately in front of eyes. Lower surface white.
Distribution: Found in coastal waters from Brazil to New Jersey, but occurs only as a straggler north of North Carolina.

Size: Largest specimen recorded was 5 feet wide. A specimen about 3 feet wide weighed 58 pounds.
General Information: Uncommon in the region north of North Carolina. It is usually found inshore in shoal water. It feeds on crabs, clams, shrimp, worms, and small fishes. Newborn young are probably about 8 inches wide.
Economic Importance: None.

Northern Sting Ray
Dasyatis centroura (Mitchill)

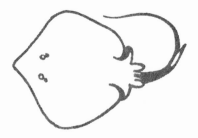

Color: Olive-brown or dark brown on upper surface of body; white on lower surface.
Distribution: Coastal waters from Georges Bank and Cape Cod to Cape Hatteras.
Size: Probably the largest sting ray in the western North Atlantic. Maximum width reported nearly 7 feet. Maximum length possibly 13–14 feet. A specimen 7 feet wide was said to weigh 350 pounds.
General Information: Often found in shoal waters near inlets and in bays but has also been taken in depths of 120–180 feet. Common in summer off the coasts of southern New England and the Middle Atlantic. Feeds on crabs, clams, squid, and worms. Little is known about its life history.
Economic Importance: None. Commonly taken by the commercial fisheries. Often caught by surf-casters along the New York and New Jersey beaches.

Stingaree
Dasyatis sabina (LeSueur)

Color: Yellow-brown or brown on upper surface of body. White below.

Distribution: Coastal waters from the Gulf of Mexico to Chesapeake Bay.

Size: A small species of sting ray. The largest specimen recorded was 2 feet wide.

General Information: Found commonly close to shore in bays and estuaries in depths of less than 8 feet. It often enters brackish waters. Main foods are small shrimp-like animals and worms. The young are probably born from spring through autumn. Young just ready for birth have been reported to be about 4 inches wide.

Economic Importance: None.

Say's Sting Ray
Dasyatis say (LeSueur)

Color: Upper surface of body red-brown, green-brown, gray-brown, or greenish gray. Lower surface white.

Distribution: Found regularly in coastal waters from Brazil to Virginia and as an occasional straggler north as far as southern Massachusetts.

Size: Maximum size reported as about 3 feet wide.

General Information: Common in depths less than 10 feet and has never been taken in depths below 30 feet. It feeds mostly on worms and shellfish but also eats shrimp, crabs, and fish. Observations in subtropical and tropical waters indicate that the young are probably born in these zones at all times of the year. They are 6–7 inches wide at birth.

Economic Importance: None.

Giant Butterfly Ray
Gymnura altavela (Linnaeus)

Color: Color very variable. Upper surface of body dark red-brown, gray-brown or coffee brown. Scattered darker or lighter dots or blotches. Lower surface white.

Distribution: Tropical and temperate waters on both sides of the Atlantic. In the western Atlantic, found from southern Massachusetts to Argentina.

Size: The maximum size reported from the western Atlantic was almost 7 feet wide.

General Information: Relatively rare on the American Atlantic Coast. Most often found in shoal water but has been taken at a depth of 180 feet. Newborn young are probably 15–18 inches wide.

Economic Importance: None.

Lesser Butterfly Ray
Gymnura micrura (Bloch and Schneider)

Color: Upper surface of body green, purple, brown, or gray with dots and markings of lighter and darker shades. Lower surface white.

Distribution: Found regularly in tropical and temperate waters from Brazil to Virginia. A summer straggler north as far as southern New England.

Size: Maximum size probably 4 feet wide.

General Information: In summer common on sandy bottoms in Chesapeake Bay. It feeds on shellfish, shrimp, and fish. The young are born from May through August in Chesapeake Bay and are 6–9 inches at birth.

Economic Importance: None.

Eagle Ray
Myliobatis freminvillii (LeSueur)

Color: Upper surface of body gray, brown, or red-brown. Lower surface pure white or tinged with color of upper surface.

Distribution: Found from Brazil to New York and as a straggler north to Cape Cod.

Size: Reaches a width of about 3 feet.

General Information: Not common at least in the northern part of its range. Feeds on crabs, lobsters, clams, and other shellfish. Young are probably 10 inches wide at birth.

Economic Importance: None.

Spotted Eagle Ray
Aetobatus narinari (Euphrasen)

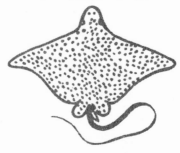

Color: Upper surface of disc greenish brown or chestnut brown; pectoral fins darker. Conspicuous white, green, or yellow spots, rings, and streaks over whole surface. Lower surface white.

Distribution: World-wide in tropical and warm temperate waters. In the western Atlantic, from Brazil to North Carolina and as a stray to Chesapeake Bay.

Size: Maximum size recorded was 7½ feet wide. A specimen between 7 and 7½ feet wide has been estimated to weigh 400–500 pounds.

General Information: Common in some years along the coast of North Carolina in summer. It is frequently seen leaping out of the water. The main foods appear to be clams and oysters. Newborn young range from 6 to 14 inches wide.

Economic Importance: Of no commercial value. This ray can be very destructive to oyster and clam beds.

Cow-nosed Ray
Rhinoptera bonasus (Mitchill)

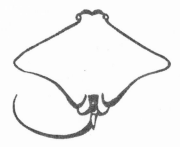

Color: Upper surface of body light to dark brown. Lower surface white or yellow-white.
Distribution: Coastal waters from Cape Cod to Brazil.
Size: The maximum size reported was 7 feet wide.
General Information: Nowhere very abundant. In various years in different localities throughout its range large schools have been sighted. It feeds on such shellfish as clams, oysters, and large snails as well as on crabs and lobsters. Shellfish buried in the bottom are said to be stirred up by the flapping of the pectoral fins. Newborn young are probably 14 inches wide.
Economic Importance: None.

Lesser Devil Ray
Mobula hypostoma (Bancroft)

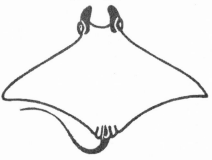

Color: Upper surface of body black or dark blue. Gray-white or yellow-white below.

Distribution: Found regularly from Brazil to North Carolina and as a straggler farther north.

Size: Maximum size recorded was 4 feet wide.

General Information: Nowhere abundant, although they have been described as swimming in schools on the coast of North Carolina. They often leap out of the water high above its surface. Chief foods are small shrimp-like animals and small fishes.

Economic Importance: None.

Giant Devil Ray
Manta birostris (Donndorff)

Color: Upper surface of body red-brown, green-brown, or black. Lower surface white.

Distribution: Found regularly from Brazil to South Carolina and as a straggler as far north as southern New England.

Size: Maximum size reported was a specimen 20 feet wide and weighing 3,502 pounds.

General Information: The Giant Devil Ray is probably most numerous in the Gulf of Mexico and off southeastern Florida. It is most often seen in the shoal water near shore, but specimens are also frequently found swimming at the surface of the water far offshore over deep water. This ray frequently occurs in pairs or schools. At times it may leap clear of the water. This ray probably feeds on small shrimp-like animals and small fish. While an inoffensive animal if left alone, the Giant Devil Ray can capsize or smash a small boat if angered. The fact that the two projecting head fins automatically close together on anything that may touch the head region between these fins may explain the stories of divers being smothered by Giant Devil Rays which grasp the air hose and cut off the air supply.

Economic Importance: Of no commercial importance. Harpooning of this ray by sportsmen, a frequent occurrence, usually results in a frenzied flight of the animal towing the boat behind it, often for several hours.

TRUE FISHES

Characters: The true fishes are a diverse group of aquatic vertebrates which, like the sharks, sawfish, skates, and rays, have well-developed jaws and respire by means of gills. They differ from the sharks and their relatives in the following characters:

1. The skeleton is formed of bone in most species. Exceptions are the primitive fishes like the sturgeons whose

skeleton is composed mostly of cartilage. However, some true bone is always present.

2. There is only one gill opening on each side of the head.

3. The fins are supported by bony rays.

General Information: Although water covers about 71 per cent of the earth's surface to an average depth of over 2 miles, not all of it is teeming with fish. Most of the fish are concentrated in the relatively shoal waters adjacent to the continental land masses, on the Continental Shelf and along the edges of the Shelf as it dips into the depths of the ocean, the Continental Slope. In these areas two major categories of fish exist: the demersal or bottom-dwelling forms such as the flounder, cod, and haddock, and the pelagic or midwater and surface forms such as the herrings and bluefish.

Beyond the edge of the Continental Slope on the ocean floor live the abyssal or deep-sea forms, frequently grotesque in appearance and possessing special light organs. Over these great depths are found the pelagic oceanic species, such as the ocean sunfish and tunas, some of which commonly enter the waters over the Continental Shelf and Slope.

Just as fish are not equally abundant from the coastal areas to the ocean depths, they are also unequally distributed from the equator to the poles. In terms of numbers the most fish are found in the subpolar and temperate zones. Here the great commercial fisheries of the world are concentrated. But it is in the subtropical and tropical zones that the greatest number of different species occur.

Within the expanse of water extending from the shore to the ocean depths and from the North to the South Pole there exists as wide a variety of environments as on land. The land beneath the sea has its hills and mountains, valleys, broad fertile plains, and desert-like regions. Rivers are replaced by ocean currents. In the fertile coastal plain of the sea, land vegetation finds its counterpart in the seaweeds and even more in the stationary plant-like animal forms such as the sea fans and pens, the sea anemones, sponges, and corals. In the bottom ooze are millions of small organisms: bacteria, protozoa, worms, molluscs, and crustaceans comparable to the bacteria, protozoa, worms, and insects found in earth on land.

Over the whole ocean bottom as over the whole land mass hovers an atmosphere containing the vital element of life, oxygen. In the sea the oxygen is dissolved in the water, while in the air it is mixed with various other gases. It has been found that a given amount of air has over 30 times as much oxygen as the same quantity of sea water. Further, water is about 800 times as dense as air at the same temperature.

As a group, fish have adapted to the relatively low concentration of oxygen in water both by requiring less of this element in respiring as compared with the land vertebrates and by the development of very efficient respiratory organs, the gills. To overcome the impediment to movement imposed by the dense water medium, faster-swimming fishes have developed streamlined bodies.

The physiology and shape of the body, the form of the mouth, teeth, and fins, and other external as well as internal structures have been modified in the various species of fishes for adaptation to a particular type of environment. As a result, these fishes are not distributed throughout the ocean waters but are restricted to a particular area or habitat.

In most fishes the eggs are fertilized after extrusion and develop and hatch in the water. However, in some species the eggs are fertilized while inside the fish, as for example in the guppi and other "live-bearers," and are carried by the female throughout development. Depending on the species and the size of the fish the number of eggs released may vary from less than a hundred to millions. In the species that protect their eggs in some manner, such as the "live-bearers," nest builders, and mouth breeders, far fewer eggs are produced by each female than in species that broadcast their eggs throughout the water.

The eggs of most fishes are less than an eighth of an inch in diameter; they are usually shaped like a sphere but sometimes may be elliptical in form. There are two types of eggs, pelagic and demersal. Pelagic eggs are buoyant and are found floating at various depths. They contain oil globules which serve as food for the developing embryo. The pelagic egg develops rapidly and the young hatch in a relatively few days. Demersal eggs sink to the bottom. They are frequently heavily yolked and may take several weeks or even months to hatch. However, some demersal eggs resemble the pelagic egg in appearance and hatch quickly. Demersal eggs often have a sticky surface or sticky threads or other structures when extruded. As a result they become attached to each other, plant and animal growths, particles of sand, and other solid objects along the bottom. For the most part newly hatched fish are entirely different in appearance from the adult and can be identified only by the specialist.

Fishes eat a wide variety of foods including the microscopic plants and animals, seaweeds, invertebrates, and aquatic vertebrates. Some fish live almost exclusively on the small plants and animals floating in the water (plankton). Others are flesh eaters, feeding mostly on larger invertebrates or fish, including members of their own species. The majority of species are covered with scales, but in some forms scales are absent or are replaced, either completely or in part, by bony plates, protuberances, prickles, or spines. A few types have developed special organs such as poisonous spines and electric dischargers for defense or for assistance in capturing food.

Economic Importance: Fish is an important source of animal protein. In some countries it is the major source of this essential component of the diet. Technological improvements in preservation and processing of fish developed since World War I have encouraged a greatly expanded international trade in salt, smoked, canned, and, more recently, frozen fish. As the world population increases the fisheries are being more heavily exploited.

Classification: The scientific classification of the true fishes found in the area from Cape Cod to Cape Hatteras is as follows:

Class: Osteicthyes (True Fishes or Bony Fishes)

Family: Acipenseridae (Sturgeons)
Acipenser oxyrhynchus—common sturgeon
Acipenser brevirostrum—short-nosed sturgeon

Family: Elopidae (Ten-Pounders)
Elops saurus—ten-pounder

Family: Megalopidae (Tarpons)
Tarpon atlanticus—tarpon

Family: Albulidae (Bonefishes)
Albula vulpes—bonefish

Family: Dussumieriidae (Round Herrings)
Etrumeus sadina—round herring

Family: Clupeidae (Herrings)
Sardinella anchovia—Spanish sardine
Clupea harengus—sea herring
Pomolobus mediocris—hickory shad
Pomolobus aestivalis—blueback
Pomolobus pseudoharengus—alewife
Alosa sapidissima—shad
Opisthonema oglinum—thread herring
Brevoortia tyrannus—menhaden

Family: Dorosomidae (Gizzard Shads)
Dorosoma cepedianum—gizzard shad

Family: Engraulidae (Anchovies)
Anchoa mitchilli—common anchovy
Anchoa hepsetus—striped anchovy
Anchoa argyrophanus—silvery anchovy

Family: Salmonidae (Salmons)
Salmo salar—Atlantic salmon
Salmo gairdnerii—rainbow trout

Family: Osmeridae (Smelts)
Osmerus mordax—smelt

Family: Ariidae (Sea Catfishes)
Galeichthys felis—sea catfish
Bagre marinus—gaff-topsail catfish

Family: Anguillidae (Eels)
Anguilla rostrata—common eel
Conger oceanica—American conger eel

Family: Synodontidae (Lizard Fishes)
Synodus foetens—lizard fish

Family: Poeciliidae (Killifishes)
Fundulus heteroclitus—common killifish
Fundulus majalis—striped killifish
Cyprinodon variegatus—sheepshead minnow
Lucania parva—rain-water fish
Fundulus luciae—Lucy's killifish
Fundulus ocellaris—ocellated killifish
Fundulus diaphanus—fresh-water killifish
Gambusia holbrooki—top minnow

Family: Belonidae (Billfishes)
Tylosurus marinus—billfish
Tylosurus acus—agujon
Ablennes hians—flat billfish

Family: Hemiramphidae (Halfbeaks)
Hyporhamphus unifasciatus—halfbeak
Hemiramphus brasiliensis—balao
Euleptorhamphus velox—flying halfbeak
Hyporhamphus hildebrandi—pajarito

Family: Scomberesocidae (Needlefishes)
Scomberesox saurus—needlefish

Family: Exocoetidae (Flying Fishes)
Cypselurus heterurus—Atlantic flying fish
Parexocoetus mesogaster—short-winged flying fish
Cypselurus furcatus—spot-fin flying fish

Family: Merlucciidae (Silver Hakes)
Merluccius bilinearis—whiting
Merluccius albidus—offshore whiting

Family: Gadidae (Cods)
Gadus callarias—cod
Melanogrammus aeglifinus—haddock
Pollachius virens—pollock
Microgadus tomcod—tomcod
Urophycis regius—spotted hake
Urophycis tenuis—white hake
Urophycis chuss—red hake
Brosme brosme—cusk
Enchelyopus cimbrius—four-bearded rockling

Family: Hippoglossidae (Halibuts)
Hippoglossus hippoglossus—Atlantic halibut

Family: Pleuronectidae (Flounders)
Hippoglossoides platessoides—dab
Pseudopleuronectes americanus—blackback flounder
Liopsetta putnami—smooth flounder
Limanda ferruginea—yellowtail flounder
Glyptocephalus cynoglossus—gray sole

Family: Paralichthyidae (Flukes)
Paralichthys dentatus—northern fluke
Paralichthys oblongus—four-spotted fluke

Family: Bothidae (Turbots)
Lophopsetta maculata—sundial
Etropus microstomus—small-mouth flounder
Platophrys ocellatus—eyed flounder

Family: Achiridae (Soles)
Trinectes maculatus—hogchoker

Family: Cynoglossidae (Tonguefishes)
Symphurus plagiusa—tonguefish

Family: Atherinidae (Silversides)
Menidia menidia—northern silverside

Menidia beryllina—tide-water silverside
Membras vagrans—rough silverside

Family: Mugilidae (Mullets)
Mugil curema—white mullet
Mugil cephalus—striped mullet

Family: Sphyraenidae (Barracudas)
Sphyraena borealis—northern barracuda
Sphyraena barracuda—great barracuda

Family: Gasterosteidae (Sticklebacks)
Apeltes quadracus—four-spined stickleback
Gasterosteus aculeatus—three-spined stickleback
Gasterosteus wheatlandi—two-spined stickleback
Pungitius pungitius—nine-spined stickleback

Family: Syngnathidae (Pipefishes)
Syngnathus fuscus—northern pipefish
Syngnathus floridae—Florida pipefish

Family: Hippocampidae (Sea Horses)
Hippocampus hudsonius—northern sea horse

Family: Fistulariidae (Cornet fishes)
Fistularia tabacaria—trumpet fish

Family: Mullidae (Goatfishes)
Mullus auratus—northern goatfish

Family: Scombridae (Mackerels)
Scomber scombrus—common mackerel
Pneumatophorus colias—chub mackerel
Auxis thazard—frigate mackerel
Sarda sarda—common bonito
Katsuwonus pelamis—ocean bonito
Euthynnus alleteratus—little tuna
Thunnus thynnus—bluefin tuna
Thunnus atlanticus—blackfin tuna
Thunnus albacares—yellowfin tuna
Thunnus alalunga—albacore

Scomberomorus maculatus—Spanish mackerel
Scomberomorus regalis—cero'
Scomberomorus cavalla—king mackerel

Family: Trichiuridae (Cutlass fishes)
Trichiurus lepturus—cutlass fish

Family: Istiophoridae (Marlins, Sailfishes)
Makaira ampla—blue marlin
Makaira albida—white marlin
Istiophorus americanus—Atlantic sailfish

Family: Xiphiidae (Swordfishes)
Xiphias gladius—swordfish

Family: Coryphaenidae (Dolphins)
Coryphaena hippurus—dolphin

Family: Stromateidae (Butterfishes)
Poronotus triacanthus—butterfish
Peprilus alepidotus—harvest fish

Family: Centrolophidae (Rudder Fishes)
Palinurichthys perciformis—black rudder fish

Family: Carangidae (Scads, Jacks, Pompanos)
Trachurops crumenopthalmus—goggle-eyed scad
Decapterus punctatus—round scad
Decapterus macarellus—mackerel scad
Trachurus trachurus—rough scad
Caranx hippos—common jack
Caranx crysos—hardtail
Caranx latus—horse-eye jack
Alectis crinitus—threadfish
Vomer setapinnis—moonfish
Chloroscombrus chrysurus—bumper
Selene vomer—look-down
Seriola zonata—banded rudder fish
Seriola dumerili—amber jack
Naucrates ductor—pilot fish
Oligoplites saurus—leatherjacket

Trachinotus carolinus—common pompano
Trachinotus falcatus—round pompano

Family: Pomatomidae (Bluefishes)
Pomatomus saltatrix—bluefish

Family: Rachycentridae (Cobias)
Rachycentron canadus—cobia

Family: Moronidae (White Basses)
Roccus saxatilis—striped bass
Morone americana—white perch

Family: Serranidae (Sea Basses, Groupers)
Centropristes striatus—common sea bass
Polyprion americanus—wreckfish

Family: Priacanthidae (Big-eyes)
Pseudopriacanthus altus—deep big-eye
Priacanthus arenatus—common big-eye

Family: Lobotidae (Tripletails)
Lobotes surinamensis—tripletail

Family: Lutianidae (Snappers)
Lutianus griseus—gray snapper

Family: Haemulidae (Grunts)
Orthopristis chrysopterus—pigfish
Haemulon plumieri—white grunt

Family: Sparidae (Porgies)
Stenotomus chrysops—northern porgy
Stenotomus aculeatus—southern porgy
Diplodus holbrookii—Holbrook's porgy
Archosargus probatocephalus—sheepshead
Lagodon rhomboides—pinfish

Family: Kyphosidae (Chubs)
Kyphosus sectatrix—Bermuda chub

Family: Otolithidae (Weakfishes)
Cynoscion regalis—gray sea trout

Cynoscion nebulosus—spotted sea trout
Cynoscion nothus—white sea trout

Family: Sciaenidae (Croakers, Drums)

Menticirrhus saxatilis—northern kingfish
Menticirrhus americanus—southern kingfish
Menticirrhus littoralis—gulf kingfish
Leiostomus xanthurus—spot
Micropogon undulatus—croaker
Pogonias cromis—black drum
Sciaenops ocellatus—channel bass
Larimus fasciatus—banded croaker
Bairdiella chrysura—sand perch

Family: Chaetodontidae (Butterfly fishes)
Chaetodon ocellatus—common butterfly fish
Chaetodon capistratus—four-eyed butterfly fish

Family: Ephippidae (Spadefishes)
Chaetodipterus faber—spadefish

Family: Branchiostegidae (Tilefishes)
Lopholatilus chamaeleonticeps—tilefish

Family: Cottidae (Sculpins)
Myoxocephalus aeneus—little sculpin
Myoxocephalus scorpius—shorthorn sculpin
Myoxocephalus octodecimspinosus—longhorn sculpin

Family: Hemitripteridae (Sea Ravens)
Hemitripterus americanus—sea raven

Family: Cyclopteridae (Lumpfishes)
Cyclopterus lumpus—lumpfish

Family: Liparidae (Sea Snails)
Neoliparis atlanticus—sea snail
Liparis liparis—striped sea snail

Family: Cephalacanthidae (Flying Gurnards)
Cephalacanthus volitans—flying gurnard

Family: Triglidae (Sea Robins)
Prionotus carolinus—common sea robin
Prionotus evolans—striped sea robin

Family: Labridae (Wrasses)
Tautoga onitis—tautog
Tautogolabrus adspersus—cunner

Family: Gobiidae (Gobies)
Gobiosoma bosci—naked goby
Gobiosoma ginsburgi—Ginsburg's goby
Microgobius thalassinus—sea-green goby

Family: Echeneidae (Remoras)
Echeneis naucrates—shark remora
Remora brachyptera—swordfish remora
Remora remora—offshore remora
Rhombochirus osteochir—spearfish remora

Family: Ammodytidae (Sand Launces)
Ammodytes americanus—American sand launce
Ammodytes oceanicus—ocean sand launce

Family: Uranoscopidae (Stargazers)
Astroscopus guttatus—northern stargazer

Family: Blenniidae (Blennies)
Chasmodes bosquianus—striped blenny
Hypsoblennius hentz—Carolina blenny

Family: Pholidae (Rock Eels)
Pholis gunnellus—rock eel

Family: Stichaeidae (Shannys)
Ulvaria subbifurcata—ulva fish

Family: Cryptacanthodidae (Wrymouths)
Cryptacanthodes maculatus—wrymouth

Family: Anarhichadidae (Wolf fishes)
Anarhichas lupus—common wolf fish

Family: Zoarcidae (Ocean Pouts)

Macrozoarces americanus—American ocean pout
Lycodes reticulatus—reticulated eelpout

Family: Ophidiidae (Cusk Eels)
Rissola marginata—margined cusk eel

Family: Batrachoididae (Toadfishes)
Opsanus tau—toadfish

Family: Gobiesocidae (Clingfishes)
Cotylis nigripinnis—clingfish

Family: Balistidae (Triggerfishes)
Balistes carolinensis—common triggerfish

Family: Monacanthidae (Filefishes)
Monacanthus hispidus—common filefish
Alutera schoepfii—orange filefish
Monacanthus ciliatus—fringed filefish
Alutera scripta—unicorn filefish

Family: Ostraciidae (Trunkfishes)
Lactophrys trigonus—common trunkfish
Lactophrys triqueter—smooth trunkfish
Lactophrys tricornis—cowfish

Family: Tetraodontidae (Swellfishes)
Lagocephalus laevigatus—smooth swellfish
Sphaeroides maculatus—northern swellfish
Sphaeroides spengleri—southern swellfish

Family: Diodontidae (Porcupine fishes)
Chilomycterus schoepfi—spiny boxfish
Diodon hystrix—porcupine fish

Family: Molidae (Ocean Sunfishes)
Mola mola—ocean sunfish
Masturus lanceolatus—sharp-tailed sunfish

Family: Lophiidae (Anglers)
Lophius americanus—American goosefish

Family Antennariidae (Sargassum fishes)

Histrio pictus—sargassum fish

Common Sturgeon
Acipenser oxyrhynchus Mitchill

Color: Blue-gray or olive-green above, gradually becoming lighter on the sides. White in the region from the upper side row of bony shields to the belly.
Distribution: Coastal waters from Hudson Bay to the Gulf of Mexico.
Size: Reported to reach a length of 18 feet. A fish 7½ feet long weighed 190 pounds.
General Information: The Common Sturgeon spends most of its life in salt water but ascends rivers into fresh water to spawn. Spawning takes place in spring and early summer. A large number of eggs are released by each fish. One fish has been recorded as carrying 2½ million eggs. The eggs hatch in about one week. The young remain in the rivers for several years until they reach 2½–3 feet, although some may go to mouths of the rivers in the first year when 5–6 inches long. Fish 7–8 feet long have been estimated to be 12 years old.

The Common Sturgeon is a bottom feeder. It uses the pointed snout to stir up the mud and uncover food. Barbels on the snout act as organs of touch to locate the food on the murky bottom. Principal foods are worms, small shellfish and fish, and small crustaceans. These are sucked up by the vacuum-like, toothless mouth located on the underside of the head.
Economic Importance: Both flesh and roe of the Common Sturgeon are highly esteemed foods. The flesh is commonly sold as a smoked product and the roe in a processed form

as caviar. This species, formerly common, is now relatively rare and taken only incidentally in the commercial fisheries for other species of fishes.

Short-nosed Sturgeon
Acipenser brevirostrum LeSueur

Color: Olive-black or red-brown above; sides reddish mixed with violet, sometimes with oblique black bands. Belly white.

Distribution: Coastal waters from Massachusetts to South Carolina.

Size: Largest recorded about 3 feet long. A 31-inch fish weighed 7¼ pounds.

General Information: Spawns in rivers in spring. Little is known about its life history. Uncommon throughout its range.

Economic Importance: None.

Ten-Pounder
Elops saurus Linnaeus

Color: Back bluish; sides silvery; belly slightly yellow.

Distribution: Recorded from Brazil to Massachusetts. Most abundant in southern Florida and the West Indies.

Size: Reported to reach a length of 3 feet.

General Information: Rare in the Chesapeake and Middle Atlantic regions.

Economic Importance: None.

Tarpon
Tarpon atlanticus (Cuvier and Valenciennes)

Color: Blue-silver above; sides and belly bright silver.
Distribution: Most common in the West Indies, the Gulf of Mexico, and Florida. Recorded from Brazil to Nova Scotia.
Size: Reported maximum length about 8 feet.
General Information: A rare straggler in the area from Cape Cod to Cape Hatteras.
Economic Importance: Of little value as a food fish. An important species in the recreational fisheries of Florida.

Bonefish
Albula vulpes (Linnaeus)

Color: Brilliant silver. Scales on upper surface of body with a greenish tint.
Distribution: Found in all tropical seas. Rarely reaches as far north as Cape Cod.
Size: May reach a length of over 2½ feet and a weight of 13 pounds.
General Information: Rare in the Chesapeake and Middle Atlantic regions.
Economic Importance: An important game fish in Florida waters.

Round Herring
Etrumeus sadina (Mitchill)

Color: Olive green above; sides and belly silvery.
Distribution: In the Gulf of Mexico and along the American Atlantic coast as far north as the Bay of Fundy. Rare north of Cape Cod. Most common in the south.
Size: Maximum length about 15 inches.
General Information: Little is known about this fish. In some years large schools are reported offshore along the New Jersey and New York coasts. Probably an important food for the tunas.
Commercial Importance: None.

Spanish Sardine
Sardinella anchovia Cuvier and Valenciennes

Color: Silvery.
Distribution: Cape Cod to Brazil.
Size: Maximum length about 7 inches.
General Information: Little is known about this fish. It is not common close to shore but often is abundant offshore in midwater over great depths.
Economic Importance: None.

Sea Herring
Clupea harengus Linnaeus

Color: Back green-blue or steel blue; sides and belly silvery.
Distribution: Both sides of the North Atlantic Ocean. In the western Atlantic it is most commonly found from northern Labrador to Block Island. Small numbers are sometimes taken farther south as far as Cape Hatteras.
Size: Maximum length about 1½ feet.
General Information: The Sea Herring is found in open coastal waters often in large schools comprising thousands of individuals. Usually the members of a school are fish of about the same length. Depending on locality, spawning may occur from spring to autumn in depths of 12–180 feet. A single female may lay 20–40 thousand eggs. The eggs sink to the bottom, and because they have a sticky surface they become attached in clumps and layers to particles of sand, stones, seaweeds, and other objects. Fish 10 inches long are about 4 years old, 15 inches long, about 9 years old. Specimens 20 years of age have been reported. Most fish do not spawn until they are 4 years of age or older. The food of the Sea Herring is mostly plankton. This species is an important source of food for many of the larger fishes.
Economic Importance: The Sea Herring is one of important species of food fishes. In the United States most of the catch is landed in Maine and consists primarily of small fish, 3–5 inches long, which are canned as "sardines." The larger-sized fish are sold fresh or are pickled or smoked.

Hickory Shad
Pomolobus mediocris (Mitchill)

Color: Gray-green above; sides and belly silver. A dark spot behind gill followed by a series of obscure black dots. A series of faint, dusky, horizontal stripes on sides.
Distribution: Found from the Bay of Fundy to Florida.
Size: Reaches a length of 2 feet. A 15-inch fish weighs 1 pound; an 18-inch fish, 2 pounds.
General Information: Little is known about this fish. It feeds mostly on small fish but squid, crabs, and fish eggs have also been found in its stomach.
Economic Importance: The Hickory Shad is taken mixed with other species of herrings mostly by the pound net fishery and has a limited market. While not an important sport fish it is known to strike at an artificial lure and will put up a good fight on light tackle.

Blueback, Glut Herring
Pomolobus aestivalis (Mitchill)

Color: Back blue-green; sides silvery. A dark spot in back of the gills. Faint horizontal stripes on upper part of body.
Distribution: Nova Scotia to Florida.
Size: Reaches a length of about 15 inches and a weight of 13 ounces.
General Information: Like the alewife, the Blueback enters rivers in spring to spawn. However, unlike the alewife the

Blueback does not usually go above the brackish water to lay its eggs. The young when about 2 inches long find their way to the sea, where they remain until mature.

Economic Importance: This species is not as abundant as the alewife. It is frequently sold mixed with other kinds of herrings.

Alewife
Pomolobus pseudoharengus (Wilson)

Color: Back gray-green; sides and belly silver. A dark spot behind the gill. Faint horizontal stripes on sides.

Distribution: Northern Nova Scotia to North Carolina. Races of this fish have become landlocked in certain freshwater lakes, including Lake Ontario and New York's Finger Lakes.

Size: Reaches a length of about 15 inches and a weight of 14 ounces.

General Information: The Alewife spends most of its life in the sea, but 3–4 years after birth it matures and in the spring enters the coastal rivers and streams and swims up into fresh water to spawn. Often the stream selected for spawning is the one in which the fish was born. Over 100,000 eggs may be laid by a single fish. Soon after hatching, when slightly over ½ inch in length, the young start moving to the sea, where they remain until adult size, entering the rivers and streams only to spawn. The Alewife feeds mostly on plankton, including small shrimp- and crab-like forms and small fish.

Economic Importance: The Alewife is of major importance in the pound net fishery of Chesapeake Bay. Some of the fish are eaten when fresh, but the bulk is salted or canned and sold as "river herring." The scales are a source of "pearl essence" used in the jewelry and display industries. The Alewife will readily strike at an artificial lure particularly after spawning, when it is ravenous and actively seeks food. They are frequently taken by trout fishermen in spring in the coastal streams and often mistaken for small shad.

Shad
Alosa sapidissima (Wilson)

Color: Green or dark blue above; silvery white on sides and belly. A dark spot behind the gill usually followed by a series of indistinct spots.

Distribution: Gulf of St. Lawrence to the St. Johns River in Florida. They have been introduced successfully by man to the Pacific coast of the United States.

Size: Maximum length is about 2½ feet with a weight of 13½ pounds.

General Information: The Shad enters coastal rivers in spring and early summer to spawn. Spawning occurs in both fresh and brackish water, but the latter is more favorable for development of the young fish. The eggs are deposited in shallow water over sandy or pebbly bottoms and are mostly laid in the period between sundown and midnight. An average 30 thousand eggs are laid by a single female, but large fish have been estimated to lay as many as 156 thousand eggs. Unlike the eggs of the other river herrings (alewife and blueback), the eggs of the Shad are partly buoyant and are not sticky when laid; they are therefore carried about to some degree by currents. Young Shad remain in the river until the fall, when they are 1½–

4½ inches long. They then move down to the sea, where they spend the remainder of their lives, entering the rivers only to spawn. They spawn for the first time when about 4 years old and commonly return to the river of their birth for this purpose. Like the other herrings, the Shad feeds primarily on plankton.

Economic Importance: An important food species. Construction of impassable dams on many of the rivers and streams and pollution of other rivers and streams have eliminated or reduced the runs of this fish in numerous places. When running upstream to spawn the Shad will strike readily on an artificial lure and makes an excellent adversary on light tackle. A spectacular sport fishery for Shad has been developed in Connecticut at the Enfield Dam.

Thread Herring
Opisthonema oglinum (LeSueur)

Color: Blue above; silvery sides and belly. Faint dark spot behind upper margin of gill cover. Dark horizontal streaks on upper part of body. Tips of dorsal and caudal fins black.

Distribution: Found from Brazil to North Carolina and as a stray as far north as Cape Cod.

Size: Reaches a maximum length of about one foot.

General Information: Little is known about this species. It is most abundant in the West Indies.

Economic Importance: None.

Menhaden
Brevoortia tyrannus (Latrobe)

Color: Color of upper surface of body variable, ranging from green to blue, blue-gray, or brownish blue. Sides and belly silvery. Large dark spot behind upper margin of gill cover followed by several dark spots arranged in irregular rows.

Distribution: Nova Scotia to eastern Florida.

Size: Maximum length reported is 20 inches.

General Information: Common near shore. Often seen near the surface of the water in large schools comprising thousands of fish. Spawning occurs in the sea, from June to August in the northern part of its range and in late autumn and winter in the southern part of its range. The eggs are buoyant and develop rapidly, usually hatching in less than 48 hours. The Menhaden feeds chiefly on microscopic plants and small crustaceans, which it sifts out of the water by means of highly specialized, comb-like gill rakers.

Economic Importance: The Menhaden is an extremely oily fish of little value as food. It is, however, the most important industrial fish now caught in the United States. In recent years over 1 billion pounds of Menhaden have been caught each year for conversion into fish meal and oil. This species is also a favorite food of other fishes, and it is frequently used in the recreational fisheries as a chum to attract game fishes or as a bait.

Gizzard Shad
Dorosoma cepedianum (LeSueur)

Color: Metallic blue above; sides and belly silvery.
Distribution: Found in coastal fresh and brackish waters from Cape Cod to Texas. Also occurs landlocked in ponds and lakes, including the Great Lakes.
Size: Maximum length about 15 inches.
General Information: Not common north of Virginia. Lives mostly in fresh and brackish water and is seldom found in salt water. The Gizzard Shad feeds on small animals and plants which it picks up from the bottom. Spawning takes place in early summer.
Economic Importance: A bony species of little commercial value. It is an important food for many other fishes.

Common Anchovy
Anchoa mitchilli (Cuvier and Valenciennes)

Color: Body silvery, translucent. A poorly defined silver band, narrower than the eye, running the length of the body.
Distribution: Occurs from Maine to Yucatan. Rare north of Cape Cod.
Size: Reaches a length of about 4 inches.
General Information: Commonly found in large schools in shallow waters along the shores. Sometimes it ascends into fresh-water streams. Spawns from May to August. The

principal food of the Common Anchovy is small shrimp-like animals.

Economic Importance: This species is not a food fish. However, it is an important part of the diet of other fishes. It is commonly used as a bait in the sport fisheries of some localities.

Striped Anchovy
Anchoa hepsetus (Linnaeus)

Color: Pale gray, iridescent. A bright silvery band, slightly narrower than the eye, runs the length of the body.

Distribution: Most common from Uruguay to Chesapeake Bay. A stray north as far as Nova Scotia.

Size: May reach over 6 inches in length.

General Information: Abundant in the West Indies and off the coast of Florida in shoal waters. It feeds on small shrimp-like animals.

Economic Importance: This species is not eaten. It may be an important part of the diet of fishes in some localities.

Silvery Anchovy
Anchoa argyrophanus (Cuvier and Valenciennes)

Color: Silvery, translucent. A broad silvery band, 1½ times as wide as the eye, runs the length of the body.

Distribution: Found mostly in the Gulf Stream. Specimens appear occasionally inshore from Cape Cod south.

Size: Maximum length about 6 inches.

General Information: Spawns in July and August. Not common inshore.
Economic Importance: None.

Atlantic Salmon
Salmo salar Linnaeus

Color: Back brown; sides silver; head and upper part of body have numerous spots and crosses.
Distribution: Found on both sides of the Atlantic Ocean. In the western Atlantic it occurs from northeastern Labrador to New York. Now uncommon south of Cape Cod.
Size: May reach a weight of over 50 pounds. A 3-foot specimen weighs 16–20 pounds.
General Information: The Atlantic Salmon spends most of its life at sea, but in spring it enters rivers and swims upstream to fresh water to spawn. The fish are fat and silvery when they enter the river. As they work upstream they become thin and turn a dull red or brown color. Large black spots appear on the body, and, in the male, red and orange spots form and both jaws become very elongated. In Maine, spawning occurs in October and November. The female smooths out a shallow depression in the sand or gravel and after the eggs are laid and fertilized covers them with the bottom material. Many of the adult fish die after spawning. Those that survive may drop back to sea after spawning or stay in the river throughout the winter and go back to sea the following spring.

The young fish, known as "parr," live in the fresh waters of the river for 2–3 years. Eventually they go downstream to salt water, usually from late spring to autumn.

They are about 5–6 inches long at this time, and their sides are marked with 10–11 black bars with bright red spots between the bars. When they reach salt water the "parr" lose all their color and become silvery. They are now termed "smolts."

The Atlantic Salmon is a heavy feeder living chiefly on fish and various types of shrimp-like animals. It itself is the prey of sharks, tuna, swordfish, and harbor seals. Growth of the Atlantic Salmon is rapid while at sea. A 45-pound fish has been reported to be 8 years old.

Economic Importance: An excellent food fish. As with the shad, impassable dams and pollution have reduced the runs or eliminated them in numerous localities. A favorite species of the angler in Maine and Canada.

Rainbow Trout
Salmo gairdnerii Gibbons

Color: Silvery when in salt water.
Distribution: Found occasionally in salt water where it has wandered from its normal habitat in fresh-water streams.
Size: Grows to a length of about 3½ feet.
General Information: Originally the Rainbow Trout was found only in the coastal streams of California. It has been planted in fresh waters throughout the United States and in the East sometimes descends coastal fresh-water streams to the brackish water at their mouths.

Smelt
Osmerus mordax (Mitchill)

Color: Transparent olive green above; sides lighter; belly silvery. A silver band on sides along length of body.

Distribution: Found from eastern Labrador to Virginia. More common from New Jersey north. It is found land-locked in fresh-water lakes in Canada, Maine, and New Hampshire and has been successfully introduced into the Great Lakes, where it is now abundant.

Size: Reaches a length of about 14 inches.

General Information: The Smelt is found mainly close to shore, commonly about river mouths. It usually runs in schools of about the same length fish. Most of the life of this species is spent in salt water, but it runs up into fresh water to spawn. Soon after the ice goes out in the coastal streams the Smelt start to run up into the fresh water. The males appear first and are soon followed by the females. Spawning occurs from February through June, depending on water temperature. The eggs sink to the bottom and stick in masses to anything they may touch or to each other. A relatively small Smelt, 2 ounces in weight, may lay 50,000 eggs. After hatching, the young remain in the stream until some time in summer. By fall they are found in salt water. At this time they are about 1½ inches long. They remain in salt water for at least two winters before returning to the fresh-water streams to spawn. The Smelt's main food is small shrimp-like animals, but it also eats worms, small fish, and small shellfish.

Economic Importance: A fine food fish now uncommon south of Cape Cod, and less abundant to the north than in the early 1900's. As with the shad, pollution, dams, and construction near streams have destroyed spawning areas or made them inaccessible, thus eliminating or reducing populations of Smelt in many localities. This species tends to concentrate in harbors in the fall of the year, at which time it can be readily caught by the angler.

Sea Catfish
Galeichthys felis (Linnaeus)

Color: Steel blue above; sides and belly silvery.

Distribution: Found from Cape Cod to Texas but not common north of Virginia.

Size: Reaches a length of about 2 feet.

General Information: Like the gaff-topsail catfish below, the male of this species carries the fertilized eggs in its mouth until they hatch. The Sea Catfish is very common in the bays and harbors of our southern states. Like most other catfish it very actively seeks food at night.

Economic Importance: A few are marketed. It is commonly caught by anglers in our southern states.

Gaff-Topsail Catfish
Bagre marinus (Mitchill)

Color: Top of head and back steel blue; sides silvery; belly white.

Distribution: Coastal waters from Cape Cod to Panama. Not common north of Delaware.

Size: Maximum length about 2 feet.

General Information: In North Carolina waters breeding occurs in late May and June. The eggs are large and range from three-fifths of an inch to one inch in diameter. After they are laid and fertilized the male picks them up and carries them around in his mouth until they hatch. For some time after hatching the fry also are carried in the mouth of the male fish. During this period the fish does not eat. The Gaff-Topsail Catfish feeds mostly on crabs and to a lesser extent on shrimp and fish.

Economic Importance: A few are marketed. This species is frequently caught by anglers along the Florida coast.

American Eel
Anguilla rostrata (LeSueur)

Color: Brown to olive-brown above; sides tinged with yellow; belly dirty white.

Distribution: Coastal streams and inshore waters from western Greenland to Central America and rarely south to Brazil.

Size: It is said to grow to a length of over 4 feet.

General Information: Mature American Eels migrate to a region southwest of Bermuda, between Bermuda and the Bahamas, and there mate and die. The eggs hatch and develop into a floating, broad, ribbon-like, transparent animal, very unlike the adult, called a leptocephalus. Over a period of slightly less than one year the leptocephalus is carried by prevailing currents to the American Atlantic coast. Here it changes to a body form like the adult. At this time it is 2–3½ inches long, transparent and uncolored except for a single row of black spots running the length of the body. These "glass eels" enter the mouths of coastal rivers and streams by the millions and attempt to work their way upstream. There is some indication that American Eels are slow-growing, possibly maturing at anywhere from 5 to 20 years of age. When mature this fish leaves the coastal streams and rivers and the inshore waters and starts its long migration to off Bermuda. The mature fish stops feeding and the color changes. The back turns to black and the sides become silvery. The eyes of the male double in size.

The American Eel will eat almost any animal food, living or dead. It is primarily a scavenger and feeds mostly at night. During the day it mostly lies buried in the bottom, often with its head protruding.

Economic Importance: An excellent food fish, marketed fresh, pickled, or smoked. There is a small commercial fishery for this species which could be expanded if consumer demand increased. A good sport fish on light tackle frequently taken by anglers fishing from shore, wharves, and piers.

American Conger Eel
Conger oceanica (Mitchill)

Color: Blue-gray to brown-gray above; sometimes black or with a reddish tinge; dirty white below.

Distribution: Found from Cape Cod south possibly to South America.

Size: May reach a length of 8 feet.

General Information: This species occurs from close inshore in a few feet of water to depths of over 850 feet, but it is most common in depths of from 250 to 450 feet. Like the American eel, the American Conger Eel migrates offshore to spawn, probably somewhere in the West Indies. The adults die after spawning and the young pass through a leptocephalus stage as do the young of the American eel. However, the young American Conger Eel does not enter fresh-water streams but remains in the sea. Fish is its chief food, but shrimp and small shellfish are also eaten.

Economic Importance: A few are taken by commercial fishermen fishing for other species of fish. It is often taken by anglers fishing on the bottom offshore.

Lizard Fish
Synodus foetens (Linnaeus)

Color: Olive-brown above; sides and belly silvery.
Distribution: Occurs from Cape Cod to Brazil. Most common from South Carolina south.
Size: Reported to reach a length of 2 feet.
General Information: The Lizard Fish is a common species on sandy shores in the southern part of its range. It is usually uncommon in the north but in some years smaller fish, 5–7 inches long, may appear in numbers. It is reported to eat small fish, crabs, shrimp, worms, and other small aquatic animals.
Economic Importance: None. Occasionally fish are taken by anglers fishing for other species.

Common Killifish
Fundulus heteroclitus (Linnaeus)

Color: Large females brown-green above; lighter on lower sides and belly. Breeding males more silvery on lower sides; yellow on belly, anal fins, ventral fins, and edges of dorsal and caudal fins. Sides with 15 narrow, silvery, vertical bars and numerous blue-white and yellowish spots. A black spot on the rear part of the dorsal fin in both sexes. Young of both sexes have a varying number of dark bars on sides.

Distribution: Labrador to Mexico. Three races are recognized. The northern race extends commonly from Labrador to Virginia.

Size: Reaches a length of about 5 inches. Females grow to a larger size than the males.

General Information: The Common Killifish is one of the most common small fishes in shallow coastal waters. It is most often found in schools in weedy, muddy places in marshes, bays, and mouths of rivers. This species prefers brackish water but also occurs in fresh and salt water. It is a very hardy fish with a remarkable ability to survive marked changes in temperature and salinity, to live in highly polluted waters, and to live out of water for a considerable time. Spawning occurs from April to August in shallows containing heavy vegetation. The young grow rapidly and reach maturity by the following year. During the winter this fish will bury itself in the mud. It is a voracious feeder and eats almost any small plant or animal form.

Economic Importance: The Common Killifish is an important source of food for other fishes. An extensive bait fishery for it has been developed in the New York-New Jersey region for use in the sport fisheries for summer flounder (fluke) and young bluefish (snappers).

Because of its hardiness and ready availability it has become an important laboratory animal for scientific investigations.

Striped Killifish
Fundulus majalis (Walbaum)

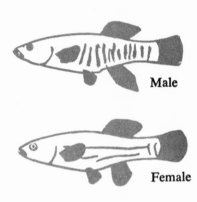

Male

Female

Color: Adult male: back olive; sides, belly, and pectoral, pelvic, and anal fins yellow; 15–20 black vertical bars on sides; black spot on last rays of dorsal fin. Adult female: back olive; silvery below; usually 2 or 3 black longitudinal stripes on sides. Young of both sexes have 7–12 vertical black bars.

Distribution: Massachusetts to Florida.

Size: Reaches a length of 8 inches.

General Information: Found in protected waters of bays and mouths of rivers, usually in small schools of several hundred fish. Spawning occurs from April to September. The Striped Killifish feeds on a variety of small aquatic animals including shellfish, small shrimp-like organisms, and fish.

Economic Importance: Probably an important source of food for other fishes in some regions.

Sheepshead Minnow, Broad Killifish
Cyprinodon variegatus Lacépède

Color: Adult females: back and sides brassy olive; belly white or yellowish; irregular black vertical bars on sides; a black spot on the rear part of the dorsal fin. Adult males: back and sides darker than in females; bars on body faint; dorsal spot lacking. Young of both sexes have markings of adult female.
Distribution: Cape Cod to Mexico.
Size: Maximum length about 3 inches.
General Information: Found in small schools in the shallow brackish waters of salt marshes, bays, and harbors where there is abundant vegetation. Spawning occurs from April to September. Only a few eggs are laid at a time by a single female, and this same fish will continue to lay a few eggs at various intervals throughout the spawning season. Newly laid eggs have numerous sticky threads on their surface with which they become attached to surrounding objects and to each other. The Sheepshead Minnow feeds on a wide variety of small aquatic plant and animal forms.
Economic Importance: Probably an important food for larger fishes in some regions. It is a hardy species suitable for brackish-water aquaria. Under favorable conditions it will spawn in aquaria and the young can be reared.

Rain-Water Fish
Lucania parva (Baird and Girard)

Color: Dark olive above; sides paler. In male, front edge of dorsal fin is black or has a black spot at the base; pelvic and anal fins orange-red in the male during the breeding season.
Distribution: Cape Cod to Key West.
Size: Maximum length about 2½ inches.
General Information: Commonly found in small schools throughout its range in brackish-water bays, ponds, and creeks containing abundant vegetation. It spawns from April to July. The maximum number of eggs produced by a single female has been reported to be 104. The Rain-Water Fish feeds on small shrimp-like animals and probably on any other small aquatic animal.
Economic Importance: A source of food for larger fishes in some areas. Like the sheepshead minnow, the Rain-Water Fish is readily kept in brackish-water aquaria.

Lucy's Killifish
Fundulus luciae (Baird)

Color: Adult female: gray-green, paler below. Adult male: olive green above; belly orange-white; sides with 11–14 dark olive-green bars; a black spot on the rear portion of the dorsal fin. Young of both sexes resemble the female.

Distribution: New York to North Carolina.
Size: Maximum length recorded is about 1½ inches.
General Information: Not abundant anywhere. It lives in shallow, brackish water together with the common killifish. Spawning occurs from April to October.
Economic Importance: None.

Ocellated Killifish
Fundulus ocellaris (Jordan and Gilbert)

Color: Adult female: olive-brown above, pale green below. Lower sides yellowish. Sides have 13 black cross bars. Body sprinkled with small black spots. Black spot on rear part of base of dorsal fin. Adult male: dark green above, paler below. Pearly spots on sides sometimes form indistinct vertical bars. Black spot on rear part of base of dorsal fin. Young colored like female.
Distribution: Chesapeake Bay to Louisiana.
Size: Reaches a length of slightly more than 2½ inches.
General Information: Most common south of Virginia. Occurs in brackish, shallow, inshore waters, often together with the common killifish. It spawns in spring. Principal foods appear to be small crustaceans, shellfish, and insects.
Economic Importance: None.

Fresh-Water Killifish
Fundulus diaphanus (LeSueur)

Color: Adult female: olive above; lower sides silvery; belly white; sides with 16–20 narrow greenish bars. Adult male: sides with 20–22 silvery bars. Young of both sexes resemble the adult female.

Distribution: Quebec to Cape Hatteras. Found in freshwater coastal streams and lakes, sometimes temporarily wandering into brackish water.

Size: Maximum length about 4½ inches.

General Information: Spawns from April to September. It feeds on miscellaneous small aquatic animals and plants.

Economic Importance: Used as a bait by anglers fishing in fresh water.

Top Minnow, Gambusia
Gambusia holbrooki (Girard)

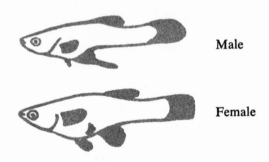

Male

Female

Color: Usually olive above; gray on sides; pale on belly. Dusky markings on scales of upper part of body form irregular dark dots.

Distribution: New Jersey to Florida. Most common from Chesapeake Bay south.

Size: Maximum length about 2½ inches. The males are smaller than the females and seldom reach a length of 1½ inches.

General Information: The Top Minnow is found abundantly in localized protected areas in both fresh and brackish water. The anal fin of the male has been modified as a copulatory organ. Fertilization of the eggs is internal and the young are born alive. Broods of young are produced from May to September and a brood may consist of from just a few fish to over 200 fish. Several broods may be produced by a single female in one year. Newborn young are about one-third of an inch long. The Top Minnow feeds mostly on the surface and eats a wide variety of foods including insects and small shrimp-like animals.

Economic Importance: This fish and closely related forms are widely used both in the United States and in other countries, where they have been introduced, to assist in the control of mosquitoes. The Top Minnow feeds voraciously on the aquatic larval stages of mosquitoes and therefore helps to reduce the mosquito population.

Billfish, Garfish
Tylosurus marinus (Walbaum)

Color: Greenish above; silver on sides; white below. A dark green stripe on the central line of the back. A blue-silver stripe along the sides.

Distribution: Cape Cod to Texas. Infrequently to Maine.

Size: Grows to a length of about 4 feet.

General Information: Common in bays and mouths of rivers in some years, frequently going up coastal rivers to fresh water. It is often seen swimming near the surface of the water singly or in small schools. It feeds on small fishes.

Economic Importance: None. An edible species not often used. It frequently takes the bait of the angler fishing near the surface of the water.

Agujon
Tylosurus acus (Lacépède)

Color: Back blue; sides silver; belly white.
Distribution: A West Indian species sometimes straying
north as far as Massachusetts.
Size: Reaches a length of 4½ feet.
General Information: Rare north of the West Indies.
Economic Importance: None.

Flat Billfish
Ablennes hians (Cuvier and Valenciennes)

Color: Back green; sides and belly silvery.
Distribution: Found in tropical seas. In the American
Atlantic it occurs from Brazil to Chesapeake Bay and,
rarely, to the north as far as Cape Cod.
Size: Reaches a length of 4 feet.
General Information: Spawns in spring. Feeds on small fish.
Economic Importance: None.

Halfbeak
Hyporhamphus unifasciatus (Ranzani)

Color: Green above with three dark streaks running along
the middle of the back; silvery on sides and belly. A darker
silver horizontal band on each side. Tip of lower jaw
crimson.
Distribution: It occurs on both coasts of the Americas and
in the Gulf of Mexico. On the American Atlantic coast it
ranges from Brazil to Cape Cod and as a straggler to
Maine. This fish is most abundant south of Chesapeake
Bay.
Size: Reaches a length of about one foot.

General Information: The Halfbeak spawns in summer.
The very young have no long lower jaw, but fish slightly
over half an inch show the beginning of elongation of this
jaw. The principal foods of this species are small shrimp-
like animals, shellfish, and plant life. They are commonly
seen darting about near the surface of the water.
Economic Importance: None.

Balao
Hemirhamphus brasiliensis (Linnaeus)

The Balao is a West Indian species sometimes found as far
north as Cape Cod but rare north of Florida.

Flying Halfbeak
Euleptorhamphus velox (Poey)

The Flying Halfbeak is a West Indian species sometimes
drifting as far north as Cape Cod. It is rare in the area
from Cape Cod to Chesapeake Bay.

Pajarito
Hyporhamphus hildebrandi Jordan and Evermann

The Pajarito is a West Indian species which occasionally
drifts as far north as Cape Cod. It is rare in the area from
Cape Cod to Chesapeake Bay.

Needlefish
Scomberesox saurus (Walbaum)

Color: Olive green above; sides and belly silvery; a dark silver horizontal band on each side; a dark green spot above the base of each pectoral fin.

Distribution: Found in temperate waters of the Indian, Pacific, and Atlantic Oceans. On the American Atlantic coast it has been reported from North Carolina to southern Newfoundland, but it is most common north of Cape Cod.

Size: Reaches a length of about 1½ feet.

General Information: The Needlefish is found chiefly offshore swimming in large schools near the surface. It is fed on by larger fish, such as pollock and tuna, and sometimes is driven up on the shores by these fishes. Spawning occurs in the open sea. The long jaws are not present in the young but develop when the fish is slightly over 1½ inches long. The lower jaw grows faster than the upper one so that a fish 4–6 inches long has a much longer lower than upper jaw and looks very much like a halfbeak. The principal foods of the Needlefish are the small floating young stages of various species of crabs and their relations and small crustaceans and fishes.

Economic Importance: This species is salable when marketed, but it is caught too irregularly to be of much commercial importance.

Atlantic Flying Fish
Cypselurus heterurus (Rafinesque)

Color: Back a dark bluish gray; sides and belly silvery.
Distribution: Found in warm waters on both sides of the Atlantic. In the American Atlantic it strays as far north as Newfoundland.
Size: Reaches a length of about 1¼ feet.
General Information: Common in the Gulf Stream. The Atlantic Flying Fish is the most common species of flying fish in the area from Cape Cod to Chesapeake Bay.
Economic Importance: Not utilized for food in the United States. The various species of flying fishes are used in our southern recreational fisheries for bait for larger game fishes.

Short-winged Flying Fish
Parexocoetus mesogaster (Bloch)

The Short-winged Flying Fish occurs in tropical seas. It is common in the Gulf Stream as far north as Cape Hatteras but is rare farther north. It seldom reaches over 7 inches in length.

Spot-Fin Flying Fish
Cypselurus furcatus (Mitchill)

Occurs in the warmer waters of the Atlantic Ocean, sometimes straying north to Cape Cod. Rare in northern waters. Reaches a length of 6 inches.

Whiting, Silver Hake
Merluccius bilinearis (Mitchill)

Color: Silvery over entire body with a dark brownish cast on upper surface.
Distribution: Newfoundland to North Carolina and in deep water as far south as the Bahamas. Common from Delaware north.
Size: Reaches a length of about 2½ feet and a weight of 5 pounds.
General Information: This species occurs in large numbers at various depths, from a few feet of water to about 400 feet. In this deeper water it is found together with the offshore whiting.

The Whiting spawns in late spring and summer. The eggs are buoyant and may hatch in 48 hours in water of favorable temperature. The young reach 1–3 inches in length at the end of the first year. This fish is a voracious feeder, preying on smaller fishes, squid, and shrimp. Frequently it will drive schools of fish on shore and itself become stranded in the excitement of the chase.
Economic Importance: A good food fish which has become increasingly important to the commercial fisheries. It is commonly caught by anglers.

Offshore Whiting
Merluccius albidus (Mitchill)

The Offshore Whiting was but recently discovered along our eastern coast in depths from 400 feet down to more than 3,600 feet.

Cod
Gadus callarias Linnaeus

Color: Variable; back and upper sides various shades of gray, green, brown, or red; belly white tinged with the general body color.

Distribution: Occurs on both sides of the North Atlantic. In the western Atlantic it ranges from western Greenland south to Virginia but is most abundant from Labrador to southern Massachusetts.

Size: The largest fish recorded was over 6 feet long and weighed 211¼ pounds. Most fish caught are less than 75 pounds.

General Information: The Cod is found from the shallow, inshore waters down to depths of 1,500 feet or more. It lives mostly near the bottom but will rise to the surface while pursuing smaller fishes. Spawning occurs in winter and early spring. It has been estimated that a fish 4⅓ feet long and weighing 51 pounds produces almost 9 million eggs at one spawning. The eggs are buoyant and hatch in about 2 weeks at a water temperature of 43 degrees. A

Cod 3 feet long is 7–8 years old. The Cod feeds on a wide variety of aquatic animals including shellfish, crabs, lobsters and other crustaceans, squid, and fish. Inedible objects such as sticks, rope, stones, and jewelry are frequently found in Cod stomachs.

Economic Importance: An important commercial species north of Cape Cod throughout the year. From Cape Cod south to New Jersey, of some commercial importance in winter: the Cod is readily taken on hook and line and supports a thriving recreational fishery in late autumn and winter south of Cape Cod, particularly in the New York area.

Haddock
Melanogrammus aeglifinus (Linnaeus)

Color: Back and upper sides dark gray; lower sides silvery; belly white. Lateral line black. A dark patch just above the pectoral fin.

Distribution: Both sides of the North Atlantic. In the American Atlantic it occurs from West Greenland to Virginia but is most abundant from the Grand Banks off Newfoundland to Cape Cod.

Size: The largest fish reported was 3⅔ feet long and weighed 37 pounds.

General Information: The Haddock is a cold-water fish usually found in depths of 150–600 feet. It is a typical ground fish living close to the bottom. Spawning occurs in late winter and early spring. It has been estimated that a fish 2⅓ feet long and weighing about 9½ pounds produced over 1,750,000 eggs. The eggs are buoyant and hatch in about 2 weeks at a water temperature of 41 degrees. The Haddock feeds on a wide variety of invertebrates, including crabs, worms, starfish, and shellfish as well as small fishes.

Economic Importance: This species is one of the most important commercial fishes north of Cape Cod. In some winters it is caught in limited amounts by the commercial fisheries from Cape Cod south to New Jersey.

Pollock
Pollachius virens (Linnaeus)

Color: Brown-green above; sides yellow-gray or light gray; belly silver-gray. A conspicuous white or light gray lateral line.

Distribution: Found in cool waters on both sides of the Atlantic. In the American Atlantic it occurs commonly from the Gulf of St. Lawrence to New Jersey but has been reported as far north as Labrador and as far south as North Carolina.

Size: Reaches a length of 3½ feet and a weight of about 35 pounds.

General Information: The Pollock is one of the most active members of the cod family. It occurs in large schools, which may be found at any level between the surface of the water and the bottom, down to depths of 600 feet or more. The Pollock spawns in late autumn and early winter. The average number of eggs produced by a single female is about 225 thousand, but larger fish may produce over four million eggs. The eggs are buoyant and hatch in 6 days at a water temperature of 49 degrees. A Pollock 2 feet long may be 4½–5½ years old. This species feeds mostly on fish and floating, shrimp-like animals as well as other crustaceans. It is a voracious feeder and consumes large quantities of both small bait fishes and the young of food fishes.

Economic Importance: A common species in the commercial fisheries, particularly in the area north of Cape Cod. Pollock will strike at an artificial lure and are caught by both commercial and recreational fishermen trolling spoons or feathers.

Tomcod
Microgadus tomcod. (Walbaum)

Color: Olive green on back and upper sides, tinged with yellow; dark blotches on sides; belly gray or yellowish white.

Distribution: Northern Newfoundland to Virginia.

Size: Reaches a length of 1¼ feet and a weight of 1¼ pounds.

General Information: This species lives in shoal waters close to shore and is mostly found in harbors and bays and around the mouths of rivers. Spawning occurs in winter, and the eggs are laid at the mouths of rivers or streams in salt or brackish water. The eggs are sticky when extruded and sink to the bottom, where they adhere to various objects and to each other. They hatch in 24 days at a water temperature of 43 degrees. The Tomcod feeds mostly on small crustaceans but will also eat worms, small shellfish, and small fishes.

Economic Importance: A good food fish not abundant enough to be of commercial importance. It is frequently caught by anglers in areas where it is locally numerous.

Spotted Hake
Urophycis regius (Walbaum)

Color: Brown above; white below; a row of white spots connected by black lines along the lateral line; first dorsal fin edged with white and with a distinct black spot.
Distribution: Occurs from Nova Scotia to Florida, but it is rare north of Cape Cod and south of Cape Hatteras.
Size: Reaches a length of 1¼ feet and a weight of 1 to 1½ pounds.
General Information: Little is known about this fish. Spawning probably takes place in winter. The principal foods of the Spotted Hake are fish and small crustaceans.
Economic Importance: None.

White Hake
Urophycis tenuis (Mitchill)

Color: Purple-brown or gray-brown above; belly yellow-white or gray-white.
Distribution: Newfoundland to Cape Hatteras.
Size: Reaches a length of about 4 feet and a weight of 40 pounds.
General Information: Occurs on the bottom from shoal waters inshore to depths down to over 3,200 feet. The White Hake is commonly found on soft, muddy bottoms and feeds largely on small crustaceans, squid, and small fishes. Spawning probably takes place from late winter to late summer. The eggs are probably buoyant.

Economic Importance: Large quantities of this species are taken by the commercial fisheries, particularly north of Cape Cod. The larger fish are mostly marketed as fresh or frozen fillets, while the small ones may be sold mixed with the smaller-sized red hake for use as mink, cat, and poultry feed. Both species of hake are commonly caught by anglers.

Red Hake, Ling
Urophycis chuss (Walbaum)

Color: Back and sides brown, red-brown, or olive-brown; lower sides silvery with a yellow tinge; belly gray, white, or yellow.

Distribution: Newfoundland to Virginia.

Size: Reaches a length of about 2½ feet and a weight of 8 pounds.

General Information: Both the Red Hake and the white hake occupy the same type of environment and are often taken together. Spawning occurs in spring and summer. The eggs are buoyant. The young are 2–3 inches long by the end of the first year and the adults are about 1⅓–1½ feet long when 3 years old. The Red Hake feeds on small crustaceans and fishes.

Economic Importance: The larger specimens of Red Hake are marketed together with the larger specimens of white hake for human consumption. Quantities of Red Hake are caught for use as mink, cat, and poultry feed. Both species of hake are commonly taken by anglers bait-fishing on the bottom.

Cusk
Brosme brosme (Müller)

Color: Variable: Back and upper sides dark gray, red-brown, or pale yellow; lower sides gray; belly gray-white. Dorsal, anal, and caudal fins have black margins edged with white.

Distribution: Occurs on both sides of the North Atlantic. In the American Atlantic it is found from Newfoundland to Cape Cod and as a stray as far south as New Jersey.

Size: Reaches a length of about 3½ feet. A fish 3⅓ feet long weighed 27 pounds.

General Information: The Cusk is a bottom species seldom found in depths of water shoaler than 60 feet, but it occurs down to depths of more than 1,800 feet. Spawning occurs in spring and summer. The eggs are buoyant. The Cusk feeds on crustaceans and shellfish.

Economic Importance: A good food fish common in the commercial fisheries north of Cape Cod.

Four-bearded Rockling
Enchelyopus cimbrius (Linnaeus)

Color: Back dark olive-yellow or brown; sides paler; belly white dotted with brown. Lining of mouth blue or dark purple.

Distribution: Occurs on both sides of the North Atlantic. In the American Atlantic it is found from Newfoundland to New York in coastal waters, and as far south as North Carolina in the deep waters of the Continental Slope.

Size: Reaches a length of about one foot.

General Information: The Four-bearded Rockling is a bottom species found in water depths ranging from a few feet down to over 4,300 feet. The eggs are buoyant and very similar in appearance to those of the red hake. The principal foods of the Four-bearded Rockling are probably small crustaceans and small fishes.

Economic Importance: None.

Atlantic Halibut
Hippoglossus hippoglossus (Linnaeus)

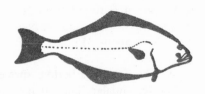

Color: Gray-brown, olive-brown, or dark brown on eyed or upper side. Blind or lower side white in smaller fish and blotched with gray in larger ones.

Distribution: Occurs regularly in the subarctic Atlantic. On the American coast it is found from Labrador to Cape Cod, and as a rare straggler south of Cape Cod to Virginia.

Size: Reported to reach a length of over 9 feet and a weight of about 700 pounds.

General Information: The Atlantic Halibut lives on the bottom and has been taken in depths ranging from less than 180 feet down to depths over 3,000 feet. The larger fish are found in the deeper water. Spawning occurs in spring. This is a prolific species, a female of about 200 pounds has been estimated to have produced over two million eggs. The eggs are buoyant and hatch in 16 days at a water temperature of 43 degrees. The Atlantic Halibut is a voracious feeder, preying mostly on other fishes but also eating crabs, lobsters, clams, and other crustaceans and shellfish.

Economic Importance: An excellent food fish but no longer abundant enough to be of great importance in the commercial fisheries.

Dab
Hippoglossoides platessoides (Fabricius)

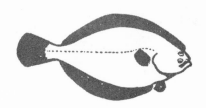

Color: Eyed side: gray-brown or red-brown. Blind side: white.

Distribution: Occurs on both sides of the North Atlantic. In the American Atlantic it is found from Labrador to Cape Cod and as a straggler south of Cape Cod to New York.

Size: Maximum length reported was about 2⅔ feet, with a weight of 14 pounds.

General Information: The Dab is a cold-water species found on the bottom from the shallow waters near shore down to depths of over 2,300 feet. It spawns in spring and 30,000 to 60,000 eggs are produced by each female. The eggs are buoyant and hatch in about 2 weeks at a water temperature of 39 degrees. The Dab feeds on a wide variety of bottom forms of animals, including worms, crustaceans, and sea urchins.

Economic Importance: A good food fish common in the catch of the otter trawl fishery north of Cape Cod.

Blackback or Winter Flounder
Pseudopleuronectes americanus (Walbaum)

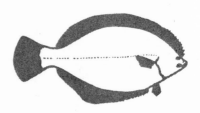

Color: Eyed side: dark gray, gray-brown, or olive green. Blind side: white.

Distribution: Labrador to Georgia.

Size: Reaches a length of about 2 feet. A fish 20 inches long was reported to weigh 5 pounds.

General Information: The Blackback is a bottom-dwelling form found in depths ranging from the shallow waters in bays, harbors, and estuaries down to 300 feet. Spawning occurs in winter and early spring. An average of half a million eggs is laid by a fish each year. The eggs sink to the bottom, where they stick to various objects and to each other. They hatch in about 2 weeks at a water temperature of 37–38 degrees. The main foods of the Blackback are small invertebrates, including shellfish, seaworms, shrimps, and small crabs. It does not eat when ready to spawn.

Economic Importance: An excellent food fish important in the catch of the small otter trawlers. The Blackback supports an extensive recreational fishery, particularly in the Middle Atlantic area.

Smooth Flounder
Liopsetta putnami (Gill)

Color: Eyed side: gray, gray-brown, black-brown. Blind side: white.

Distribution: Labrador to Cape Cod and as a stray south to Rhode Island.

Size: Reaches a length of about one foot and a weight of 1½ pounds.

General Information: The Smooth Flounder is most commonly found living on the bottom in sheltered bays, harbors, and river mouths, usually in depths of from 10 to 30 feet. It spawns in winter and like the blackback flounder probably feeds mostly on small invertebrates.

Economic Importance: A good food fish, but neither large nor plentiful enough to be important in the commercial fisheries.

Yellowtail Flounder
Limanda ferruginea (Storer)

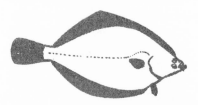

Color: Eyed side: brown or olive-gray tinged with red, with scattered large irregular brown-red spots. Blind side: white, yellowish about caudal peduncle.

Distribution: Labrador to Virginia.

Size: Reaches a length of about 2 feet.

General Information: The Yellowtail Flounder occurs commonly on the bottom in depths of 30–300 feet. Spawning takes place in spring and summer. The eggs are buoyant and hatch in 5 days at a water temperature of 50–52 degrees. The principal foods of this species are small crustaceans, small shellfish, and worms.

Economic Importance: A good food fish and one of the most valuable of the flatfishes in the commercial catch from southern New England north.

Gray Sole, Witch Flounder
Glyptocephalus cynoglossus (Linnaeus)

Color: Eyed side: brown-gray. Blind side: white.

Distribution: Occurs on both sides of the North Atlantic. In the American Atlantic it is found from Newfoundland to Virginia but is most abundant north of Cape Cod.

Size: Reaches a length of about 2 feet and a weight of about 4 pounds.

General Information: The Gray Sole is a bottom species seldom found in waters shoaler than 60 feet and most common in depths between 360 and 900 feet. It has been taken in depths down to more than 5,000 feet. Spawning occurs in late spring and summer. The eggs are buoyant and hatch in about one week at a water temperature of 46–49 degrees. The Gray Sole feeds on a wide variety of small invertebrates.

Economic Importance: A good food fish common in the catch of otter trawlers particularly north of Cape Cod.

Sundial, Windowpane Flounder
Lophopsetta maculata (Mitchill)

Color: Eyed side: pale olive green, red-brown, or gray-brown, mottled in appearance and dotted with irregular brown spots. Blind side: white.

Distribution: Gulf of St. Lawrence to South Carolina but most common south of Cape Cod.

Size: Reaches a length of 1½ feet and a weight of 2 pounds.

General Information: The Sundial is a shoal-water, bottom-inhabiting species. It is found commonly from just below the tide mark down to a depth of about 150 feet. Spawning occurs in late spring and summer. The eggs are buoyant and hatch in about one week at a water temperature of 51–56 degrees. Fish one foot in length are about 7 years old. The Sundial feeds on a wide variety of invertebrates including shrimps, crabs, and small fishes.

Economic Importance: A good food fish mostly discarded because of its small size and relatively thin body. The bigger fish are sometimes marketed. The Sundial is often caught by anglers fishing for other species.

Northern Fluke, Summer Flounder
Paralichthys dentatus (Linnaeus)

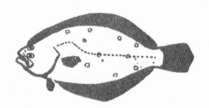

Color: Eyed side: color variable, commonly brown or gray. Most specimens marked with dark spots surrounded by white margins. Blind side: white.

Distribution: Occurs from Maine to South Carolina. Most common south of Cape Cod.

Size: Maximum length reported almost 4 feet, with a weight of 26 pounds. A 30-pound fish has also been reported.

General Information: This species is found on the Continental Shelf in depths of 150–500 feet during the winter and early spring. In late spring and summer large numbers of Northern Fluke move inshore close to the beaches and also enter bays and harbors. The Northern Fluke spawns from late autumn to early spring. The eggs are probably buoyant. The principal foods of this species are small fishes, crustaceans, and shellfish. The Northern Fluke is an active, predaceous species; it will follow small fish to the surface and jump clear of the water in the excitement of the chase.

Economic Importance: An excellent food fish of considerable importance in the commercial fisheries, particularly in the otter trawl fishery of the Middle Atlantic and Chesapeake regions. The Northern Fluke bites readily on natural baits or artificial lures and is subject to an intensive recreational fishery from Cape Cod south to Virginia, particularly in the New York-New Jersey area.

Four-spotted Fluke
Paralichthys oblongus (Mitchill)

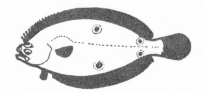

Color: Eyed side: mottled gray or brown with four large black eyespots edged with pinkish white. Blind side: white.
Distribution: Massachusetts to South Carolina.
Size: Reaches a length of about 1⅓ feet.
General Information: The Four-spotted Fluke is not as abundant as the northern fluke and seldom enters the shoal waters of bays and harbors. It is commonly found in depths of 40–900 feet. Spawning occurs from May through July. The eggs are buoyant. It feeds chiefly on small fishes, squid, crustaceans, shellfish, and worms.
Economic Importance: Of little importance in the commercial fisheries. A few Four-spotted Fluke are marketed mixed with the catch of the northern fluke. Occasionally this species is caught by the angler and mistaken for the northern fluke.

Small-Mouth Flounder
Etropus microstomus (Gill)

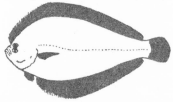

Color: Eyed side: light brown mottled with darker brown. Blind side: white.
Distribution: Occurs from New York to Virginia and possibly further south.

Size: Reaches a length of about 6 inches.
General Information: The Small-Mouth Flounder is locally common in summer in shallow waters adjacent to beaches and in bays and harbors. Little is known about this species.
Economic Importance: None.

Eyed Flounder
Platophrys ocellatus (Agassiz)

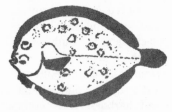

Color: Eyed side: light gray with a reddish tinge, covered with small dark gray spots and light rings enclosing areas of the ground color.
Distribution: Found from Brazil to Cape Cod but uncommon north of Cape Hatteras.
Size: Reaches a length of about 8 inches.
General Information: Little is known about this species.
Economic Importance: None.

Tonguefish
Symphurus plagiusa (Linnaeus)

Color: Eyed side: brownish with 6–7 dark crossbars. Blind side: white.
Distribution: Gulf Coast of Florida to North Carolina and as a straggler to Chesapeake Bay.

Size: Reaches a length of about 8 inches.
General Information: Little is known about this species.
Economic Importance: None.

Hogchoker
Trinectes maculatus (Bloch and Schneider)

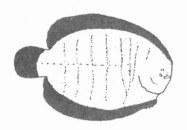

Color: Eyed side: gray-green to dark brown; a varying number of dark bars, usually 7–8, extend from the dorsal to the anal fin; a dark longitudinal stripe along the lateral line. Blind side: dirty white, usually with dark spots variable in size and number.
Distribution: Occurs from Massachusetts Bay to Panama. It is common from Cape Cod to Virginia but is most abundant from Virginia south.
Size: Reaches a length of about 8 inches.
General Information: The Hogchoker is a bottom species commonly found in the shallow, brackish waters of bays and estuaries. It spawns in late spring and summer. A 6½-inch fish has been estimated as producing 54,000 eggs at one spawning. Fish 2–3 inches long are one year old. The chief foods of the Hogchoker are worms and small crustaceans.
Economic Importance: None. An interesting species readily adaptable to the brackish-water home aquarium.

Northern Silverside
Menidia menidia (Linnaeus)

Color: Greenish above, silvery on sides and below; sides have a dark silvery band bounded above by a narrow black line. Scales on upper part of sides and back have many dark brown dots.

Distribution: Occurs from Nova Scotia to Chesapeake Bay, where it mixes with the southern silverside, a closely related form.

Size: Reaches a length of 6 inches.

General Information: The Northern Silverside is found in salt and brackish waters in protected bays, coves, and river mouths, usually on sand or gravel bottoms. It occurs in schools and is one of the most abundant species of our small fishes. It is particularly numerous in the channels running through salt marshes, where large schools may often be seen swimming near the surface of the shallow water. Spawning takes place from April to August and the eggs, like those of the tide-water silverside below, have sticky threads on their surfaces with which they adhere to various objects on the bottom and to each other. The food of the Northern Silverside consists of a wide variety of small aquatic animals and plants.

Economic Importance: A good food fish but marketed for such purpose in only limited quantities. It is used extensively in our recreational fisheries as a bait.

Tide-Water Silverside
Menidia beryllina (Cope)

Color: Back pale green; sides and belly silvery; silvery band along each side bordered above by a dark line; back scales with many brown dots. Often the body has a distinct yellow cast.

Distribution: Occurs from Cape Cod to South Carolina.

Size: Reaches a length of about 3 inches.

General Information: The Tide-Water Silverside is found in fresh, brackish, and salt water but is not common in strictly salt water. It occurs in large schools in the protected waters of bays and estuaries, often among heavy vegetation. Spawning takes place in spring and summer. The eggs have sticky threads on their surface. Newly laid eggs adhere by these threads to each other, the bottom sand, vegetation, and other objects in the water. The Tide-Water Silverside feeds on small crustaceans, shellfish, worms, and other small animals, as well as seaweed.

Economic Importance: When fried crisp this fat little fish can be eaten whole. It is considered a delicacy in some areas, where it is marketed under the name "whitebait."

Rough Silverside
Membras vagrans (Goode and Bean)

Color: Back greenish; lower sides and belly silvery; sides have broad silvery band bounded above with a dark line; numerous dark spots on scales of back.

Distribution: New York to Mexico.

Size: Grows to a length of about 5 inches.

General Information: This species is most often found in salt water but is sometimes taken in brackish water. It frequently occurs together with the common silverside, with which it is easily confused. Spawning takes place from spring through summer. The Rough Silverside feeds on small crustaceans and other small aquatic animals, fish eggs, and seaweed.

Economic Importance: None. Probably a source of food for larger fishes in some areas.

White Mullet
Mugil curema Cuvier and Valenciennes

Color: Back dark green; sides silvery, belly paler. Bluish-black spot at base of pectoral fin.

Distribution: Occurs in warm and temperate seas. In the western Atlantic it is found from Cape Cod to Brazil.

Size: In the southern part of its range it may reach a length of 3 feet, but fish less than 14 inches are more common. In the north the fish taken are usually less than 6 inches long.

General Information: The habits of this species are very similar to those of the striped mullet. However, the White Mullet spawns in the spring, while the striped mullet spawns in autumn and winter.

Economic Importance: This species is caught by the commercial fisheries south of Virginia, but it is not as important as the striped mullet because of its smaller size. It is frequently used as a bait in the marine recreational fisheries of our southern states. Both the white and striped mullet are hardy, active fishes in the brackish-water home aquarium.

Striped Mullet
Mugil cephalus Linnaeus

Color: Blue-gray and green above; silvery below. Scales on sides with dusky centers forming longitudinal lines along sides. A bluish spot at base of pectoral fin.

Distribution: Occurs in temperate and warm water on both sides of the Atlantic, in the Mediterranean, and in parts of the Pacific Ocean. In the western Atlantic it is found from Brazil to Cape Cod and as a straggler north to Nova Scotia.

Size: This species may grow to 2½ feet in the southern part of its range but seldom is over one foot and is usually smaller in the north.

General Information: The Striped Mullet is a common shore species in the Middle Atlantic and Chesapeake regions, particularly in the smaller sizes. Large schools are frequently seen near the surface of the water. When frightened these fish will leap from the water in a follow-the-leader fashion. Spawning occurs offshore in late fall and winter. The young come in to shore when about one inch long. At this time they are a shiny silver in color and are so unlike the adult that they were classified by early ichthyologists as a different species. The Striped Mullet feeds mostly on algae and to a lesser extent on microscopic plants and animals.

Economic Importance: An important species in the commercial fisheries of our southern states.

Northern Barracuda
Sphyraena borealis DeKay

Color: Olive green above; sides and belly silvery. Young have dusky blotches along sides and back.

Distribution: Cape Cod to Panama.

Size: Reaches a length of about one foot but is seldom over 7 inches in the north.

General Information: This species is most plentiful in the southern part of its range but in some years is very common in the north. Frequently it may be found along sandy shores in bays not far from ocean inlets. It is a voracious species feeding largely on small fishes.
Economic Importance: None.

Great Barracuda
Sphyraena barracuda (Shaw)

The Great Barracuda is a West Indian species rarely reaching farther north than South Carolina. Stray specimens have been reported as far north as Massachusetts.

Four-spined Stickleback
Apeltes quadracus (Mitchill)

Color: Greenish brown above; belly silvery; dark, irregular patches on back and sides.
Distribution: Found from Nova Scotia to Virginia in salt and brackish water and sometimes in fresh water.
Size: Reaches a length of 2½ inches.
General Information: This species is a common inhabitant of salt marshes and is usually found among dense masses of seaweed. Unlike the three-spined stickleback, the Four-spined Stickleback is never found floating on the surface at sea. The Four-spined Stickleback spawns in spring and early summer. Its spawning habits are similar to those of the three-spined stickleback below, but the nest is not

nearly so elaborate. This species feeds mostly on small crustaceans.

Economic Importance: None. The Four-spined Stickleback is a hardy though pugnacious species easily kept in the salt- or brackish-water home aquarium.

Three-spined Stickleback
Gasterosteus aculeatus Linnaeus

Color: Dark green above, sometimes blue; back and upper sides have faint dark bars. In breeding season red on sides.

Distribution: Occurs in salt and fresh waters along the coasts in the northern hemisphere. In the western Atlantic it is found from Labrador to Virginia.

Size: Reaches a length of 4 inches.

General Information: This is a very variable species differing in appearance according to locality. The number of bony plates on the sides varies, and sometimes no plates are present. The dorsal spines may be short or long, and a keel may or may not be present on the caudal peduncle.

The Three-spined Stickleback is mostly a shore fish living in the protected waters of coastal bays and estuaries, but it has been taken on the surface offshore floating among seaweed. It enters creeks and streams in spring to spawn. The male builds a barrel-shaped nest of bits of vegetation which are cemented together with sticky threads secreted from his kidneys. The nest is weighted down with pebbles. The male lures one or more females into the nest, where each lays from 100 to 150 eggs. After laying her eggs the female is driven away. The nest is guarded by the male for 6–10 days, after which time the eggs hatch. The nest is then destroyed, but the male continues to guard the young until they are able to fend for themselves. The food of the Three-spined Stickleback is mostly small crustaceans and other small animals, including fish fry as well as fish eggs and microscopic plants.

Economic Importance: None. A hardy but pugnacious species easily kept in the brackish- or salt-water home aquarium.

Two-spined Stickleback
Gasterosteus wheatlandi Putnam

Color: Green above; sides of head and body golden and with dark blotches; breast silvery.

Distribution: Newfoundland to New York.

Size: Grows to a length of about 4 inches.

General Information: Most common north of Cape Cod, usually in salt water. This species occurs regularly in shoal inshore waters, often in company with the three-spined stickleback, but it has also been caught on the surface in offshore waters. The Two-spined Stickleback is often confused with the three-spined stickleback.

Economic Importance: None.

Nine-spined Stickleback
Pungitius pungitius (Linnaeus)

Color: Olive brown above; sides have faint bars or blotches; belly silvery. During the breeding season the undersurface of the head becomes tinted with red and the belly greenish. In the male the undersurface of the body becomes rosy.

Distribution: This species occurs in both fresh and salt water in the northern parts of both the eastern and western hemispheres. In the western Atlantic it is found from the Arctic Ocean to New Jersey.

Size: Reaches about 3 inches in length.

General Information: The Nine-spined Stickleback is a shallow-water species most often found in the sheltered waters of harbors, bays, and salt marshes or in coastal fresh-water lakes and ponds. Spawning occurs in early spring. The male usually builds a nest of vegetation among the water plants and guards the eggs until they hatch.

Economic Importance: None. A hardy aquarium fish like most of its relatives.

Northern Pipefish
Syngnathus fuscus Storer

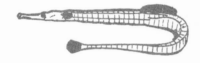

Color: Various, depending on surroundings. May be olive green, shades of brown, or shades of red.

Distribution: Occurs from Nova Scotia to South Carolina.

Size: Reaches a length of about one foot.

General Information: The Northern Pipefish is found in quiet coastal salt and brackish waters among seaweeds and eelgrass. Sometimes it is found offshore near the surface of the water, usually under floating seaweed. Breeding occurs in spring and summer. The Northern Pipefish, like the other pipefishes and sea horses, carries its eggs and developing young in a sac located on the lower, rear part of the body. Only the male carries the young. The female deposits its eggs into the brood sac of the male, where they are fertilized. In about 10 days the young hatch and leave the pouch. They are now about half an inch long and are miniature copies of the adults. The food of the Northern Pipefish is mostly small crustaceans or other small animals. Despite its hard, seemingly indigestible body of rings of bony plates, the Northern Pipefish has been frequently observed in the stomachs of larger fish and has been seen being eaten by a blue crab.

Economic Importance: None. An interesting species in the home salt-water aquarium.

Florida Pipefish
Syngnathus floridae (Jordan and Gilbert)

Color: Varies with environment; frequently brown above, silvery beneath; gray speckles along the side.
Distribution: Virginia to Texas.
Size: Reaches a length of about 9 inches.
General Information: The life history of this species is very similar to that of the northern pipefish.
Economic Importance: None. A good fish in the home marine aquarium.

Northern Sea Horse
Hippocampus hudsonius DeKay

Color: Variable according to surroundings; gray, yellow, or brown mottled with darker and paler markings.
Distribution: Occurs from South Carolina to Cape Cod and as a straggler to Nova Scotia.
Size: Maximum length recorded is 7½ inches.
General Information: The Northern Sea Horse is found in dense vegetation in protected areas along our shores. It is often found clinging by its flexible tail to the netting of commercial fish traps and eel pots. It breeds in summer, and as in the case of the pipefishes the male carries the developing eggs in a pouch. The young are ⅓–½ inch long at birth and resemble the adults in appearance. As many as 150 young may be born at one time. Unlike the pipefishes the sea horses have a flexible, prehensile tail which they use to hold on to vegetation, branches, and other objects in the water. The food of the Northern Sea Horse consists mostly of small crustaceans and other small animals.
Economic Importance: Sea horses are in considerable demand by the salt-water aquarists.

Trumpet Fish
Fistularia tabacaria Linnaeus

Color: Greenish brown above; lower surface silvery; back and sides have 10 dark crossbars and large pale blue spots. Tail filament deep blue.
Distribution: A tropical species, ranging from Brazil to Cape Cod and as a stray to Nova Scotia. Common in the West Indies.
Size: Reaches a length of 6 feet in the West Indies but northern specimens are usually under one foot.
General Information: Little is known about this species.

Economic Importance: None.

Northern Goatfish
Mullus auratus Jordan and Gilbert

The Northern Goatfish is a West Indian species common north to Florida. Occasional specimens, usually less than 4 inches in length, are found as far north as Cape Cod.

Common Mackerel
Scomber scombrus Linnaeus

Color: Steel blue above; sides silvery with coppery reflections; belly silvery white. Upper portion of sides of body have dark, transverse, irregular bands.
Distribution: Occurs in temperate waters on both sides of the Atlantic Ocean. In the western Atlantic it is found from the Gulf of St. Lawrence to North Carolina.
Size: This species may reach a length of almost 2 feet.
General Information: The Common Mackerel is often found in large schools swimming near the surface offshore. While the larger fish are mostly found offshore, the smaller younger fish are common in the protected waters of bays and river mouths. This species has been found at various depths, from the surface down to 600 feet. Spawning occurs in spring and early summer and over 500,000 eggs may be laid by one fish. The eggs float. Fish 7–8 inches

long are called "tacks" or "spikes," those 10–11 inches long, "tinkers." The Common Mackerel grows rapidly in its first two years, reaching 12–13 inches at the end of the second year of life. After that growth is slow, and fish 8 years old are less than 17 inches long. The food of this species is mostly small crustaceans and fish, but it also eats a wide variety of other small animals including microscopic forms. Its stomach is often found packed with a small crustacean, *Calanus,* called "red feed" by the commercial fisherman.

Economic Importance: The Common Mackerel is an important commercial species which fluctuates widely in abundance from year to year and over periods of years. It is an active fish and strikes readily at a moving bait or artificial lure; in periods of abundance it is intensively fished for by anglers.

Chub Mackerel
Pneumatophorus colias Gmelin

Color: Steel blue above; sides silvery; belly silvery white. Transverse irregular bands on upper portion of sides of body but thinner and more broken than in the common mackerel. Lower parts of the sides covered with hazy, irregular spots.

Distribution: Occurs on both sides of the Atlantic Ocean in temperate waters. In the western Atlantic it is found from Nova Scotia to New Jersey and sometimes to Virginia.

Size: Reaches a length of 14 inches.

General Information: Like the common mackerel, this species fluctuates widely in abundance from year to year or over periods of years. When it is abundant, large schools are often visible swimming near the surface offshore and close to inlets of bays. The Chub Mackerel eats much the same food as the common mackerel.

Economic Importance: A good food fish often taken, together with the common mackerel, by commercial fishermen. When abundant it is an important species in the sport fishery, as it will strike readily at a moving bait or artificial lure. It is often confused with the common mackerel.

Frigate Mackerel
Auxis thazard (Lacépède)

The Frigate Mackerel is commonly found offshore in warm seas. In the western Atlantic it is a rare straggler in the area from Cape Cod to Cape Hatteras. Specimens taken in this area are usually less than one foot long.

Common Bonito
Sarda sarda (Bloch)

Color: Blue-black above; lower sides and belly silvery. Upper parts of sides have parallel dark blue bands running obliquely from the edge of the back toward the rear of the gill opening. The young have dark blue vertical bars on the sides which disappear in the adult.

Distribution: Occurs in warm waters on both sides of the Atlantic Ocean and in the Mediterranean. In the western

Atlantic it has been reported as far north as Nova Scotia.
Size: This species may grow to a length of 3 feet and a
weight of 12 pounds.
General Information: The Common Bonito is found travel-
ing in large schools offshore. It feeds ravenously on fish
and squid and is often seen leaping out of the water while
in pursuit of its prey. Spawning takes place in spring.
Economic Importance: Although a good food fish, the
Common Bonito has but a limited market in the United
States. It is often taken by sport fishermen on trolled
artificial lures.

Ocean Bonito
Katsuwonus pelamis (Linnaeus)

Color: Blue-black above; sides and belly silvery. Lower
sides have parallel dark blue-black bands running from
under pectoral fin to caudal peduncle.
Distribution: The Ocean Bonito occurs in warm and temperate waters of all oceans. In the western Atlantic it has
been recorded as far north as Cape Cod.
Size: Reaches a length of over 2 feet.
General Information: This species is mostly found offshore
in small schools. In some years it is very abundant. It
feeds mostly on fishes, especially the flying fishes.
Economic Importance: The Ocean Bonito is frequently
taken on artificial lures by sport fishermen trolling offshore.

Little Tuna, False Albacore
Euthynnus alleteratus (Rafinesque)

Color: Steel blue above; silvery white on lower sides and belly. Upper sides marked with irregular oblique bands sloping from the top edge of the back toward the head.

Distribution: Occurs in the warmer waters of all oceans. In the western Atlantic it straggles as far north as Cape Cod.

Size: Reaches a length of about 2½ feet.

General Information: Often occurs in large schools offshore. It feeds on fish.

Economic Importance: The Little Tuna is not an important commercial species. It is frequently taken by the angler trolling offshore.

Bluefin Tuna
Thunnus thynnus (Linnaeus)

Color: Back dark blue; sides and belly silvery gray tinged with glistening pink, green, and other iridescent colors.

Distribution: Occurs in warm and temperate waters on both sides of the Atlantic Ocean, in the Mediterranean, and in the Pacific and Indian Oceans. In the American Atlantic it is found as far north as the southeast coast of Newfoundland.

Size: The Bluefin Tuna is said to reach a length of over 14 feet and a weight of 1,600 pounds.

General Information: The Bluefin Tuna is mostly found offshore in clear water. Fish of 3–500 pounds may often be seen in small schools, splashing and jumping near the surface. Each school usually consists of fish of about the same size. The large tuna usually do not school. Age studies show that this fish is 2 feet long by the middle of the second summer of life and almost 4 feet long by the fifth summer. The Bluefin Tuna feeds primarily on fish, including herrings, mackerels, sand launces, and a wide variety of other species.

Economic Importance: This species is of relatively little importance in the commercial fisheries of the American Atlantic, but attempts are now being made to develop a profitable fishery for it. The Bluefin Tuna is important in the recreational fisheries. Small fish strike at artificial lures trolled in the foamy wake of a vessel. Larger fish are attracted to the vessel by scattered ground menhaden and caught on hooks baited with whole fish such as butterfish, mackerel, or menhaden. Fish weighing over 900 pounds have been taken by rod and reel.

Blackfin Tuna
Thunnus atlanticus (Lesson)

The Blackfin Tuna is known only from the tropical western Atlantic Ocean. It sometimes strays as far north as Cape Cod but is most common in the Caribbean and in southern Florida, where it is caught by the sport fishermen.

Yellowfin Tuna
Thunnus albacares (Bonnaterre)

The Yellowfin Tuna occurs in the offshore tropical waters of the Atlantic Ocean. It is uncommon from Virginia north but has recently been caught in the Gulf Stream track far off the coast of Massachusetts.

Albacore
Thunnus alalunga (Gmelin)

The Albacore is found in all warm seas. In the western Atlantic it is rare north of Florida.

Spanish Mackerel
Scomberomorus maculatus (Mitchill)

Color: Dark blue above; silvery below. Sides have oval orange or yellow spots irregularly arranged both above and below lateral line. Front part of first dorsal fin black.
Distribution: Occurs on both coasts of North America. In the western Atlantic it is found from Brazil to Maine. It is common north of Chesapeake Bay but most abundant off our southern states.
Size: Reaches a length of 3 feet and a weight of 10 pounds.
General Information: This species appears in schools in the Middle Atlantic region in spring and autumn. It was formerly very common in this area but in recent years has been relatively scarce. Spawning occurs in spring and summer. The eggs are buoyant. The Spanish Mackerel feeds mostly on fish.

Economic Importance: This species is an excellent food fish of high market value. It is frequently taken by the angler in the southern part of its range.

Cero
Scomberomorus regalis (Bloch)

Color: Dark blue above; silvery sides. Sides have yellow dots arranged in rows and mostly below the lateral line. A brown stripe goes from the pectoral fin to the base of the tail. The front part of the first dorsal fin is blue.

Distribution: Occurs from Cape Cod to Brazil but most common off southern Florida and the West Indies.

Size: Fish 6 feet long have been reported. It is said to reach a weight of 35 pounds.

General Information: This species is uncommon north of Chesapeake Bay.

Economic Importance: An excellent food and game fish.

King Mackerel, Cavalla
Scomberomorus cavalla (Cuvier and Valenciennes)

Color: Dark gray above; silvery on sides and belly. Sides of small fish marked with dark gray or yellow spots which disappear in larger fish.

Distribution: Occurs in the warm waters of the North Atlantic. In the western Atlantic it is found regularly from Brazil to North Carolina and frequently as far north as Cape Cod. A rare straggler north of Cape Cod.

Size: Reported to reach 5 feet in length and 100 pounds in weight.

General Information: This species was formerly common north of the Carolinas but is now only occasionally seen in the Middle Atlantic region.

Economic Importance: A good food and game fish.

Cutlass Fish
Trichiurus lepturus Linnaeus

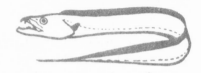

Color: Entire body silvery.

Distribution: Occurs in warm seas. In the western Atlantic it is fairly common from North Carolina south and is abundant in the Gulf of Mexico and the West Indies. Single specimens are often taken in the Middle Atlantic region. It is a rare straggler north of Cape Cod.

Size: This species is said to grow to a length of 5 feet.

General Information: The Cutlass Fish probably spawns in spring. It is a predaceous species living chiefly on fish.

Economic Importance: An edible fish but not marketed in quantity.

Blue Marlin
Makaira ampla (Poey)

Color: Back and upper sides dark blue with a copper tint. Lower sides and belly pale gray-blue. Vertical, hazy violet-blue bars on the sides.

Distribution: Occurs in the warm waters of the western Atlantic. It is most common off Cuba and the Bahamas. While it is found frequently in the Middle Atlantic region, it is not as common as the white marlin.

Size: The Blue Marlin is said to reach a length of 26 feet. Fish of 1,000 pounds have reportedly been harpooned.

General Information: This species is never very abundant. Usually only a single fish or a pair of fish are seen in a locality.

Economic Importance: The Blue Marlin is of limited commercial value but it is an important game fish in southern waters.

White Marlin
Makaira albida (Poey)

Color: Back and upper sides dark blue; lower sides and belly white. Vertical, hazy, violet-blue bands on the sides of the body.

Distribution: Occurs in the western Atlantic. It is common off Florida, Cuba, and the Bahamas and is found regularly to southern Massachusetts in summer.

Size: Fish up to 9 feet in length and over 160 pounds have been reported.

General Information: The White Marlin feeds on fish and squid. Single fish, pairs, or sometimes small schools are encountered offshore.

Economic Importance: This species is of little value commercially although it is sometimes eaten. It is an important game fish.

Atlantic Sailfish
Istiophorus americanus (Cuvier and Valenciennes)

The Sailfish occurs in the warmer waters of the American Atlantic and is common off southern Florida and in the West Indies. It is a rare straggler in the Middle Atlantic region but has been reported as far north as Cape Cod.

Swordfish
Xiphias gladius Linnaeus

Color: Black, dark purple, or blue above. Silvery below.
Distribution: Cosmopolitan in warm seas. In the western Atlantic it ranges as far north as the coast of Newfoundland.
Size: This species may grow to 16 feet in length and weigh 1,100 pounds.
General Information: The Swordfish is found offshore in the ocean but sometimes approaches close to the shore to feed. It is often seen, singly or in pairs, resting quietly near the surface of the water. It has been taken on lines at depths of 1,200 feet. The Swordfish feeds mostly on fish and squid, and deep-sea fish found in their stomachs indicate that they will go to great depths in search of food. The sword is used to strike at the prey, either killing or stunning it before it is eaten. Harpooned Swordfish have been known to attack boats, driving their swords into the hulls.

Economic Importance: An excellent food fish commercially taken by harpoon. A recreational fishery using both harpoon and trolled baits or artificial lures has developed in recent years.

Dolphin
Coryphaena hippurus Linnaeus

Color: Background silvery; iridescent colors over sides with blues and golden yellows predominating.

Distribution: Cosmopolitan in warm, open seas. In the western Atlantic it is found north to Cape Cod and as a straggler to Nova Scotia.

Size: Attains a length of about 6 feet.

General Information: The Dolphin is a fast-swimming species most common in the blue waters of the open sea. It feeds largely on fish, particularly the flying fishes. This animal is a true fish, although its name is often applied to certain sea mammals which are also known as porpoises.

Economic Importance: This species is frequently taken by the sport fisherman while offshore.

Butterfish
Poronotus triacanthus (Peck)

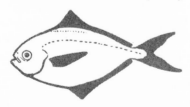

Color: Silvery gray or blue above; sides paler; silvery below. Numerous irregular dark spots on the sides of live fish, which fade soon after death.

Distribution: Occurs from Florida to Nova Scotia. It is most abundant in the Middle Atlantic and New England regions.

Size: Grows to a length of one foot and a weight of 1¼ pounds.

General Information: The Butterfish is often found close inshore in the shallow waters of coves and bays over sandy bottoms. It is also encountered offshore, particularly in winter, in depths down to 700 feet. Spawning occurs in spring and early summer. The eggs are buoyant. Young Butterfish frequently are found swimming among the stinging tentacles of jellyfishes, where they are protected from larger fishes. The Butterfish feeds on a wide variety of animals including small fish, crustaceans, squid, and worms.

Economic Importance: A good pan fish and important in the commercial fisheries of the Middle Atlantic and southern New England. It is frequently caught by anglers fishing from shore in favorable local areas.

Harvest Fish, Starfish
Peprilus alepidotus (Linnaeus)

Color: Silvery green above; sides silvery or with a yellow tinge.

Distribution: Occurs from Florida to Cape Cod. It is most common in the Chesapeake Bay region.

Size: Reaches a length of about 11 inches and a weight of 1¼ pounds.

General Information: The Harvest Fish is mostly a bay species, often found living together with the butterfish. Spawning takes place in late spring and early summer. Like the butterfish this species eats small fish, crustaceans, squid, and worms.

Economic Importance: A good pan fish. The Harvest Fish is taken commercially in the greatest quantity by the pound net fisheries in Chesapeake Bay.

Black Rudder Fish
Palinurichthys perciformis (Mitchill)

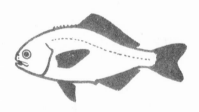

Color: Blackish green.

Distribution: Found from Cape Hatteras to Nova Scotia but most common south of Cape Cod.

Size: Reaches a length of almost 14 inches and a weight of 1½ pounds.

General Information: The Black Rudder Fish is often found under floating wreckage, boxes, barrels, or masses of drifting seaweed. In New York it commonly congregates around the offshore traps in the vicinity of Fire Island Inlet. This species feeds on a wide variety of animals including small crustaceans, shellfish, and small fishes.

Economic Importance: A good food fish but not plentiful enough to be of commercial importance.

Goggle-eyed Scad
Trachurops crumenopthalmus (Bloch)

Color: Olive-blue above; silvery below; a faint spot near the rear margin of the gill cover.

Distribution: Cosmopolitan in warm seas. In the western Atlantic it occurs as a stray as far north as Nova Scotia.

Size: Grows to a length of 2 feet.

General Information: Fish caught from Virginia north are usually less than 7 inches long. This species probably feeds on fish and worms.

Economic Importance: None.

Round Scad
Decapterus punctatus (Agassiz)

Color: Bluish above; silvery below. A dark spot near the rear edge of the gill cover. Spots along the lateral line.

Distribution: Occurs from Brazil to Cape Cod and is common in the West Indies and off Florida.

Size: Reaches a length of about one foot.

General Information: Feeds on small crustaceans and worms.

Economic Importance: None.

Mackerel Scad
Decapterus macarellus (Cuvier and Valenciennes)

Color: Slate blue above; silvery below. A black spot near rear margin of gill cover.
Distribution: Occurs in the warmer waters of the Atlantic, straying north to Nova Scotia.
Size: Reaches a length of one foot.
General Information: Uncommon in the northern part of its range but in some years fairly numerous in the fall of the year.
Economic Importance: None.

Rough Scad
Trachurus trachurus (Linnaeus)

The Rough Scad is found in warm and temperate seas and is common off the Florida Keys. It is rare in the region from Cape Hatteras north. The maximum length of this species is about one foot.

Common Jack, Crevalle
Caranx hippos (Linnaeus)

Color: Bluish or bronze-green above; lower parts silvery, often blotched with golden yellow. A distinct spot on hind edge of gill flap. Young have 5–6 vertical dark bars.

Distribution: Occurs in warm seas. It is common on both coasts of the Atlantic and the eastern coast of the Pacific. In the western Atlantic it is taken regularly to Cape Cod and as a straggler to Nova Scotia.

Size: Reaches a length of 2½ feet and a weight of 20 pounds.

General Information: Usually only fish less than one foot long are taken north of Cape Hatteras, and in some years the young 2–5 inches in length are very common.

Economic Importance: Important as a food and game fish only along the southern Atlantic and Gulf Coast.

Blue Runner, Hardtail
Caranx crysos (Mitchill)

Color: Greenish bronze above; silvery bronze below. Usually a spot on the rear part of the gill cover.

Distribution: Found regularly from Brazil to Cape Cod and as a stray to Nova Scotia.

Size: Reaches a length of almost 2 feet and a weight of about 4 pounds.

General Information: As with the common jack, only small Hardtails, usually fish less than one foot long, are found north of Cape Hatteras.

Economic Importance: This species is important as a food fish only along the southern Atlantic and Gulf coasts.

Horse-Eye Jack, Jurel
Caranx latus Agassiz

The Horse-Eye Jack is a West Indian species which reaches as far south as Brazil. It is common on the east coast of Panama. It is found along the coasts of the south Atlantic states and occasionally as far north as Chesapeake Bay.

Threadfish
Alectis crinitus (Mitchill)

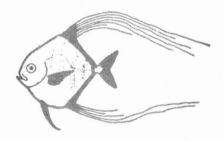

The Threadfish is a warm-water species found on both coasts of tropical America. It is found as a stray commonly as far north as Cape Cod. For a long time this fish was considered a different species from the Cuban jack, but recent findings indicate that it is the young of the Cuban jack. Specimens taken north of Cape Hatteras are usually less than 8 inches long.

Moonfish
Vomer setapinnis (Mitchill)

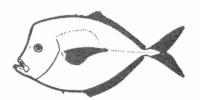

Color: Blue-green above; sides silvery.
Distribution: Found from Uruguay to Cape Cod and straying north as far as Nova Scotia.
Size: Reaches a length of one foot.
General Information: This species is most common from Chesapeake Bay south. Young less than 4 inches long are frequently caught north of Chesapeake Bay.
Economic Importance: The Moonfish is used as food in some localities in the southern part of its range.

Bumper
Chloroscombrus chrysurus (Linnaeus)

The Bumper ranges from Brazil to Cape Cod and as a straggler into the Gulf of Maine. It is not common north of North Carolina. It is a small species, seldom over 8 inches long, not highly valued as food.

Look-down
Selene vomer (Linnaeus)

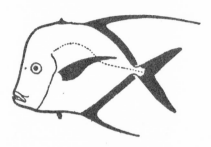

Color: Blue-green above; bright silvery sides; young have four or more dusky vertical bars on sides.

Distribution: Occurs in warm waters on both American coasts. In the Atlantic it is common from Uruguay to Chesapeake Bay, and the young are frequently taken north of Chesapeake Bay to Cape Cod and occasionally north to the Gulf of Maine.

Size: Reaches a length of one foot.

General Information: The Look-down is less common north of Chesapeake Bay than the moonfish. Only young fish, mostly under 4 inches in length, are taken in the northern area.

Economic Importance: The Look-down is considered a good food fish in some sections of its southern range.

Banded Rudder Fish
Seriola zonata (Mitchill)

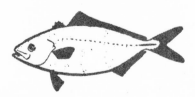

Color: Silvery brown or blue above; sides paler; white below. Young fish has 5–6 dark brown or blue vertical bands on body.

Distribution: Occurs from the Gulf of Mexico to Cape Cod and as a straggler north to Nova Scotia.

Size: Reaches a maximum length of about 3 feet.

General Information: Only the young fish in the banded stage and less than one foot in length are taken with any frequency from Cape Hatteras north.

Economic Importance: This species is considered a good food and game fish in the southern part of its range. North of Cape Hatteras the banded smaller sizes are sometimes caught by the angler fishing for other species.

Amber Jack
Seriola dumerili (Risso)

Color: Bluish above; bluish silver below; a bronze stripe along the length of the side. Young have dark brown or blue vertical bars.

Distribution: Occurs in the tropical Atlantic. In the western Atlantic it is found from Brazil to Massachusetts.

Size: Reaches a length of 5–6 feet and a weight of at least 120 pounds.

General Information: This species is most common in southern waters. Fish taken north of Cape Hatteras are usually less than one foot long. At this size they are easily confused with the smaller-sized banded rudder fish.

Economic Importance: A good food and game fish.

Pilot Fish
Naucrates ductor (Linnaeus)

Color: Bluish; 5–7 dark vertical bands on sides of body. Tail white-tipped.

Distribution: Cosmopolitan in warm seas. In the American Atlantic it strays as far north as Nova Scotia.

Size: Reaches a length of about 2 feet.

General Information: The Pilot Fish accompanies sharks in their wanderings, feeding on scraps left by these larger animals and on the many parasites present on the bodies of the sharks.

Economic Importance: None.

Leatherjacket
Oligoplites saurus (Bloch and Schneider)

The Leatherjacket occurs on both coasts of tropical America. In the Atlantic it reaches as far north as Cape Cod, but it is uncommon from Chesapeake Bay north. This fish grows to a length of about one foot.

Common Pompano
Trachinotus carolinus (Linnaeus)

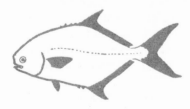

The Common Pompano is found from Brazil to Cape Cod, but specimens found north of Virginia are usually the young, less than 4–5 inches long. It is said to reach a weight of 8 pounds, but fish weighing 2 pounds and about

1½ feet long are more common in the southern part of its range. This fish is highly prized for food.

Round Pompano
Trachinotus falcatus (Linnaeus)

The Round Pompano is found from Brazil to Cape Cod, but mostly young fish, less than 5 inches in length, are taken in the area from Chesapeake Bay north. This species is reported to reach a weight of 3 pounds. It is an excellent food fish.

Bluefish
Pomatomus saltatrix (Linnaeus)

Color: Greenish above; silvery below.
Distribution: Irregularly distributed in warmer seas. In the western Atlantic it is found from Argentina north to Cape Cod and as a straggler to Nova Scotia.
Size: Reaches a length of almost 4 feet and a weight of at least 27 pounds.
General Information: The Bluefish is an oceanic species found both inshore and offshore. It travels in large schools following the schools of menhaden, mackerel, and other fishes, upon which it relentlessly preys. Spawning occurs in spring and summer, probably offshore. The young Bluefish called "snappers" enter the shoal, protected, coastal

waters in early spring and throughout the summer. In autumn they move offshore. Bluefish are very abundant in some years and relatively scarce in other years.

Economic Importance: The Bluefish is an excellent food fish and is subject to both extensive commercial and recreational fisheries. It is caught regularly by the offshore angler trolling a feather or other artificial lure or by the bait fisherman who attracts the fish to the boat by "chumming" with ground menhaden. This species is also commonly taken by the surf caster and in the "snapper" sizes by bank and pier sport fishermen.

Cobia
Rachycentron canadus (Linnaeus)

Color: Black above; grayish white below. Young have a black band on sides extending from the snout to the base of the tail fin.

Distribution: Cosmopolitan in warm seas. Common from Chesapeake Bay south. It is an occasional visitor north of Chesapeake Bay as far as Cape Cod.

Size: Reaches a length of 5 feet. A fish of 84 pounds has been reported.

General Information: This species is uncommon north of Chesapeake Bay. It feeds on fish and crustaceans and for the latter reason is known in some areas as the "crabeater."

Economic Importance: The Cobia is marketed for food in the southern part of its range.

Striped Bass, Rockfish
Roccus saxatilis (Walbaum)

Color: Dark green above; silvery on sides and belly. Scales have 7–8 distinct, sometimes broken, longitudinal black stripes.

Distribution: Occurs from the Gulf of St. Lawrence to Florida. It has been introduced successfully on the Pacific coast of the United States.

Size: Grows to a length of over 6 feet. The largest recorded weighed 125 pounds.

General Information: The Striped Bass is a powerful species common along the shores of the Middle Atlantic and Chesapeake regions. Smaller fish up to 10–15 pounds often school in large numbers. The larger fish are more often found singly or in small schools. Spawning occurs in spring and the adult fish run up rivers to brackish and fresh waters to lay their eggs. A 3-pound fish was reported to contain 14,000 eggs, while a 75-pound fish was estimated to have about ten million eggs. The eggs are heavier than fresh water and hatch in 48 hours at a water temperature of 64 degrees. Recently it has been found that there are various races of Striped Bass along its range. Most of the fish caught from New England south to Virginia are probably spawned in Chesapeake Bay and its tributaries, although some spawning also takes place in various other localities in the Middle Atlantic and southern New England regions. The Striped Bass is a voracious fish, feeding mostly on a wide variety of fishes and crustaceans, shellfish, and sea worms.

Economic Importance: A good food fish important in the

commercial fisheries from Cape Cod to Cape Hatteras, particularly in Chesapeake Bay. This species is one of the major marine game fishes eagerly sought after by anglers casting in the surf from shore or trolling or still-fishing in boats close to shore.

White Perch
Morone americana (Gmelin)

Color: Olive, gray-green, or blackish above; sides and belly silvery, sometimes brassy. Pale longitudinal stripes on smaller fish, usually disappearing in larger fish.
Distribution: Occurs from Nova Scotia to South Carolina.
Size: Grows to about 15½ inches in length and a weight of about 2 pounds.
General Information: The White Perch is most plentiful in brackish-water ponds, bays, and estuaries. It is often landlocked in fresh-water ponds. This species reproduces in both fresh and brackish water, but in fresh water the average size of the fish decreases after several generations. Spawning occurs in spring. The eggs are adhesive and stick together in clumps or to any object they touch. The White Perch feeds on small fishes, crustaceans, and other small animals as well as on fish eggs.
Economic Importance: A commercial species where abundant. It is most important in the commercial fisheries of Chesapeake Bay. The White Perch is frequently taken by anglers in some localities.

Common Sea Bass
Centropristes striatus (Linnaeus)

Color: Brown, dark gray, or blue-black. Young under 3 inches with a dark brown or black stripe from eye to base of tail fin and frequently with hazy dark vertical bands on sides.

Distribution: Occurs from Florida to Cape Cod and as a straggler to Maine.

Size: Reaches a length of over 2 feet and a weight of more than 8 pounds.

General Information: The Common Sea Bass is found mostly in salt water in depths ranging from a few feet down to 420 feet. In summer it is common inshore on rocky bottoms and near wrecks and wharves. Spawning takes place in spring. The eggs are buoyant. The adult males have a fatty hump on their backs in front of the dorsal fin. Older females regularly change sex and become fertile males. The Common Sea Bass is a bottom feeder and its main foods are crustaceans and shellfish, squid, and small fishes.

Economic Importance: A valuable food fish caught in large numbers by the commercial fisheries in the Middle Atlantic region. It is frequently taken in its smaller sizes by anglers fishing in bays and other inshore waters. Larger fish are an important part of the catch of the "deep-sea," recreational boat fisheries.

Wreckfish
Polyprion americanus (Bloch and Schneider)

Color: Black or grayish brown. Tail fin edged with white.
Distribution: Known from temperate waters on both coasts
of the Atlantic, the Mediterranean, and the Indian Ocean.
Size: Reaches a length of at least 5 feet and a weight of
more than 100 pounds.
General Information: The Wreckfish is said to be mostly
found in wrecks. Adults are not uncommon on the bottom
in depths greater than 1,800 feet. Small fish are occasionally found under floating wreckage and debris in the
coastal waters from Virginia to Cape Cod.
Economic Importance: None.

Deep Big-Eye
Pseudopriacanthus altus (Gill)

This red, roundish fish is a West Indian species commonly
found in the Caribbean and the Gulf of Mexico north to
South Carolina. The young stray north to Cape Cod and

sometimes into the Gulf of Maine. The Deep Big-Eye reaches a length of 11 inches but is usually less than 4 inches in northern waters.

Common Big-Eye
Priacanthus arenatus Cuvier and Valenciennes

This bright red fish occurs in the tropical Atlantic south to Brazil. Young fish are occasionally taken northward as far as Cape Cod. The Common Big-Eye reaches a length of one foot in the southern part of its range.

Tripletail
Lobotes surinamensis (Bloch)

Color: Brownish black; dark blotches below base of dorsal and anal fins.
Distribution: Occurs from Uruguay to Cape Cod.
Size: Reaches a length of about 3 feet and a weight of well over 25 pounds.
General Information: The Tripletail is never very abundant anywhere but is most common from Virginia south.
Economic Importance: Not abundant enough to be of importance in the fisheries.

Gray Snapper
Lutianus griseus (Linnaeus)

The Gray Snapper is one of several species of snappers common off Florida. The young of this fish and possibly of some of the other species sometimes stray into the coastal waters from Cape Hatteras to Cape Cod.

Pigfish
Orthopristis chrysopterus (Linnaeus)

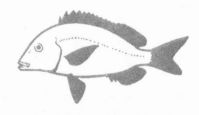

Color: Bluish with purple reflections above; sides silvery; golden stripes on back.
Distribution: New York to Mexico.
Size: Reaches a length of 15 inches. The maximum weight recorded is 2 pounds.
General Information: The Pigfish is not taken in large numbers north of Chesapeake Bay. Spawning occurs in spring. This species feeds on worms and to a lesser extent on crustaceans, shellfish, insect larvae, and fish.
Economic Importance: A good food fish. It is important in the southern commercial fisheries. Large numbers are taken in North Carolina.

White Grunt
Haemulon plumieri (Lacépède)

The White Grunt is a West Indian species occurring only as a straggler north of South Carolina.

Northern Porgy
Stenotomus chrysops (Linnaeus)

Color: Silver-blue above; iridescent silvery below. Young have about 6 dusky, indistinct, vertical bars.

Distribution: North Carolina to Cape Cod and occasionally to Maine.

Size: Grows to a length of 18 inches and a weight of 4 pounds.

General Information: The Northern Porgy is a very abundant species in the Middle Atlantic region, where it is found in large schools usually over sandy bottoms. In the spring the adults come close to shore, often into the protected waters of deeper bays, to spawn. The eggs float. By the end of the first summer the young are about 4 inches long. During the winter the Northern Porgy moves offshore and to the south off the coasts of Virginia and North

Carolina into depths of 120–500 feet or more. This fish is mostly a bottom feeder, eating crustaceans and worms and other small bottom forms.

Economic Importance: An important commercial species, particularly in the Middle Atlantic area. The northern porgy is a good pan fish and is eagerly sought after by recreational fishermen. It is a vigorous antagonist on light tackle.

Southern Porgy
Stenotomus aculeatus (Cuvier and Valenciennes)

The Southern Porgy replaces the northern porgy from Virginia southwards. An occasional stray Southern Porgy may be taken off Virginia and more rarely north of Virginia.

Holbrook's Porgy
Diplodus holbrookii (Bean)

Holbrook's Porgy is not uncommon from the Gulf of Mexico north to North Carolina but is rare in Virginia. It reaches a length of 14 inches.

Sheepshead
Archosargus probatocephalus (Walbaum)

Color: Greenish yellow; sides have 7 dark vertical bars.
Distribution: Occurs from Texas to Cape Cod and as a stray to the Bay of Fundy.
Size: Reaches a length of 2½ feet. The maximum weight recorded was 30 pounds.
General Information: The Sheepshead was formerly common from Virginia to New York. It is now rare in this region. Spawning occurs in spring and the eggs float. This species feeds mostly on crustaceans and shellfish.
Economic Importance: An excellent food fish common in the commercial catches of the south Atlantic and Gulf coast states. This species is often caught by the angler in areas where it is abundant.

Pinfish
Lagodon rhomboides (Linnaeus)

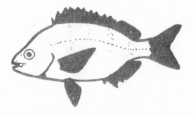

Color: Dark green above; silvery below. Sides have light blue and yellow longitudinal stripes. From 4 to 6 hazy vertical bars on sides.

Distribution: Occurs from Massachusetts to Texas but is most common from Virginia southward.

Size: Reaches a length of about 13 inches.

General Information: The Pinfish spawns in late autumn and winter. It feeds on fish, shellfish, worms, crustaceans, and seaweed.

Economic Importance: A good food fish of some importance in the commercial fisheries of Florida.

Bermuda Chub
Kyphosus sectatrix (Linnaeus)

The Bermuda Chub is a tropical species common about Bermuda and the Florida Keys. It is found from Panama to Cape Cod but occurs only rarely, and usually as smaller-sized young, from North Carolina northward. It reaches a length of about 1½ feet.

Gray Sea Trout, Weakfish
Cynoscion regalis (Bloch and Schneider)

Color: Greenish above; silvery below. Back and sides with a metallic glitter of blue, green, purple, and gold. Upper sides have oblique, wavy lines composed of blotches of black, bronze, and dark green.

Distribution: Found from the east coast of Florida to Massachusetts and straying northward to the Bay of Fundy.

Size: Reaches a weight of 30 pounds. A fish 2½ feet long weighs 9–10 pounds.

General Information: The Weakfish was formerly very abundant from North Carolina as far north as Massachusetts. In recent years it has declined in abundance and larger fish have become rare. Schools of this species approach the inshore waters in spring to spawn. While some spawning occurs in the northern part of the range of this fish, the bulk of the successful spawning seems to take place in the vicinity of Chesapeake Bay. The eggs float. In the autumn the fish leave the inshore waters and most of them move south to offshore waters in the vicinity of Chesapeake Bay and Cape Hatteras. The male Weakfish can make a drumming sound by vibrating the special thickened muscles in the belly wall against the air bladder. The Weakfish feeds both on the bottom and in the upper levels of the water and eats a wide variety of animals including shellfish, crustaceans, and small fishes.

Economic Importance: The Weakfish is one of the important species in the commercial fisheries of the Chesapeake and Middle Atlantic regions. It is a popular game fish and will readily rise to the surface of the water in pursuit of a moving bait or artificial lure.

Spotted Sea Trout, Spotted Weakfish
Cynoscion nebulosus (Cuvier and Valenciennes)

Color: Dark gray above with a metallic blue glitter; silvery below. Numerous black spots on upper part of sides and on the dorsal and caudal fins.

Distribution: Found from Texas to New York but uncommon north of Delaware.

Size: The largest fish recorded weighed 16 pounds. A fish

2¼ feet long weighed almost 8½ pounds.
General Information: This species is not as numerous as the weakfish. It feeds on fish and crustaceans.
Economic Importance: A good food fish, caught in commercial quantities from Virginia south to Florida on both the Atlantic and Gulf coasts. It is an excellent game fish.

Silver or White Sea Trout
Cynoscion nothus (Holbrook)

The White Sea Trout is most abundant in the Gulf of Mexico but is found occasionally as far north as Virginia and Maryland.

Northern King Whiting or Kingfish
Menticirrhus saxatilis (Bloch and Schneider)

Color: Dusky above with a metallic silver glitter; silvery below; sides with brown-black oblique bars running toward the rear and upward except for two oblique bars near the head which run obliquely forward and upward. The second of these anterior bars forms a V with the first of the body bars.
Distribution: Occurs from Florida to Cape Cod and as a stray to Maine. It is most common from Chesapeake Bay to New York.

Size: Reaches a length of 17 inches and a weight of 3 pounds.

General Information: The Northern Kingfish is found in small schools near ocean beaches and in bays and estuaries, usually on sandy bottoms. It spawns in the protected waters of the bays in late spring and summer. The eggs are buoyant. This species is a bottom feeder and eats crustaceans, small shellfish, worms, and young fishes.

Economic Importance: A prime food fish readily marketed but not as abundant as many other commercial species. The Northern Kingfish is a good game fish frequently caught by the surf angler.

Southern King Whiting or Kingfish
Menticirrhus americanus (Linnaeus)

Color: Silvery gray above; white below and often with dusky markings. Sides with 7–8 obscure, oblique bands running upward and backward; band sometimes absent.

Distribution: Occurs from New York to Texas, but it is not common north of Chesapeake Bay.

Size: This species reaches a length of at least 16 inches and a weight of about 2½ pounds.

General Information: The Southern Kingfish is similar in its habits to the northern kingfish.

Economic Importance: An excellent food fish. It is the most common species in the commercial catches of the south Atlantic states and is frequently caught by anglers fishing in waters from Chesapeake Bay south.

Gulf Kingfish or King Whiting
Menticirrhus littoralis (Holbrook)

The Gulf Kingfish is common on the Gulf coast and along
the shores of the south Atlantic states north to North
Carolina. It occurs as a stray in Chesapeake Bay. This species is silvery gray above, paler beneath; it has no dark
markings on its sides. It is a good food and game fish.

Spot, Lafayette
Leiostomus xanthurus Lacépède

Color: Blue-gray above with a golden glitter; silvery below.
Sides with 12–15 yellow oblique bars, indistinct in very
large fish. Large yellow-black spot just behind upper edge
of gill slit.
Distribution: Occurs in coastal waters from Texas to Cape
Cod and as a rare stray to Massachusetts Bay.
Size: Maximum length about 13½ inches with a weight of
about 1½ pounds. Most fish are usually less than 10 inches
long and weigh one-quarter to three-quarters of a pound.
General Information: The Spot is common in the coastal
salt and brackish waters of protected bays, coves, and
estuaries. It is most numerous in the Chesapeake area. In
periods of abundance, large numbers of Spot appear off
the shores of northern New Jersey and New York. Spawn-

ing takes place in autumn and winter, probably at sea. This species feeds on small crustaceans and worms and to a lesser extent on small shellfish and fishes.

Economic Importance: The Spot is a major species in the commercial fisheries of Chesapeake Bay and the Carolinas. It is a good pan fish and is regularly fished for by the shore and small-boat angler.

Croaker, Hardhead
Micropogon undulatus (Linnaeus)

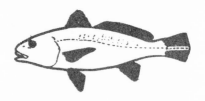

Color: Silvery green or gray above; silvery white below; back and sides have brownish oblique wavy bars less distinct in larger fish.

Distribution: Found from Texas to Cape Cod but not common north of New Jersey.

Size: The largest fish reported was 20 inches long and weighed slightly over 4 pounds. Most fish taken are less than one foot long and under a pound in weight.

General Information: The Croaker is found commonly on shallow sandy shores in summer; and offshore, in deeper waters, in winter. Spawning occurs from late summer through early winter. This species is a bottom feeder and eats small crustaceans, shellfish, and worms. Both sexes are able to produce croaking sounds, whence the name Croaker. There has been a drastic reduction in the abundance of Croakers in recent years.

Economic Importance: The Croaker is important in the commercial fisheries of the Chesapeake region. It is a good pan fish and supports a heavy recreational fishery, particularly in the waters of southern New Jersey and in Chesapeake Bay.

Black Drum, Sea Drum
Pogonias cromis Linnaeus

Color: Back and sides silvery with a brassy luster turning to a dark gray soon after death; belly grayish white. Small fish have 4–5 black vertical bars on sides.

Distribution: Found from Argentina to Cape Cod and as a stray to Massachusetts Bay.

Size: The largest specimen recorded weighed 146 pounds. A fish 4⅓ feet long weighed 87½ pounds.

General Information: The Black Drum is most common from New Jersey southward. It is a bottom feeder and eats mostly shellfish and crustaceans. It is reported to be very destructive on oyster beds, and as a result in New York State the conservation law stipulates that any specimen of this fish caught must not be returned to the water alive.

Economic Importance: A coarse-fleshed fish taken in small quantities by the commercial fisheries from New Jersey south. The Black Drum is a favorite species of the surf-caster.

Channel Bass, Red Drum
Sciaenops ocellatus (Linnaeus)

Color: Metallic greenish bronze above; white below. Scales on sides with dark centers forming stripes. Usually one jet black spot at base of tail fin; sometimes several black spots instead of one.

Distribution: Occurs on sandy shores from Texas to New Jersey and rarely to New York and Cape Cod.

Size: Reaches a length of about 5 feet and a weight of 75 pounds.

General Information: The Channel Bass spawns in autumn and early winter in the area south of Cape Hatteras. It feeds on crustaceans and shellfish. The name Red Drum has been given this species because some of the fish turn to a reddish color after death.

Economic Importance: This is an important food fish in the south Atlantic and Gulf regions. It is sought after by the surf-caster from New Jersey shores south.

Banded Croaker
Larimus fasciatus Holbrook

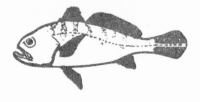

Color: Gray-green above; silvery beneath. A yellow tinge over body. Sides have 7–9 vertical black bars.

Distribution: Found from Texas to Chesapeake Bay and as a rare straggler north to Cape Cod.

Sizes: Reaches a length of 10 inches.

General Information: The Banded Croaker is most common south of Cape Hatteras, where it is often taken in the otter trawls of shrimp fishermen. It is a small fish usually less than 8 inches long and is generally discarded.

Economic Importance: None.

Silver or Sand Perch
Bairdiella chrysura (Lacépède)

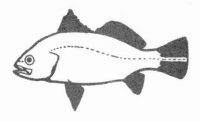

Color: Green or blue-gray above; lower sides and belly silvery.

Distribution: Occurs from New York to Texas.

Size: Reported to reach a length of one foot. Usually it is less than 9 inches.

General Information: The Sand Perch is common in summer in New York bays, particularly fish under 6 inches in length. Adults are more abundant from New Jersey south. This fish spawns in spring and early summer. The eggs are buoyant. The main foods of the Sand Perch are small crustaceans, worms, and fishes.

Economic Importance: Because of its small size only a few of the species are marketed.

Common Butterfly Fish
Chaetodon ocellatus Bloch

The Common Butterfly Fish is a West Indian species the young of which occasionally stray north as far as Cape

Cod. This fish reaches a length of about 8 inches, but specimens taken north of Cape Hatteras are usually less than 4 inches long.

Four-eyed Butterfly Fish
Chaetodon capistratus Linnaeus

The Four-eyed Butterfly Fish is a West Indian species the young of which are sometimes taken as far north as Cape Cod. This species reaches a length of 6 inches, but fish taken north of Cape Hatteras are usually younger fish of a smaller size.

Spadefish
Chaetodipterus faber (Broussonet)

Color: Variable; gray, green, or yellow; sides have 4–6 black vertical bands sometimes obscure in larger fish.
Distribution: Found from Brazil to Cape Cod but rare north of Chesapeake Bay. Common in the West Indies.

Size: Reaches a length of 3 feet.

General Information: The Spadefish lives on rocky bottoms and in wrecks. It spawns in summer. The principal food of this species is invertebrates.

Economic Importance: The Spadefish is a commercially important food fish in the tropics.

Tilefish
Lopholatilus chamaeleonticeps Goode and Bean

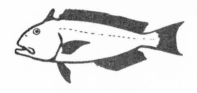

Color: Back and upper sides olive green or bluish; lower sides yellow or rose; belly white with a rosy tint.

Distribution: This fish is found along the edge of the Continental Shelf from Nova Scotia to the Gulf of Mexico.

Size: Reaches a weight of 50 pounds. A fish 3½ feet long weighed 35½ pounds.

General Information: The Tilefish is found in depths of 270–1,200 feet. It appears to be most abundant in the deep waters from off Nantucket to off Delaware Bay. Spawning occurs in summer. The eggs are buoyant: This species feeds on a wide variety of bottom-dwelling invertebrates of which crabs appear to be the most important item.

Economic Importance: A good food fish of limited importance in the commercial fisheries from Cape Hatteras to Cape Cod.

Little Sculpin
Myoxocephalus aeneus (Mitchill)

Color: Variable; usually a shade of gray or green-gray above; sides mottled light and dark; belly white or light gray.

Distribution: Newfoundland to New Jersey but most common south of Cape Cod.

Size: Reaches a length of about 8 inches.

General Information: The Little Sculpin is common from the tide mark down to depths of about 90 feet. It is the common sculpin in the shoal waters of the southern New England and the Middle Atlantic regions. Spawning occurs in winter and early spring. The sticky eggs sink to the bottom, where they adhere to various objects and to each other. The Little Sculpin feeds on all types of bottom animals as well as fish.

Economic Importance: Of no commercial value. This species is frequently caught by anglers while fishing for other species.

Shorthorn Sculpin
Myoxocephalus scorpius (Linnaeus)

Color: Upper surface of body variable shades of brown; broad black bars. Lower sides spotted with yellow. Belly yellow or white in females, orange spotted with white in males.

Distribution: Occurs on both sides of the North Atlantic. In the American Atlantic it is found from northern Labrador to southern New England and as a stray south to New Jersey. It is most common north of Cape Cod.

Size: This species is reported to grow to a length of 3 feet, but it usually is less than 2 feet long.

General Information: The Shorthorn Sculpin is a cold-water fish living on the bottom and most common in waters shoaler than 60 feet. It spawns in winter and the eggs, which are sticky, are deposited among the seaweed, in crevices between rocks and even in old tin cans and other debris. The eggs hatch in 4 to 12 weeks, depending on the temperature of the water. The principal foods of this fish are crabs and other crustaceans, but worms and small fishes are also eaten.

Economic Importance: An edible species of no commercial importance.

Longhorn Sculpin
Myoxocephalus octodecimspinosus (Mitchill)

Color: Variable, depending on surroundings. Ground tint of back and sides yellow-green to dark olive, green-brown or dark gray. Four irregular, dark crossbars; these crossbars often indistinct or broken up into blotches.

Distribution: Occurs in coastal waters from Newfoundland to New Jersey and in deep waters south to Virginia.

Size: Reaches a length of 1½ feet, but most fish taken are less than one foot.

General Information: The Longhorn Sculpin is common in cool waters from the shoals in harbors, bays, and estuaries down to depths of over 600 feet. Spawning occurs in late autumn and winter. The eggs are adhesive when laid, and they stick together in clumps and attach to any object that they may touch. Fish 10 inches long are 4 years old; 11–12 inches long, 6 years old. This species eats a wide variety of foods including shrimps, crabs, and other crustaceans, worms, shellfish, and small fishes. It grunts when removed from the water.

Economic Importance: None. The Longhorn Sculpin is frequently caught by anglers fishing for winter flounders.

Sea Raven
Hemitripterus americanus (Gmelin)

Color: Variable; red, reddish purple, yellow-brown to chocolate. Paler on lower sides than on back and upper sides. Belly yellow. Body colors may be solid or have mottled shades of the general ground color.

Distribution: Newfoundland south to Chesapeake Bay.

Size: Reaches a length of about 2 feet and a weight of about 7 pounds.

General Information: The Sea Raven is most common in depths of 15–300 feet. Spawning occurs in late autumn and winter and 15,000–40,000 eggs are laid by a single fish. The eggs are sticky and are deposited mostly on certain species of northern sponges, to which they adhere. The Sea Raven is a voracious feeder and eats a wide variety of invertebrates and fishes. It is capable of swallowing a fish almost as large as itself.

Economic Importance: None.

Lumpfish
Cyclopterus lumpus (Linnaeus)

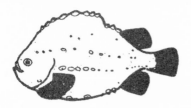

Color: Variable; gray-blue, slate blue, yellow-green, olive, shades of brown; belly a paler shade of same color or white. Some fish have dark blotches or black dots on the back and sides.

Distribution: Occurs on both sides of the North Atlantic. In the western Atlantic it is found from Davis Strait southward to New Jersey and as a stray to Chesapeake Bay.

Size: Reaches a length of about 2 feet. The heaviest fish reported weighed 20 pounds.

General Information: The Lumpfish is mostly a bottom species but is often found floating among masses of seaweed. It is common in cool, shoal waters over rocky bottoms. This fish will frequently attach itself to the sides of lobster cars, poles of fish traps, or stones by the ventral sucker-like disc. Spawning occurs in late winter and spring. The eggs are sticky and sink to the bottom where they adhere to each other in a large spongy mass. The male Lumpfish guards the eggs until they hatch. The Lumpfish feeds on small crustaceans, small fishes, and jellyfishes.

Economic Importance: None.

Sea Snail
Neoliparis atlanticus Jordan and Evermann

Color: Ground color green to reddish brown; lighter or darker dots of same color scattered over body.

Distribution: Occurs from Newfoundland to southern New England and as a straggler as far south as New Jersey. Rare south of Cape Cod.

Size: Reaches a length of about 5 inches.

General Information: North of Cape Cod the Sea Snail has been taken in depths of a few feet down to 300 feet. It is frequently found under stones or attached to seaweed or lobster pots by the sucking disc on the undersurface of the body. Very little is known about the life history of this fish. It is believed to spawn in winter.

Economic Importance: None.

Striped Sea Snail
Liparis liparis (Linnaeus)

Color: Variable; ground color gray, brown, red, or dark green. Longitudinal stripes of lighter or darker shades of the ground color may or may not be present.

Distribution: Occurs in the boreal and temperate waters of the North Atlantic. In the American North Atlantic it has been found from Greenland to Virginia but is rare south of Cape Cod.

Size: Reported to reach a length of 10 inches in Arctic waters but seldom over 5 inches in temperate waters.

General Information: The Striped Sea Snail lives on rocky bottoms, usually among masses of attached seaweed (kelp) to which it is frequently found clinging by the ventral sucking disc. Spawning occurs in winter and spring. The eggs sink and form sticky bunches which adhere to seaweed and other objects. The main food of this fish appears to be small crustaceans, but small shellfish, fish fry, and algae are also eaten.

Economic Importance: None.

Flying Gurnard
Cephalacanthus volitans (Linnaeus)

The Flying Gurnard occurs in the warm waters of both sides of the Atlantic. It reaches a length of about one foot. Rare north of North Carolina. Strays as far north as Cape Cod.

Common Sea Robin
Prionotus carolinus (Linnaeus)

Color: Red-brown or gray above; 5 dark, saddle-like blotches along back; pale yellow or white below. A black spot between the fourth and fifth spines of the first dorsal fin.

Distribution: Occurs in the coastal waters from the Bay of Fundy to South Carolina, but it is most common south of Cape Cod.

Size: Reaches a length of about 16 inches but is usually less than one foot.

General Information: The Common Sea Robin is a bottom species found from tide mark down to depths of 250 feet or more. It is common inshore in summer but in winter moves offshore into deep water. Spawning occurs in spring and summer. The eggs are buoyant and hatch in 60 hours at a water temperature of 72 degrees. The Common Sea Robin is a voracious feeder and eats a wide variety of crustaceans as well as worms, shellfish, and small fish.

Economic Importance: An edible species marketed in limited quantities. It strikes readily at artificial lures or natural baits and is frequently caught by anglers fishing for other species.

Striped Sea Robin
Prionotus evolans (Linnaeus)

Color: Pale green or light brown above; white below. Four to five dark saddle-like blotches on back. A prominent dark brown stripe along lower part of side. Lateral line a blackish brown streak. A black blotch extends from the fourth to sixth spines on the first dorsal fin.

Distribution: Found in coastal waters from South Carolina to Cape Cod and as a stray into the Gulf of Maine.

Size: Reaches a length of about 1½ feet.

General Information: The Striped Sea Robin is similar in its habits to the common sea robin.

Economic Importance: An edible species marketed in limited quantities. Like the common sea robin it is often caught by anglers fishing for other species.

Tautog, Blackfish
Tautoga onitis (Linnaeus)

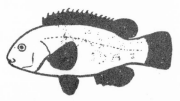

Color: Brown, black, or greenish black above and on sides; belly paler. Irregular blackish blotches or bars on the sides of smaller fish, frequently disappearing in larger fish.

Distribution: Nova Scotia to South Carolina, but most common south of Cape Cod to Delaware.

Size: Grows to a length of about 3 feet and a weight of 22 pounds, but fish over 11 pounds are not common.

General Information: This species is common on rocky shores and musselbeds, near wrecks, and around piers in company with the cunner. Spawning occurs in spring and early summer. The eggs are buoyant. The Tautog feeds on a wide variety of invertebrates, especially mussels, barnacles, and crabs.

Economic Importance: A good food fish marketed in moderate quantities. The Tautog is a favorite of the shore and small-boat angler and one of the species regularly taken by the recreational "deep-sea" fisheries of New York and New Jersey.

Cunner, Bergall
Tautogolabrus adspersus (Walbaum)

Color: Varies with the environment; brown, black-brown, olive green, blue, or reddish, or a mixture of these colors.

Distribution: Newfoundland to New Jersey and as a straggler south to Chesapeake Bay.

Size: Reaches a length of about 15 inches and a weight of 2½ pounds.

General Information: The Cunner is an abundant coastal species commonly found around rocks, wrecks, and the pilings of wharves and bridges. In New England and parts of New York it is found close to shore in bays, sounds, and inlets. South of New York it frequents wrecks and the rocky ledges offshore. Spawning occurs in spring and early summer. The eggs are buoyant. The Cunner eats a wide variety of foods including invertebrates, small fish, and eel grass, and it is an avid scavenger.

Economic Importance: The Cunner was formerly of some importance as a commercial species in northern New England, but now few are landed. It is a good pan fish esteemed by New England anglers but regarded as a nuisance by sport fishermen in the New York-New Jersey area because of its ability to steal the bait offered for other species of fishes.

<h3 style="text-align:center">Naked Goby
Gobiosoma bosci (Lacépède)</h3>

Color: Greenish to dusky above; pale below. Sides have narrow pale crossbars.

Distribution: Occurs from Massachusetts to Florida.

Size: Reaches a length of about 2½ inches.

General Information: The Naked Goby is locally abundant in protected waters close to shore. It is found commonly in brackish water and has been caught in fresh water. Spawning takes place in spring and summer. The eggs are sticky when first laid and are heavier than water. This fish feeds mostly on small invertebrates.

Economic Importance: A good fish in the brackish-water home aquarium.

Ginsburg's Goby
Gobiosoma ginsburgi Hildebrand and Schroeder

Color: Greenish to dusky above; pale below. Sides have narrow pale crossbars. Lateral line usually has longitudinally elongated dark spots.
Distribution: Occurs from New York to Virginia.
Size: Reaches a length of about 2 inches.
General Information: Ginsburg's Goby is found not only in shoal water, together with the naked goby, but also in deeper water down to depths of 150 feet or more. It spawns in spring. The principal food of this species appears to be small crustaceans.
Economic Importance: None.

Sea-green Goby
Microgobius thalassinus Jordan and Gilbert

Color: Pale green or blue; bluish vertical bars on sides above abdomen in the male.
Distribution: Chesapeake Bay to North Carolina.
Size: Reaches a length of about 2 inches.
General Information: This is a relatively rare species. It probably spawns in spring and summer. It feeds mostly on small crustaceans.
Economic Importance: None.

Shark Remora
Echeneis naucrates Linnaeus

Color: Body color slate gray or brown-gray. Sides marked by a broad dark brown or grayish stripe with white edge.
Distribution: Cosmopolitan in warm seas. In the western Atlantic it is taken occasionally as far north as Cape Cod and, rarely, north of Cape Cod.
Size: Reaches a length of over 3 feet.
General Information: This species clings to ships or to sharks by the sucker-like disc on its head. It feeds on fragments of fish killed by the shark to which it is attached.
Economic Importance: None.

Swordfish Remora
Remora brachyptera (Lowe)

Color: Light reddish brown above, darker below.
Distribution: Cosmopolitan in warm seas. In the western Atlantic it is found as far north as Maine.
Size: Reaches a length of about one foot.
General Information: This species is frequently found attached to the shoulder of the swordfish, but it also has been taken from the gill cavity of the ocean sunfish and the mouths and gill cavities of larger sharks.
Economic Importance: None.

Offshore Remora
Remora remora (Linnaeus)

Color: A uniform dark gray, black, or brown color over entire body.

Distribution: Cosmopolitan in tropical seas. In the western Atlantic it is common in the West Indies, but it is sometimes found north to Cape Cod and as a rare stray north of Cape Cod.

Size: Reaches a length of about 1½ feet.

General Information: This species appears to be more offshore in habit than the shark remora and is frequently found attached to sea turtles and larger sharks.

Economic Importance: None.

Spearfish Remora
Rhombochirus osteochir (Cuvier)

Color: Light brown.

Distribution: West Indies north to Cape Cod.

Size: Reaches a length of about 8½ inches.

General Information: This is a West Indian species most commonly found attached to sailfishes and marlins.

Economic Importance: None.

American Sand Launce
Ammodytes americanus De Kay

Color: Olive, blue, or brownish green above; sides silvery; belly dull white.

Range: Hudson Bay to Cape Hatteras.

Size: May reach a length of 7 inches.

General Information: This fish is abundant in the surf off sandy beaches or near inlets. It is commonly seen offshore in large schools swimming near the surface and being preyed on by larger fishes beneath and sea birds above. When frightened it darts into the bottom sand and frequently, while so buried, is left stranded on bars and flats which are exposed as the tide falls. The American Sand Launce feeds mostly on small crustaceans, as well as a wide variety of other small aquatic animals.

Economic Importance: This is an abundant species of great importance as a food for larger fishes. Small quantities are sold for food and some are used for bait by both the commercial and recreational fisheries. A large commercial fishery has developed in Europe for a related species of sand launce, primarily for processing into fish meal and oil.

Ocean Sand Launce
Ammodytes oceanicus

This species, discovered by the author and as yet undescribed, has been found from New York to Cape Cod. In the past it has been confused with the American sand launce. Little is known about this fish.

Northern Stargazer
Astroscopus guttatus (Abbott)

Color: Dusky; many irregular white spots on upper sides; hazy dark blotches on lower sides. Dirty white below. Upper part of caudal peduncle has 5 irregular white blotches; a dark longitudinal band on the side of the caudal peduncle.

Distribution: New York to Virginia.

Size: Reaches a length of about one foot.

General Information: This fish is not abundant anywhere. It frequently buries itself in the bottom with only its eyes and lips showing. The Northern Stargazer is capable of producing a shock by means of electric organs situated just back of the eyes. Whether these electric organs are used to capture food or for defense, or both, is not known. Crustaceans and fish have been found in the stomachs of this species.

Economic Importance: None.

Striped Blenny
Chasmodes bosquianus (Lacépède)

Color: Male: olive green with about 9 horizontal, narrow, irregular blue lines converging backward. A broad deep orange-yellow stripe through first dorsal fin. Female: dark olive green with a network of narrow pale green lines and several broad dark bars most distinct posteriorly. A dusky spot at the base of the caudal fin in both sexes.

Distribution: Found from Florida to New York but rare north of Maryland.

Size: Reaches a length of about 4 inches.

General Information: The Striped Blenny is most common close to shore in shoal water but has been taken down to depths of 90 feet. It spawns in spring and summer. The eggs are sticky when first laid and are frequently found attached to shells. This fish feeds on small crustaceans, small shellfish, and insect larvae.

Economic Importance: None.

Carolina Blenny
Hypsoblennius hentz (LeSueur)

Color: Olive, covered with scattered, irregularly shaped brown spots; spots on posterior part of body tend to form vertical bars. Some individuals have fewer spots and more vertical bars on sides of body and extending onto the dorsal fin.

Distribution: Found from Chesapeake Bay to Florida.

Size: Maximum length about 4 inches.

General Information: The Carolina Blenny is found in depth from tide mark down to 150 feet. It spawns in summer. The principal foods of this fish appear to be small crustaceans, shellfish, and probably seaweeds.

Economic Importance: None.

Rock Eel
Pholis gunnellus (Linnaeus)

Color: Variable; upper part of body yellow, olive brown or red. Belly pale gray to yellow-white. An oblique streak from the eye to the angle of the jaw. A row of 10–14 round black spots along the middle of the back and spreading onto the dorsal fin.

Distribution: Occurs on both sides of the North Atlantic. In the western Atlantic it is found from Hudson Strait to the deep waters off Delaware Bay but is most common from southern Massachusetts north.

Size: Maximum length is about one foot, but specimens over 8 inches are not common.

General Information: The Rock Eel has been caught in depths from the low-tide mark down to 600 feet. It is locally common on stony bottoms, living in the crevices between the rocks. Spawning takes place in winter. The eggs are sticky when laid. This fish feeds on small crustaceans and worms.

Economic Importance: None.

Ulva Fish, Radiated Shanny
Ulvaria subbifurcata (Storer)

Color: Back and upper sides dull brown with obscure bars or blotches. An oblique dark bar runs downward and backward from the eye. Belly pale brown or yellow-white. A large black blotch on the front portion of the dorsal fin.

Distribution: Newfoundland to Cape Cod and as a rare straggler further south.

Size: Maximum length about 6½ inches.

General Information: The Ulva Fish is a bottom species living from low-tide mark down to depths of at least 180 feet.

Economic Importance: None.

Wrymouth
Cryptacanthodes maculatus Storer

Color: Various shades of brown. Upper sides marked with 2–3 irregular rows of dark brown spots running from head to tail.

Distribution: Found from Labrador to New Jersey.
Size: Maximum length about 3 feet.
General Information: The Wrymouth is a bottom species found from the intertidal zone down to a depth of at least 600 feet. It lives in burrows in the mud. Spawning probably occurs in winter and spring. This fish feeds on crustaceans and fish.
Economic Importance: None.

Common Wolf Fish
Anarhichas lupus Linnaeus

Color: Variable; usually purple-brown but may be olive green or bluish gray. Sides have 10 or more irregular, broken dark bands or blotches. Throat and belly a dirty white with a tinge of the color of the upper parts.
Distribution: Occurs on both sides of the North Atlantic. In the western Atlantic it is found from Davis Strait to Cape Cod and less commonly south of Cape Cod to New Jersey.
Size: Maximum length about 5 feet. Usually fish that are caught are less than 4 feet. A specimen slightly over 3 feet long weighed 16–17 pounds.
General Information: The Common Wolf Fish is a bottom species found from shoal waters close to shore down to depths of over 500 feet. It is a cool-water fish, solitary in habit and not found in schools. Spawning takes place in winter. The eggs are sticky when laid and attach in loose clumps to seaweeds, stones, and other objects. The Common Wolf Fish feeds on shellfish, crustaceans, sea urchins, and starfish, which it crushes in its heavy molar-like teeth.

Economic Importance: A good food fish common in the commercial catch of the fisheries north of Cape Cod.

American Ocean Pout, Eelpout
Macrozoarces americanus (Bloch and Schneider)

Color: Ground color variable; upper surface and sides of body muddy yellow, reddish brown, olive green, pale gray. Belly same color as rest of body or white, yellow, or pink. Sides dotted with dark spots clustered in irregular crossbars going out onto dorsal fin. A dark brown stripe goes from the eye to the edge of the gill cover.

Distribution: Newfoundland south to Delaware.

Size: Reaches a length of 3½ feet and a weight of 12 pounds.

General Information: The American Ocean Pout is a bottom species. It is common in depths of 50–250 feet and has been caught down to depths of over 600 feet. Spawning takes place in autumn. A fish almost 3 feet long contained over 4,000 eggs. The eggs are laid in masses and are held together on the bottom by a gelatinous material. In southern New England, fish one foot long are 3 years old; 2 feet long, 6–7 years old; 3 or more feet long, 12–16 years old. This species feeds on a wide variety of invertebrates, including shellfish, crustaceans, sea urchins, and brittle stars.

Economic Importance: The American Ocean Pout was marketed in quantities for the first time during World War II. Discovery of a parasite in the flesh which resulted in the condemnation of large amounts of fish discouraged the fishery, and commercial landings are now negligible.

Reticulated or Arctic Eelpout
Lycodes reticulatus Reinhardt

Color: Brown with a network of black lines on the head and body.
Distribution: Occurs on both sides of the Arctic Atlantic. In the western Atlantic it has been reported as far south as southern Massachusetts, but it is rare south of Cape Cod.
Size: Reaches a length of 1¼ feet.
General Information: This is a bottom species. Little is known about its life history.
Economic Importance: None.

Margined Cusk Eel
Rissola marginata (De Kay)

Color: Grayish green; sides golden; belly white. Dorsal and anal fins margined with black.
Distribution: New York to Texas.
Size: Maximum length about 9 inches.
General Information: Occurs on sandy shores. It has not been found abundantly anywhere. This fish probably stays burrowed in the bottom during the day and comes out at night to feed.
Economic Importance: None.

Toadfish
Opsanus tau (Linnaeus)

Color: Ground color of body variable; olive green, yellow, or brown. Back and sides darker than belly. Body irregularly marked with dark brown bars and patches.
Distribution: Found from Cuba to Cape Cod and as a stray north to Maine.
Size: Maximum length about 1¼ feet.
General Information: The Toadfish is a shoal water species common on sandy or muddy bottoms. It spawns in late spring and summer. The adhesive eggs are laid under stones, logs, shells, in tin cans, or in other objects. The male guards the eggs for about 3 weeks until they hatch. This fish commonly hides under stones, darting out suddenly to seize passing prey. It is a voracious feeder and will eat almost anything, including crustaceans, worms, and fishes. The Toadfish is able to make grunting noises and does so when handled.
Economic Importance: None. The Toadfish is often caught by anglers. It is a pugnacious species when caught and will erect the sharp spines on its dorsal fin and operculum and snap at anything near its mouth. Both the spines and powerful jaws and teeth can inflict a painful wound.

Clingfish
Cotylis nigripinnis Peters

Color: Mostly olive with a little red; sometimes banded with darker or paler shades of the same colors.
Distribution: Chesapeake Bay to at least as far south as Florida.
Size: Maximum length about 4 inches.
General Information: This species attaches itself to shells, rocks, and other objects by means of the large sucking disc located between the pelvic fins. It has been taken in waters of 1–110 feet deep. Spawning occurs in spring.

The Clingfish feeds on small crustaceans and worms.

Common Triggerfish
Balistes carolinensis Gmelin

The Common Triggerfish is common in tropical and sub-tropical waters but may occasionally be found as a straggler north to Nova Scotia. It reaches about a foot in length.

Common Filefish
Monacanthus hispidus (Linnaeus)

The Common Filefish is most abundant in the West Indies and along the South Atlantic coast of the United States. Small fish are not uncommon north to Cape Cod but are rare in the Gulf of Maine and off Nova Scotia. Although this fish may reach a length of 10 inches, fish in the north are usually less than 6 inches.

Orange Filefish
Alutera schoepfii (Walbaum)

Color: Variable; brown, yellow-orange, white, or gray, mottled with darker hues of the same color. Yellow and orange spots on sides. Small fish are black or gray with dusky or brownish spots on the sides.
Distribution: Found from Brazil to Cape Cod and as a rare straggler north to Maine.
Size: Reaches a length of 2 feet.
General Information: The Orange Filefish is not uncommon in the region from Chesapeake Bay to Cape Cod. It eats small invertebrates and seaweeds, frequently standing on its head while feeding.
Economic Importance: None.

Fringed Filefish
Monacanthus ciliatus (Mitchill)

The Fringed Filefish is common in Florida waters but rare in the north. It has been reported as a straggler as far north as Newfoundland. This fish reaches a length of about 8 inches.

Unicorn Filefish
Alutera scripta (Gmelin)

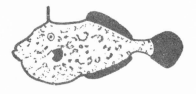

The Unicorn Filefish is found in tropical seas. It is a rare straggler from Chesapeake Bay north. It reaches a length of 3 feet, but specimens taken north of Chesapeake Bay are usually less than 6 inches long.

Common Trunkfish
Lactophrys trigonus (Linnaeus)

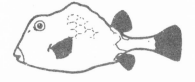

The Common Trunkfish is a West Indian species common as far north as southern Florida. This fish reaches a length of 9 inches. Small fish, less than one inch long, are not uncommon in the region from Cape Hatteras to Cape Cod.

Smooth Trunkfish
Lactophrys triqueter (Linnaeus)

The Smooth Trunkfish is a West Indian species reaching north to Florida. Small individuals may occur as rare stragglers north to Cape Cod. Maximum size in the south is about 10 inches.

Cowfish
Lactophrys tricornis (Linnaeus)

The Cowfish inhabits the tropical parts of the Atlantic. It is common to North Carolina, and the young are found as rare stragglers in the region from Cape Hatteras to Cape Cod. This fish grows to about one foot in length.

Smooth Swellfish, Rabbit Fish
Lagocephalus laevigatus (Linnaeus)

Color: Dark green above; sides bright silver; belly white.
Distribution: Brazil to Cape Cod but seen only occasionally north of Cape Hatteras.
Size: Reaches a length of about 2 feet.
General Information: The Smooth Swellfish is the largest species of this group of fishes.
Economic Importance: This fish is sometimes caught by anglers fishing for other species of fish.

Northern Swellfish or Puffer
Sphaeroides maculatus (Bloch and Schneider)

Color: Dusky, brown, or olive green above; sides greenish yellow or orange; belly white; 6–8 indefinite vertical dark bands on sides.

Distribution: Occurs from Florida to Cape Cod and as a stray into the Gulf of Mexico.

Size: Maximum size about 14 inches.

General Information: The Northern Swellfish is an abundant inshore species common in shoal waters on sandy shores. It spawns in spring and summer. The principal foods of this fish are small crustaceans and shellfish. The Northern Swellfish regularly inflates when frightened by gulping water or, when taken from the water, by gulping air. It frequently burrows in the sand, at which time only the eyes and a small part of the upper surface of the head are visible.

Economic Importance: This species was formerly of no commercial value and considered a nuisance by anglers. In recent years it has become a valued food fish. The sandpaper-like skin is removed by the fisherman and the chunk of white body meat remaining is marketed under the name "sea squab." A small recreational fishery has also developed for this swellfish.

Southern Swellfish or Puffer
Sphaeroides spengleri (Bloch)

The Southern Swellfish is a tropical Atlantic species common north to Florida. It is a rare straggler from Cape Hatteras north to Cape Cod. The maximum size is about one foot.

Spiny Boxfish
Chilomycterus schoepfi (Walbaum)

Color: Ground, yellow-green to olive above; belly white heavily tinted with yellow or orange. Upper part of body has dark brown or black irregular longitudinal stripes somewhat parallel to one another. A dark irregular patch on each side of the base of the dorsal fin; a smaller one between the bases of the dorsal and anal fins; a dark patch at the base of the pectoral fin and another behind the pectoral fin.

Distribution: Occurs from Florida to Cape Cod and as a rare stray in the Gulf of Maine. It is most abundant south of Cape Hatteras.

Size: Maximum length about 10 inches.

General Information: Both young and adults are not uncommon inshore from Cape Hatteras to New York. The main foods of the Spiny Boxfish are small crustaceans and shellfish.

Economic Importance: None. This is an interesting and colorful species in the home marine aquarium.

Porcupine Fish
Diodon hystrix Linnaeus

The Porcupine Fish is found in all tropical seas. In the western Atlantic it is common north to Florida and occurs as a rare straggler from Cape Hatteras north. Its maximum length is about 3 feet.

Ocean Sunfish
Mola mola (Linnaeus)

Color: Dark gray above; sides paler with silvery reflections; belly dusky white.

Distribution: Cosmopolitan in the open seas in temperate and tropical waters.

Size: Grows to a weight of over one ton. A fish slightly over 8 feet long weighed 1,800 pounds.

General Information: The Ocean Sunfish is an oceanic species often found drifting at the surface of the water. It is reported to groan when hauled from the water. Fish taken along our coast have been found to be feeding on jellyfish.

Economic Importance: None.

Sharp-tailed Ocean Sunfish
Masturus lanceolatus (Liénard)

Like the ocean sunfish, the Sharp-tailed Sunfish is cosmopolitan in the open seas in temperate and tropical waters. Along the American Atlantic coast no adults of this fish have been reported north of North Carolina (possibly because of confusion between the two species of sunfish).

American Goosefish, Monkfish, Angler
Lophius americanus Cuvier and Valenciennes

Color: Chocolate brown above, mottled with paler and darker browns. Belly dirty white.
Distribution: Found from Newfoundland south to at least North Carolina.

Size: Reaches a length of 4 feet and a weight of over 50 pounds. A fish slightly over 3 feet long weighed 32 pounds.
General Information: The American Goosefish is found from the tide mark down to depths of more than 2,000 feet. It is a bottom species. Spawning takes place in spring and early summer. The eggs are laid in a ribbon of mucous to form a broad, jelly-like sheet containing a single layer of eggs. These sheets or veils of eggs may be from 25 to 35 feet long and 2 to 3 feet wide and float near the surface of the water. Veils of eggs have been estimated to contain over 1,250,000 eggs. The American Goosefish is a voracious feeder. The flap of skin at the end of the first dorsal spine is used as a bait to attract small fish. The Goosefish remains quietly resting on the bottom waving the flap until a small fish comes close, at which time it darts rapidly forward with open mouth and engulfs the prey. Larger fish, sea birds, and a wide variety of invertebrates are also eaten.
Economic Importance: A good food fish only relatively recently marketed in limited quantities. This species is sometimes caught by the angler fishing for other fishes.

Sargassum Fish
Histrio pictus (Cuvier and Valenciennes)

The Sargassum Fish is a tropical and subtropical species drifting north with the Gulf Stream and occasionally found in the region from Cape Hatteras to Cape Cod, usually in the drifting seaweed offshore. This species reaches a length of about 6 inches.

INDEX

INDEX TO COMMON NAMES

c = classification page

A

agujon, 276c, 309
albacore, 278c, 348
    false (little tuna), 278c, 345
alewife, 275c, 290
amber jack, 279c, 362
American conger eel, 276c, 301
American eel, 276c, 300
    goosefish, 283c, 413
    ocean pout, 283c, 403
    sand launce, 282c, 397
anchovy, common, 275c, 294
    silvery, 275c, 295
    striped, 275c, 295
angel shark, 231c, 252
angler (American goosefish), 283c, 413
Arctic (reticulated) eelpout, 283c, 404
Atlantic flying fish, 276c, 312
    halibut, 277c, 322
    sailfish, 279c, 352
    salmon, 275c, 296

B

balao, 276c, 311
banded croaker, 281c, 382
    rudder fish, 279c, 361
barn-door skate, 255c, 260
barracuda, great, 278c, 336
    northern, 278c, 335
basking shark, 230c, 235
bass, channel, 281c, 381
    common sea, 280c, 368
    striped, 280c, 366
bergall (cunner), 282c, 393
Bermuda chub, 280c, 375
big-eye, common, 280c, 370
    deep, 280c, 369
big skate, 255c, 261

billfish, 276c, 309
    flat, 276c, 310
blackback flounder, 277c, 324
black dogfish, 231c, 250
    drum, 281c, 381
black rudder fish, 279c, 355
black-tipped shark, small, 231c, 245
blackfin tuna, 278c, 347
blackfish (tautog), 282c, 393
blenny, Carolina, 282c, 400
    striped, 282c, 399
blueback, 275c, 289
bluefin tuna, 278c, 346
bluefish, 280c, 364
blue marlin, 279c, 350
    runner (hardtail), 279c, 358
    shark, 230c, 241
bonefish, 275c, 286
bonito, common, 278c, 344
    ocean, 278c, 345
bonnet shark, 231c, 247
boxfish, spiny, 283c, 411
brier (clear-nosed) skate, 255c, 258
broad killifish (sheepshead minnow), 276c, 305
brown shark, 231c, 246
bull shark, 231c, 244
bumper, 279c, 360
butterfish, 279c, 353
butterfly fish, common, 281c, 383
    four-eyed, 281c, 384
butterfly ray, giant, 255c, 266
    lesser, 255c, 267

C

Carolina blenny, 282c, 400
catfish, gaff-topsail, 276c, 299
    sea, 276c, 299

cat shark, deep-water, 230c, 238
  false, 230c, 239
  cavalla (king mackerel), 279c, 349
cero, 279c, 349
chain dogfish, 230c, 238
channel bass, 281c, 381
chub, Bermuda, 280c, 375
chub mackerel, 278c, 343
clear-nosed skate, 255c, 258
clingfish, 283c, 405
cobia, 280c, 365
cod, 277c, 315
common anchovy, 275c, 294
  big-eye, 280c, 370
  bonito, 278c, 344
  butterfly fish, 281c, 383
  filefish, 283c, 406
  hammerhead shark, 231c, 249
  jack, 279c, 357
  killifish, 276c, 302
  mackerel, 278c, 342
  pompano, 280c, 363
  sawfish, 255c, 256
  sea bass, 280c, 368
  sea robin, 282c, 391
  sturgeon, 275c, 284
  thresher shark, 230c, 235
  triggerfish 283c, 406
  trunkfish, 283c, 408
  wolf fish, 282c, 402
conger eel, American, 276c, 301
cowfish, 283c, 409
cow-nosed ray, 255c, 269
crevalle (common jack), 279c, 357
croaker, 281c, 380
  banded, 281c, 382
cub shark, 231c, 244
cunner, 282c, 393
cusk, 277c, 321
cusk eel, margined, 283c, 404
cutlass fish, 279c, 350

D

dab, 277c, 323
deep big-eye. 280c, 369
deep-water cat shark, 230c, 238
devil ray, giant, 256c, 270
  lesser, 256c, 270
dogfish, black, 231c, 250
  chain, 230c, 238
  smooth, 230c, 239
  spiny, 231c, 249
dolphin, 279c, 353
drum, black, 281c, 381
  red (channel bass), 281c, 381
  sea (black), 281c, 381
dusky shark, 231c, 247

E

eagle ray, 255c, 267
  spotted, 255c, 268
eel, American (common), 276c, 300
  American conger, 276c, 301
  margined cusk, 283c, 404
  rock, 282c, 400
eelpout (American ocean pout), 283c, 403
  Arctic (reticulated), 283c, 404
  reticulated, 283c, 404
electric ray, 255c, 257
eyed flounder, 277c, 330

F

false albacore (little tuna), 278c, 345
  cat shark, 230c, 239
filefish, common, 283c, 406
  fringed, 283c, 407
  orange, 283c, 407
  unicorn, 283c, 408
flat billfish, 310
Florida pipefish, 340
flounder, blackback, 277c, 324
  eyed, 277c, 330

flounder (*cont.*):
small-mouth, 277c, 329
smooth, 277c, 325
summer (northern fluke), 277c, 328
windowpane (sundial), 277c, 327
winter (blackback), 277c, 324
witch (gray sole), 277c, 326
yellowtail, 277c, 325
fluke, four-spotted, 277c, 329
northern, 277c, 328
flying fish, Atlantic, 276c, 312
short-winged, 276c, 313
spot-fin, 276c, 313
flying gurnard, 281c, 391
halfbeak, 276c, 311
four-bearded rockling, 277c, 321
four-eyed butterfly fish, 281c, 384
four-spined stickleback, 278c, 336
four-spotted fluke, 277c, 329
fresh-water killifish, 276c, 307
frigate mackerel, 278c, 344
fringed filefish, 283c, 407

G

gaff-topsail catfish, 276c, 299
gambusia (top minnow), 276c, 308
garfish (billfish), 276c, 309
giant butterfly ray, 255c, 266
devil ray, 256c, 270
Ginsburg's goby, 282c, 395
gizzard shad, 275c, 294
glut herring (blueback), 275c, 289
goatfish, northern, 278c, 342
goby, Ginsburg's, 282c, 395
naked, 282c, 394
sea-green, 282c, 395
goggle-eyed scad, 279c, 356
goosefish, American, 283c, 413

gray sea trout, 280c, 375
snapper, 280c, 371
sole, 277c, 326
great barracuda, 278c, 336
Greenland shark, 231c, 251
ground shark, 231c, 244
spot-fin, 231c, 245
grunt, white, 280c, 372
Gulf king whiting (kingfish), 281c, 379
kingfish, 281c, 379
gurnard, flying, 281c, 391

H

haddock, 277c, 316
hake, red, 277c, 320
silver (whiting), 277c, 314
spotted, 277c, 319
white, 277c, 319
halfbeak, 276c, 310
flying, 276c, 311
halibut, Atlantic, 277c, 322
hammerhead shark, common, 231c, 249
southern, 231c, 248
hardhead (croaker), 281c, 380
hardtail, 279c, 358
harvest fish, 279c, 354
herring glut (blueback), 275c, 289
round, 275c, 287
sea, 275c, 288
thread, 275c, 292
hickory shad, 275c, 289
hogchoker, 277c, 331
Holbrook's porgy, 280c, 373
horse-eye jack, 279c, 359

J

Jack, amber, 279c, 362
common, 279c, 357
horse-eye, 279c, 359
jurel (horse-eye jack), 279c, 359

K

killifish, broad (sheepshead minnow), 276c, 305
  common, 276c, 302
  fresh-water, 276c, 307
  Lucy's, 276c, 306
  ocellated, 276c, 307
  striped, 276c, 304
king mackerel, 279c, 349
king whiting (kingfish), Gulf, 281c, 379
  northern, 281c, 377
  southern, 281c, 378
kingfish, Gulf, 281c, 379
  northern, 281c, 377
  southern, 281c, 378

L

Lafayette (spot), 281c, 379
lamprey, sea, 227
launce, American sand, 282c, 397
  ocean sand, 282c, 398
leatherjacket, 279c, 363
lemon shark, 230c, 243
leopard skate, 255c, 260
lesser butterfly ray, 255c, 267
  devil ray, 256c, 270
ling (red hake), 277c, 320
little sculpin, 281c, 386
  skate, 255c, 259
  tuna, 278c, 345
lizard fish, 276c, 302
longhorn sculpin, 281c, 387
lookdown, 279c, 361
Lucy's killifish, 276c, 306
lumpfish, 281c, 389

M

mackerel, chub, 278c, 343
  common, 278c, 342
  frigate, 278c, 344
  king, 279c, 349
  Spanish, 279c, 348
mackerel scad, 279c, 357

mackerel shark, 230c, 232
  sharp-nosed (mako), 230c, 233
mako, 230c, 233
man-eater (white shark), 230c, 234
margined cusk eel, 283c, 404
marlin, blue, 279c, 350
  white, 279c, 351
menhaden, 275c, 293
minnow, sheepshead, 276c, 305
  top, 276c, 308
monkfish (American goosefish), 283c, 413
moonfish, 279c, 360
mullet, striped, 278c, 334
  white, 278c, 334

N

naked goby, 282c, 394
needlefish, 276c, 312
nine-spined stickleback, 278c, 338
northern barracuda, 278c, 335
  fluke, 277c, 328
  goatfish, 278c, 342
  kingfish, 281c, 377
  king whiting (kingfish), 281c, 377
  pipefish, 278c, 339
  porgy, 280c, 372
  puffer (swellfish), 283c, 410
  sea horse, 278c, 340
  silverside, 277c, 332
  stargazer, 282c, 398
  sting ray, 255c, 264
  swellfish, 283c, 410
nurse shark, 230c, 236

O

ocean bonito, 278c, 345
  pout, American, 283c, 403
  sand launce, 282c, 398
  sunfish, 283c, 412

ocean bonito (*cont.*):
  sunfish, sharp-tailed, 283c, 413
ocellated killifish, 276c, 307
offshore remora, 282c, 396
  whiting, 277c, 315
orange filefish, 283c, 407

P

pajarito, 276c, 311
Paragaleus, 230c, 241
perch, sand, 281c, 383
  silver (sand), 281c, 383
  white, 280c, 367
pigfish, 280c, 371
pilot fish, 279c, 362
pinfish, 280c, 374
pipefish, Florida, 278c, 340
  northern, 278c, 339
pollock, 277c, 317
pompano, common, 280c, 363
  round, 280c, 364
porbeagle (mackerel shark), 230c, 232
porcupine fish, 283c, 412
porgy, Holbrook's, 280c, 373
  northern, 280c, 372
  southern, 280c, 373
Portuguese shark, 231c, 251
pout, American ocean, 283c, 403
puffer (swellfish), northern, 283c, 410
  southern, 283c, 410

R

rabbit fish (smooth swellfish), 283c, 409
radiated shanny (ulva fish), 282c, 401
rainbow trout, 275c, 297
rain-water fish, 276c, 306
raven, sea, 281c, 388
ray, cow-nosed, 255c, 269
  eagle, 255c, 267
  electric, 255c, 257

ray (*cont.*):
  giant butterfly, 255c, 266
  giant devil, 256c, 270
  lesser butterfly, 255c, 267
  lesser devil, 256c, 270
  northern sting, 255c, 264
  Say's sting, 255c, 265
  southern sting, 255c, 263
  spotted eagle, 255c, 268
red drum (channel bass), 281c, 381
red hake, 277c, 320
remora, offshore, 282c, 396
  shark, 282c, 396
  spearfish, 282c, 397
  swordfish, 282c, 396
reticulated eelpout, 283c, 404
robin, common sea, 282c, 391
  striped sea, 282c, 392
rock eel, 282c, 400
rockfish (striped bass), 280c, 366
rockling, four-bearded, 277c, 321
rosetted skate, 255c, 260
rough scad, 279c, 357
  silverside, 278c, 333
round herring, 275c, 287
  pompano, 280c, 364
  scad, 279c, 356
rudder fish, banded, 279c, 361
  black, 279c, 355
runner, blue (hardtail), 279c, 358

S

sailfish, Atlantic, 279c, 352
salmon, Atlantic, 275c, 296
sand launce, American, 282c, 397
  ocean, 282c, 398
sand perch, 281c, 383
  shark, 230c, 231
sardine, Spanish, 275c, 287
sargassum fish, 284c, 414
sawfish, common, 255c, 256

Say's sting ray, 255c, 265
scad, goggle-eyed, 279c, 256
    mackerel, 279c, 357
    rough, 279c, 357
    round, 279c, 356
sculpin, little, 281c, 386
    longhorn, 281c, 387
    shorthorn, 281c, 386
sea bass, common, 280c, 368
sea catfish, 276c, 299
    drum (black drum), 281c,
        381
    -green goby, 282c, 395
    herring, 275c, 288
    horse, northern, 278c, 340
    lamprey, 227
    raven, 281c, 388
    robin, common, 282c, 391
        striped, 282c, 392
    snail, 281c, 389
        striped, 281c, 390
    trout, gray, 280c, 375
        silver (white), 281c, 377
        spotted, 281c, 376
        white, 281c, 377
shad, 275c, 291
    gizzard, 275c, 294
    hickory, 275c, 289
shanny, radiated (ulva fish),
    282c, 401
shark, angel, 231c, 252
    basking, 230c, 235
    blue, 230c, 241
    bonnet, 231c, 247
    brown, 231c, 246
    bull, 231c, 244
    common hammerhead,
        231c, 249
    common thresher, 230c,
        235
    cub, 231c, 244
    deep-water cat, 230c, 238
    dusky, 231c, 247
    false cat, 230c, 239
    Greenland, 231c, 251
    ground, 231c, 244
    lemon, 230c, 243

shark (*cont.*):
    mackerel, 230c, 232
    nurse, 230c, 236
    Portuguese, 231c, 251
    sand, 230c, 231
    sharp-nosed, 230c, 242
    sharp-nosed mackerel
        (mako), 230c, 233
    sickle-shape, 231c, 244
    small black-tipped, 231c,
        245
    smooth-tooth, 230c, 243
    southern hammerhead,
        231c, 248
    spot-fin ground, 231c, 245
    tiger, 230c, 240
    whale, 230c, 237
    white, 230c, 234
shark remora, 282c, 396
sharp-nosed mackerel shark
    (mako), 230c, 233
sharp-nosed shark, 230c, 242
sharp-tailed ocean sunfish,
    283c, 413
sheepshead, 280c, 374
    minnow, 276c, 305
shorthorn sculpin, 281c, 386
short-nosed sturgeon, 275c,
    285
short-winged flying fish, 276c,
    313
shovelhead, 231c, 247
sickle-shape shark, 231c, 244
silver hake (whiting), 277c,
    314
    perch (sand perch), 281c,
        383
    sea trout (white sea trout),
        281c, 377
silverside, northern, 277c, 332
    rough, 278c, 333
    tide-water, 278c, 332
silvery anchovy, 275c, 295
skate, barn-door, 255c, 260
    big, 255c, 261
    brier (clear-nosed), 255c,
        258

skate (*cont.*):
  clear-nosed, 255c, 258
  leopard, 255c, 260
  little, 255c, 259
  rosetted, 255c, 260
  smooth-tailed, 255c, 263
  thorny, 255c, 262
small black-tipped shark, 231c, 245
small-mouth flounder, 277c, 329
smelt, 276c, 297
smooth dogfish, 230c, 239
  flounder, 277c, 325
  swellfish, 283c, 409
  trunkfish, 283c, 408
  -tailed skate, 255c, 263
  -tooth shark, 230c, 243
snail, sea, 281c, 389
  striped sea, 281c, 390
snapper, gray, 280c, 371
sole, gray, 277c, 326
southern hammerhead shark, 231c, 248
southern kingfish, 281c, 378
  king whiting (kingfish), 281c, 378
  porgy, 280c, 373
  puffer (swellfish), 283c, 410
  sting ray, 255c, 263
  swellfish, 283c, 410
spadefish, 281c, 384
Spanish mackerel, 279c, 348
  sardine, 275c, 287
spearfish remora, 282c, 397
spiny boxfish, 283c, 411
  dogfish, 231c, 249
spot, 281c, 379
spot-fin flying fish, 276c, 313
  ground shark, 231c, 245
spotted eagle ray, 255c, 268
spotted hake, 277c, 319
  sea trout, 281c, 376
  weakfish (sea trout), 281c, 376

starfish (harvest fish), 279c, 354
stargazer, northern, 282c, 398
stickleback, four-spined, 278c, 336
  nine-spined, 278c, 338
  three-spined, 278c, 337
  two-spined, 278c, 338
sting ray, northern, 255c, 264
  Say's, 255c, 265
  southern, 255c, 263
stingaree, 255c, 265
striped anchovy, 275c, 295
  bass, 280c, 366
  blenny, 282c, 399
  killifish, 276c, 304
  mullet, 278c, 334
  sea robin, 282c, 392
  sea snail, 281c, 390
sturgeon, common, 275c, 284
  short-nosed, 275c, 285
summer flounder (northern fluke), 277c, 328
sundial, 277c, 327
sunfish, ocean, 283c, 412
  sharp-tailed ocean, 283c, 413
swellfish, northern, 283c, 410
  smooth, 283c, 409
  southern, 283c, 410
swordfish, 279c, 352
  remora, 282c, 396

T

tarpon, 275c, 286
tautog, 282c, 393
ten-pounder, 275c, 285
thorny skate, 255c, 262
threadfish, 279c, 359
thread herring, 275c, 292
thresher shark, common, 230c, 235
three-spined stickleback, 278c, 337

tide-water silverside, 278c, 332

tiger shark, 230c, 240

tilefish, 281c, 385

toadfish, 283c, 404

tomcod, 277c, 318

tonguefish, 277c, 330

top minnow, 276c, 308

torpedo, 255c, 257

triggerfish, common, 283c, 406

tripletail, 280c, 370

trout, gray sea, 280c, 375

rainbow, 275c, 297

silver (white) sea, 281c, 377

spotted sea, 281c, 376

white sea, 281c, 377

trumpet fish, 278c, 341

trunkfish, common, 283c, 408

smooth, 283c, 408

tuna, blackfin, 278c, 347

bluefin, 278c, 346

little, 278c, 345

yellowfin, 278c, 347

two-spined stickleback, 278c, 338

U

ulva fish, 282c, 401

unicorn filefish, 283c, 408

W

weakfish (sea trout), spotted, 281c, 376

whale shark, 230c, 237

white grunt, 280c, 372

hake, 277c, 319

marlin, 279c, 351

mullet, 278c, 334

perch, 280c, 367

sea trout, 281c, 377

shark, 230c, 234

whiting, 277c, 314

Gulf king (Gulf kingfish), 281c, 379

northern king (northern kingfish), 281c, 377

offshore, 277c, 315

southern king (southern kingfish), 281c, 378

windowpane flounder (sundial), 277c, 327

winter (blackback) flounder, 277c, 324

witch flounder (gray sole), 277c, 326

wolf fish, common, 282c, 402

wreckfish, 280c, 369

wrymouth, 282c, 401

Y

yellowtail flounder, 277c, 325

yellowfin tuna, 278c, 347

INDEX TO SCIENTIFIC NAMES

A

Ablennes hians, 276c, 310
acanthias, Squalus, 231c, 249
Acipenser brevirostrum, 275c, 285
  oxyrhynchus, 275c, 284
aculeatus, Gasterosteus, 278c, 337
  Stenotomus, 280c, 373
acus, Tylosurus, 276c, 309
adspersus, Tautogolabrus, 282c, 393
aeglifinus, Melanogrammus, 277c, 316
aeneus, Myoxocephalus, 281c, 386
aestivalis, Pomolobus, 275c, 289
Aetobatus narinari, 255c, 268
alalunga, Thunnus, 278c, 348
albacares, Thunnus, 278c, 347
albida, Makaira, 279c, 351
albidus, Merluccius, 277c, 315
Albula vulpes, 275c, 286
Alectis crinitus, 279c, 359
alepidotus, Peprilus, 279c, 354
alleteratus, Euthynnus, 278c, 345
Alopias vulpinus, 230c, 235
Alosa sapidissima, 275c, 291
altavela, Gymnura, 255c, 266
altus, Pseudopriacanthus, 280c, 369
Alutera schoepfii, 283c, 407
  scripta, 283c, 408
americana, Dasyatis, 255c, 263
  Morone, 280c, 367
americanus, Ammodytes, 282c, 397
  Hemitripterus, 281c, 388
  Istiophorus, 279c, 352
  Lophius, 283c, 413
  Macrozoarces, 283c, 403

americanus (*cont.*):
  Menticirrhus, 281c, 378
  Polyprion, 280c, 369
  Pseudopleuronectes, 277c, 324
Ammodytes americanus, 282c, 397
  oceanicus, 282c, 398
ampla, Makaira, 279c, 350
Anarhichas lupus, 282c, 402
Anchoa argyrophanus, 275c, 295
  hepsetus, 275c, 295
  mitchilli, 275c, 294
anchovia, Sardinella, 275c, 287
Anguilla rostrata, 276c, 300
Apeltes quadracus, 278c, 336
Aprionodon isodon, 230c, 243
Apristurus profundorum, 230c, 238
Archosargus probatocephalus, 280c, 374
arenatus, Priacanthus, 280c, 370
argyrophanus, Anchoa, 275c, 295
Astroscopus guttatus, 282c, 398
atlanticus, Neoliparis, 281c, 389
  Tarpon, 275c, 286
  Thunnus, 278c, 347
auratus, Mullus, 278c, 342
Auxis thazard, 278c, 344

B

Bagre marinus, 276c, 299
Bairdiella chrysura, 281c, 383
Balistes carolinensis, 283c, 406
barracuda, Sphyraena, 278c, 336

beryllina, Menidia, 278c, 332
bilinearis, Merluccius, 277c, 314
birostris, Manta, 256c, 270
bonasus, Rhinoptera, 255c, 269
borealis, Sphyraena, 278c, 335
bosci, Gobiosoma, 282c, 394
bosquianus, Chasmodes, 282c, 399
brachyptera, Remora, 282c, 396
brasiliensis, Hemirhamphus, 276c, 311
brevirostris, Negaprion, 230c, 243
brevirostrum, Acipenser, 275c, 285
Brevoortia tyrannus, 275c, 293
Brosme brosme, 277c, 321
brosme, Brosme, 277c, 321

C

callarias, Gadus, 277c, 315
canadus, Rachycentron, 280c, 365
canis, Mustelus, 230c, 239
capistratus, Chaetodon, 281c, 384
Caranx crysos, 279c, 358
  hippos, 279c, 357
  latus, 279c, 359
Carcharhinus falciformis, 231c, 244
  leucas, 231c, 244
  limbatus, 231c, 245
  milberti, 231c, 246
  obscurus, 231c, 247
Carcharias taurus, 230c, 231
carcharias, Carcharodon, 230c, 234
Carcharodon carcharias, 230c, 234
carolinensis, Balistes, 283c, 406

carolinus, Prionotus, 282c, 391
  Trachinotus, 280c, 363
cavalla, Scomberomorus, 279c, 349
Centropristes striatus, 280c, 368
Centroscyllium fabricii, 231c, 250
Centroscymnus coelolepis, 231c, 251
centroura, Dasyatis, 255c, 264
cepedianum, Dorosoma, 275c, 294
Cephalacanthus volitans, 281c, 391
cephalus, Mugil, 278c, 334
Cetorhinus maximus, 230c, 235
Chaetodipterus faber, 281c, 384
Chaetodon capistratus, 281c, 384
  ocellatus, 281c, 383
chamaeleonticeps, Lophola-tilus, 281c, 385
Chasmodes bosquianus, 282c, 399
Chilomycterus schoepfi, 283c, 411
Chloroscombrus chrysurus, 279c, 360
chrysops, Stenotomus, 280c, 372
chrysopterus, Orthopristis, 280c, 371
chrysura, Bairdiella, 281c, 383
chrysurus, Chloroscombrus, 279c, 360
chuss, Urophycis, 277c, 320
ciliatus, Monacanthus, 283c, 407
cimbrius, Enchelyopus, 277c, 321
cirratum, Ginglymostoma, 230c, 236

Clupea harengus, 275c, 288
coelolepis, Centroscymnus, 231c, 251
colias, Pneumatophorus, 278c, 343
Conger oceanica, 276c, 301
Coryphaena hippurus, 279c, 353
Cotylis nigripinnis, 283c, 405
crinitus, Alectis, 279c, 359
cromis, Pogonias, 281c, 381
crumenopthalmus, Trachurops, 279c, 356
Cryptacanthodes maculatus, 282c, 401
crysos, Caranx, 279c, 358
curema, Mugil, 278c, 334
cuvier, Galeocerdo, 230c, 240
Cyclopterus lumpus, 281c, 389
cynoglossus, Glyptocephalus, 277c, 326
Cynoscion nebulosus, 281c, 376
 nothus, 281c, 377
 regalis, 280c, 375
Cyprinodon variegatus, 276c, 305
Cypselurus furcatus, 276c, 313
 heterurus, 276c, 312

D

Dasyatis americana, 255c, 263
 centroura, 255c, 264
 sabina, 255c, 265
 say, 255c, 265
Decapterus macarellus, 279c, 357
 punctatus, 279c, 356
dentatus, Paralichthys, 277c, 328
diaphanus, Fundulus, 276c, 307
Diodon hystrix, 283c, 412
diplana, Sphyrna, 231c, 248

Diplodus holbrookii, 280c, 373
Dorosoma cepedianum, 275c, 294
ductor, Naucrates, 279c, 362
dumeril, Squatina, 231c, 252
dumerili, Seriola, 279c, 362

E

Echeneis naucrates, 282c, 396
eglanteria, Raja, 255c, 258
Elops saurus, 275c, 285
Enchelyopus cimbrius, 277c, 321
erinacea, Raja, 255c, 259
Etropus microstomus, 277c, 329
Etrumeus sadina, 275c, 287
Euleptorhamphus velox, 276c, 311
Euthynnus alleteratus, 278c, 345
evolans, Prionotus, 282c, 392

F

faber, Chaetodipterus, 281c, 384
fabricii, Centroscyllium, 231c, 250
falcatus, Trachinotus, 280c, 364
falciformis Carcharhinus, 231c, 244
fasciatus, Larimus, 281c, 382
felis, Galeichthys, 276c, 299
ferruginea, Limanda, 277c, 325
Fistularia tabacaria, 278c, 341
floridae, Syngnathus, 278c, 340
foetens, Synodus, 276c, 302
freminvillii, Myliobatis, 255c, 267

Fundulus diaphanus, 276c, 307
    heteroclitus, 276c, 302
    luciae, 276c, 306
    majalis, 276c, 304
    ocellaris, 276c, 307
    furcatus, Cypselurus, 276c, 313
fuscus, Syngnathus, 278c, 339

G

Gadus callarias, 277c, 315
gairdnerii, Salmo, 275c, 297
Galeichthys felis, 276c, 299
Galeocerdo cuvier, 230c, 240
Gambusia holbrooki, 276c, 308
garmani, Raja, 255c, 260
Gasterosteus aculeatus, 278c, 337
    wheatlandi, 278c, 338
Ginglymostoma cirratum, 230c, 236
ginsburgi, Gobiosoma, 282c, 395
gladius, Xiphias, 279c, 352
glauca, Prionace, 230c, 241
Glyptocephalus cynoglossus, 277c, 326
Gobiosoma bosci, 282c, 394
    ginsburgi, 282c, 395
griseus, Lutianus, 280c, 371
gunnellus, Pholis, 282c, 400
guttatus, Astroscopus, 282c, 398
Gymnura altavela, 255c, 266
    micrura, 255c, 267

H

Haemulon plumieri, 280c, 372
harengus, Clupea, 275c, 288
Hemirhamphus brasiliensis, 276c, 311
Hemitripterus americanus, 281c, 388

hentz, Hypsoblennius, 282c, 400
hepsetus, Anchoa, 275c, 295
heteroclitus, Fundulus, 276c, 302
heterurus, Cypselurus, 276c, 312
hians, Ablennes, 276c, 310
hildebrandi, Hyporhamphus, 276c, 311
Hippocampus hudsonius, 278c, 340
Hippoglossoides platessoides, 277c, 323
Hippoglossus hippoglossus, 277c, 322
hippoglossus, Hippoglossus, 277c, 322
hippos, Caranx, 279c, 357
hippurus, Coryphaena, 279c, 353
hispidus, Monacanthus, 283c, 406
Histrio pictus, 284c, 414
holbrooki, Gambusia, 276c, 308
holbrookii, Diplodus, 280c, 373
hudsonius, Hippocampus, 278c, 340
Hyporhamphus hildebrandi, 276c, 311
    unifasciatus, 276c, 310
hypostoma, Mobula, 256c, 270
Hypsoblennius hentz, 282c, 400
hystrix, Diodon, 283c, 412

I

isodon, Aprionodon, 230c, 243
Istiophorus americanus, 279c, 352
Isurus oxyrinchus, 230c, 233

K

Katsuwonus pelamis, 278c, 345
Kyphosus sectatrix, 280c, 375

L

Lactophrys tricornis, 283c, 409
 trigonus, 283c, 408
 triqueter, 283c, 408
laevigatus, Lagocephalus, 283c, 409
laevis, Raja, 255c, 260
Lagocephalus laevigatus, 283c, 409
Lagodon rhomboides, 280c, 374
Lamna nasus, 230c, 232
lanceolatus, Masturus, 283c, 413
Larimus fasciatus, 281c, 382
latus, Caranx, 279c, 359
Leiostomus xanthurus, 281c, 379
lepturus, Trichiurus, 279c, 350
leucas, Carcharhinus, 231c, 244
Limanda ferruginea, 277c, 325
limbatus, Carcharhinus, 231c, 245
Liopsetta putnami, 277c, 325
Liparis liparis, 281c, 390
liparis, Liparis, 281c, 390
littoralis, Menticirrhus, 281c, 379
Lobotes surinamensis, 280c, 370
Lophius americanus, 283c, 413
Lopholatilus chamaeleonticeps, 281c, 385
Lophopsetta maculata, 277c, 327
Lucania parva, 276c, 306

luciae, Fundulus 276c, 306
lumpus, Cyclopterus, 281c, 389
lupus, Anarhichas, 282c, 402
Lutianus griseus, 280c, 371
Lycodes reticulatus, 283c, 404

M

macarellus, Decapterus, 279c, 357
Macrozoarces americanus, 283c, 403
maculata, Lophopsetta, 277c, 327
maculatus, Cryptacanthodes, 282c, 401
 Scomberomorus, 279c, 348
 Sphaeroides, 283c, 410
 Trinectes, 277c, 331
majalis, Fundulus, 276c, 304
Makaira albida, 279c, 351
 ampla, 279c, 350
Manta birostris, 256c, 270
marginata, Rissola, 283c, 404
marinus, Bagre, 276c, 299
 Petromyzon, 227
 Tylosurus, 276c, 309
Masturus lanceolatus, 283c, 413
maximus, Cetorhinus, 230c, 235
mediocris, Pomolobus, 275c, 289
Melanogrammus aeglifinus, 277c, 316
Membras vagrans, 278c, 333
Menidia beryllina, 278c, 332
 menidia, 277c, 332
menidia, Menidia, 277c, 332
Menticirrhus americanus, 281c, 378
 littoralis, 281c, 379
 saxatilis, 281c, 377
Merluccius albidus, 277c, 315
 bilinearis, 277c, 314

mesogaster, Parexocoetus,
    276c, 313
microcephalus, Somniosus,
    231c, 251
microdon, Pseudotriakis, 230c,
    239
Microgadus tomcod, 277c, 318
Microgobius thalassinus, 282c,
    395
Micropogon undulatus, 281c,
    380
microstomus, Etropus, 277c,
    329
micrura, Gymnura, 255c, 267
milberti, Carcharhinus, 231c,
    246
mitchilli, Anchoa, 275c, 294
Mobula hypostoma, 256c, 270
Mola mola, 283c, 412
mola, Mola, 283c, 412
Monacanthus ciliatus, 283c,
    407
    hispidus, 283c, 406
mordax, Osmerus, 276c, 297
Morone americana, 280c, 367
Mugil cephalus, 278c, 334
    curema, 278c, 334
Mullus auratus, 278c, 342
Mustelus canis, 230c, 239
Myliobatis freminvillii, 255c,
    267
Myoxocephalus aeneus, 281c,
    386
    octodecimspinosus, 281c,
    387
    scorpius, 281c, 386

N

narinari, Aetobatus, 255c, 268
nasus, Lamna, 230c, 232
Naucrates ductor, 279c, 362
naucrates, Echeneis, 282c, 396
nebulosus, Cynoscion, 281c,
    376
Negaprion brevirostris, 230c,
    243

Neoliparis atlanticus, 281c,
    389
nigripinnis, Cotylis, 283c, 405
nobliana, Torpedo, 255c, 257
nothus, Cynoscion, 281c, 377

O

oblongus, Paralichthys, 277c,
    329
obscurus, Carcharhinus, 231c,
    247
oceanica, Conger, 276c, 301
oceanicus, Ammodytes, 282c,
    398
ocellaris, Fundulus, 276c, 307
ocellata, Raja, 255c, 261
ocellatus, Chaetodon, 281c,
    383
    Platophrys, 277c, 330
    Sciaenops, 281c, 381
octodecimspinosus, Myoxoce-
    phalus, 281c, 387
oglinum, Opisthonema, 275c,
    292
Oligoplites saurus, 279c, 363
onitis, Tautoga, 282c, 393
Opisthonema oglinum, 275c,
    292
Opsanus tau, 283c, 404
Orthopristis chrysopterus,
    280c, 371
Osmerus mordax, 276c, 297
osteochir, Rhombochirus,
    282c, 397
oxyrhynchus, Acipenser, 275c,
    284
oxyrinchus, Isurus, 230c, 233

P

Palinurichthys perciformis,
    279c, 355
Paragaleus pectoralis, 230c,
    241
Paralichthys dentatus, 277c,
    328
    oblongus, 277c, 329

Parexocoetus mesogaster, 276c, 313

parva, Lucania, 276c, 306

pectinatus, Pristis, 255c, 256

pectoralis, Paragaleus, 230c, 241

pelamis, Katsuwonus, 278c, 345

Peprilus alepidotus, 279c, 354

perciformis, Palinurichthys, 279c, 355

Petromyzon marinus, 227

Pholis gunnellus, 282c, 400

pictus, Histrio, 284c, 414

plagiusa, Symphurus, 277c, 330

platessoides, Hippoglossoides, 277c, 323

Platophrys ocellatus, 277c, 330

plumieri, Haemulon, 280c, 372

Pneumatophorus colias, 278c, 343

Pogonias cromis, 281c, 381

Pollachius virens, 277c, 317

Polyprion americanus, 280c, 369

Pomatomus saltatrix, 280c, 364

Pomolobus aestivalis, 275c, 289
    mediocris, 275c, 289
    pseudoharengus, 275c, 290

Poronotus triacanthus, 279c, 353

Priacanthus arenatus, 280c, 370

Prionace glauca, 230c, 241

Prionotus carolinus, 282c, 391
    evolans, 282c, 392

Pristis pectinatus, 255c, 256

probatocephalus, Archosargus, 280c, 374

profundorum, Apristurus, 230c, 238

pseudoharengus, Pomolobus, 275c, 290

Pseudopleuronectes americanus, 277c, 324

Pseudopriacanthus altus, 280c, 369

Pseudotriakis microdon, 230c, 239

punctatus, Decapterus, 279c, 356

Pungitius pungitius, 278c, 338

pungitius, Pungitius, 278c, 338

putnami, Liopsetta, 277c, 325

Q

quadracus, Apeltes, 278c, 336

R

Rachycentron canadus, 280c, 365

radiata, Raja, 255c, 262

Raja eglanteria, 255c, 258
    erinacea, 255c, 259
    garmani, 255c, 260
    laevis, 255c, 260
    ocellata, 255c, 261
    radiata, 255c, 262
    senta, 255c, 263

regalis, Cynoscion, 280c, 375
    Scomberomorus, 279c, 349

regius, Urophycis, 277c, 319

Remora brachyptera, 282c, 396
    remora, 282c, 396

remora, Remora, 282c, 396

reticulatus, Lycodes, 283c, 404

retifer, Scyliorhinus, 230c, 238

Rhincodon typus, 230c, 237

Rhinoptera bonasus, 255c, 269

Rhombochirus osteochir, 282c, 397

rhomboides, Lagodon, 280c, 374

Rissola marginata, 283c, 404

Roccus saxatilis, 280c, 366

rostrata, Anguilla, 276c, 300

S

sabina, Dasyatis, 255c, 265
sadina, Etrumeus, 275c, 287
salar, Salmo, 275c, 296
Salmo gairdnerii, 275c, 297
  salar, 275c, 296
saltatrix, Pomatomus, 280c, 364
sapidissima, Alosa, 275c, 291
Sarda sarda, 278c, 344
sarda, Sarda, 278c, 344
Sardinella anchovia, 275c, 287
saurus, Elops, 275c, 285
  Oligoplites, 279c, 363
  Scomberesox, 276c, 312
saxatilis, Menticirrhus, 281c, 377
  Roccus, 280c, 366
say, Dasyatis, 255c, 265
schoepfi, Chilomycterus, 283c, 411
schoepfii, Alutera, 283c, 407
Sciaenops ocellatus, 281c, 381
Scoliodon terrae-novae, 230c, 242
Scomber scombrus, 278c, 342
Scomberesox saurus, 276c, 312
Scomberomorus cavalla, 279c, 349
  maculatus, 279c, 348
  regalis, 279c, 349
scombrus, Scomber, 278c, 342
scorpius, Myoxocephalus, 281c, 386
scripta, Alutera, 283c, 408
Scyliorhinus retifer, 230c, 238
sectatrix, Kyphosus, 280c, 375
Selene vomer, 279c, 361
senta, Raja, 255c, 263
Seriola dumerili, 279c, 362
  zonata, 279c, 361
setapinnis, Vomer, 279c, 360
Somniosus microcephalus, 231c, 251
spengleri, Sphaeroides, 283c, 410

Sphaeroides maculatus, 283c, 410
  spengleri, 283c, 410
Sphyraena barracuda, 278c, 336
  borealis, 278c, 335
Sphyrna diplana, 231c, 248
  tibura, 231c, 247
  zygaena, 231c, 249
Squalus acanthias, 231c, 249
Squatina dumeril, 231c, 252
Stenotomus aculeatus, 280c, 373
  chrysops, 280c, 372
striatus, Centropristes, 280c, 368
subbifurcata, Ulvaria, 282c, 401
surinamensis, Lobotes, 280c, 370
Symphurus plagiusa, 277c, 330
Syngnathus floridae, 278c, 340
  fuscus, 278c, 339
Synodus foetens, 276c, 302

T

tabacaria, Fistularia, 278c, 341
Tarpon atlanticus, 275c, 286
tau, Opsanus, 283c, 404
taurus, Carcharias, 230c, 231
Tautoga onitis, 282c, 393
Tautogolabrus adspersus, 282c, 393
tenuis, Urophycis, 277c, 319
terrae-novae, Scoliodon, 230c, 242
thalassinus, Microgobius, 282c, 395
thazard, Auxis, 278c, 344
Thunnus alalunga, 278c, 348
  albacares, 278c, 347
  atlanticus, 278c, 347
  thynnus, 278c, 346
thynnus, Thunnus, 278c, 346
tibura, Sphyrna, 231c, 247

tomcod, Microgadus, 277c, 318

Torpedo nobliana, 255c, 257

Trachinotus carolinus, 280c, 363

falcatus, 280c, 364

Trachurops crumenopthalmus, 279c, 356

Trachurus trachurus, 279c, 357

trachurus, Trachurus, 279c, 357

triacanthus, Poronotus, 279c, 353

Trichiurus lepturus, 279c, 350

tricornis, Lactophrys, 283c, 409

trigonus, Lactophrys, 283c, 408

Trinectes maculatus, 277c, 331

triqueter, Lactophrys, 283c, 408

Tylosurus acus, 276c, 309

marinus, 276c, 309

typus, Rhincodon, 230c, 237

tyrannus, Brevoortia, 275c, 408

U

Ulvaria subbifurcata, 282c, 401

undulatus, Micropogon, 281c, 380

unifasciatus, Hyporhamphus, 276c, 310

Urophycis chuss, 277c, 320

regius, 277c, 319

tenuis, 277c, 319

V

vagrans Membras, 278c, 333

variegatus, Cyprinodon, 276c, 305

velox, Euleptorhamphus, 276c, 311

virens, Pollachius, 277c, 317

volitans, Cephalacanthus, 281c, 391

vomer, Selene, 279c, 361

Vomer setapinnis, 279c, 360

vulpes, Albula, 275c, 286

vulpinus, Alopias, 230c, 235

W

wheatlandi, Gasterosteus, 278c, 338

X

xanthurus, Leiostomus, 281c, 379

Xiphias gladius, 279c, 352

Z

zonata, Seriola, 279c, 361

zygaena, Sphyrna, 231c, 249